D0429254

Fundraising
for Libraries

25 PROVEN WAYS TO GET
MORE MONEY FOR YOUR LIBRARY

James Swan

Neal-Schuman Publishers, Inc.
NEW YORK   LONDON

Published by Neal-Schuman Publishers, Inc.
100 Varick Street
New York, NY 10013

The paper used in this publication meets the minimum requirements of American National Standard for Information Sciences—Permanence of Paper for Printed Library Materials, ANSI Z39, 48–1992.

Library of Congress Cataloging-in-Publication Data

Swan, James, 1941-
    Fundraising for libraries: 25 proven ways to get more money for your library / James Swan.
        p. cm. —
Includes bibliographical references and index.
ISBN 1-55570-433-6 (alk. paper)
    1. Library fund raising—United States—Handbooks, manuals, etc.
I. Title: Fund raising for libraries II. Title III. How-to-do-it manuals for libraries; no. 120.

Z683.2.U6 S93 2002
025.1'1'0973—dc21   2002005813

Contents

List of Figures

Preface

Fundraising for Libraries: 25 Proven Ways to Get More Money for Your Library is designed to help you find all of the library funding you need and want. The book examines how fundraising for libraries is done most effectively and where to turn for help, drawing from examples of the hits and misses of actual library fundraising campaigns. Most importantly, you will learn how to select the right technique for your particular project. The best fundraising strategy is to know what you want to buy, build, or fund, and then find the most suitable way to raise the needed dollars.

The critical skill of asking for money in ways that get results is carefully examined here. Remember that fundraisers are like salespeople. Some are better at closing a deal than others. This guide will share techniques that will help you become an expert at asking for and getting the gifts you want.

Fundraising for Libraries explores methods of creating effective and efficient fundraising committees. Let's be honest—often these committees are made up of anyone who will volunteer to ask for money. Consider innovative ways to be more selective like the librarians discussed in this book. You want the people who will be effective at getting the money to fund your project. People who will give to the cause before they ask others to give are key. There are important factors to keep in mind in order to best select and organize volunteers and committees.

The book examines successful communications techniques, as well. You will find views on how to turn your ideas into exciting visions that sell themselves. A colorful drawing of the new library will make it easier to sell the dream. Would your effort be even more effective if you had a three-dimensional model of the new or renovated library?

Other library fundraisers are always willing to lend a hand, but the assistance of a professional is sometimes crucial. They can help you do a feasibility study, find a lead gift, and help organize the campaign. Here you will find the ways to locate the additional help you may need.

DRAMATIC DEVELOPMENTS IN FUNDRAISING

I have been involved in fundraising for libraries for over thirty years. In the last decade, as I gave presentations at state and regional library conferences, I discovered that not all library fundraising was created equal. Some techniques take a lot of effort and produce little return. Other activities take a long time to develop, but have the potential to produce a high return—if the donors are properly cultivated. I could also see fundraising efforts being organized into a continuum of effort from aggressively seeking large donations for a building project to passively waiting for people to give money.

Regardless of the size of their library, I want librarians and other fundraisers to ask a powerful question. What are the ways to get some real money for your library? If librarians could understand how to go for the "pie in the sky" and get it, they might not have to worry about bake sales and spaghetti suppers. That is why after discussing the big ideas of fundraising in the first part of the book, I turn in the second part to the specific 25 proven ways to actually get more money for your library. These ways are ordered by their potential to bring in enough money to make a BIG difference to the library—even if it takes several years.

HOW TO READ THIS GUIDE

As you read, think of yourself brainstorming with your colleagues in a "Fundraising for Libraries 101" workshop. To be more precise, the title of the workshop might also encompass "Fundraising 102 and 103," because this guide embraces the basics, provides essential detail, and also tells you where to get more help. Feel free to tailor this workshop to your particular needs and interests. *Fundraising for Libraries* is organized so you can read it from cover to cover and develop a clear understanding of basics of fundraising. Those who would prefer to "get the juices flowing" by reading the specific suggestions first and then filling in with the background later, are welcome to do so.

Part I, "Fundamentals of Fundraising" is designed to give a basic overview of fundraising. It starts with increasing regular funding, which has the best chance of producing the most money, and once it is in place, it is sustainable with little or no effort. This part of the book concludes with passive fundraising ideas that require little more than just doing a good job of running a library. In between, it moves from capital campaigns to soliciting donations to moneymaking projects to get money from nonconstituents.

I have included a bibliography at the end of each chapter. The short annotations will help you decide if you can use the resource or not. Most of the books and other materials deal specifically with the topic they address, all of which makes up the business of fundraising. If your budget is limited, borrow the books on interlibrary loan. When you have them in your hands you can decide if they are worth buying.

PART I: FUNDAMENTALS OF FUNDRAISING

Chapter 1 discusses key elements in the fundamentals of fundraising. How do you develop the right attitudes about fundraising, ask for money, give before asking, and select the fundraising activity to match the project? It also discusses the importance of the library's image and performance as they relate to funding. Other ideas in the first chapter include brainstorming, selling and closing the sale, getting help, and developing a gift policy. These fundamentals build the foundation for the rest of the book. Everything else leads back to the concepts examined in this first chapter.

Chapter 2 reviews the methods for increasing regular funding. If all libraries had all the money they needed from regular sources, librarians wouldn't have to fundraise. With that thought in mind, this chapter tackles the business of getting more money from taxes. Passing a referendum and appealing to the governing body are the most common avenues for increasing regular funding. Chapter 2 examines creating a budget, gathering statistics, planning, and arguments to use in the appeal. It also suggests ways to win the support of members of the governing body and the voters. If it is successful, increasing regular funding could be the best way of all to get more money for your library. This doesn't mean that you shouldn't seek funding from other sources. You should. That is why you need to read the rest of the book.

Chapter 3 explores funding through successful grant writing. Writing a grant is the first way people think of when they need more money for their library. Grant funding is a good source of extra income, but it doesn't cure all ills. Grant applications succeed because the grant writer has started by aligning the purposes of the grants to the objectives of the funding agency. This chapter considers the various elements of a successful grant, including a succinct introduction, clearly documented needs, attainable goals and objectives, logical methodologies, a realistic budget, commitments for future funding, and qualitative and quantitative methods of evaluation. There is also a discussion of how to find grant opportunities.

Chapter 4 discusses ways to find funds for capital improvements. In detail, it reviews how to pass a bond issue, conduct a capital campaign, solicit large gifts from individuals, and write large grants. It also covers using telephone surveys, focus groups, hiring professional consultants, feasibility studies, interviewing community leaders, and strategies for winning a bond election. Getting enough money to build a new library could be your biggest challenge. It could also be the most rewarding work you will do.

Chapter 5 gives you the how-to-do-it of soliciting money. The most effective way to raise money from private sources is to ask individuals for it. You don't have to sell them anything. You just contact them and ask, "Will you give $100 to the library?" or whatever amount you determine. Helping you get to *yes* is the main purpose of this chapter. The chapter outlines how to recruit, organize, and train volunteers. Next you learn how to evaluate potential donors by assessing their interest in the library and their capability to give. It shows you who to ask for money first and the best ways to ask. You learn critical selling techniques that you didn't learn in library school, like being silent after asking for the gift. Soliciting money from people is not easy, but ordinary people can do it, if they will follow the suggestions in this chapter.

Chapter 6 reviews selling goods to make money for the library. They are called moneymaking projects, not fundraising. The only reason to sell products to raise money is to get money from nonconstituents (I define everyone who lives in the community or uses the library as a constituent of the library.). This chapter reviews the best things to sell and the selling opportunities to avoid. It is better to sell something we get for free than to pay retail for a product and then try to charge more than it is worth to make money. Chapter 6 ends with a sampler of moneymaking ideas discovered over the years. Just remember one thing. If you have to sell something to get money from people, include some fun in the deal.

Chapter 7 explains the principles of passive fundraising. Passive fundraising is doing something positive and letting people figure out that your library needs money. Passive fundraising lets what you do on a day-to-day basis speak for you. This includes being friendly to people, going the extra mile to help them, and being interested in them and their families. Passive techniques include creating a memorial giving flyer and then putting it on the circulation desk for people to take. A letter to Santa in the local newspaper, a page on the library's Web site, or a Christmas tree decorated with ornaments that suggest a book to give the library are all passive fundraising ideas. Passive fundraising could bring in some of the best gifts your library will ever receive. It may just require patience.

Chapter 8 is the last chapter in Part I. It discusses enlisting help from other sources. This section of *Fundraising for Libraries* points you toward other sources for more help. It shows how to find a professional, and explains how that person can help you. It explores the benefits of having a Friends of the Library group, and talks about having a foundation to build an endowment for the library. Finally, it suggests ways of getting help from professional colleagues.

PART II: 25 PROVEN FUNDRAISING TECHNIQUES

The second part of this guide includes the 25 proven ways to get more money for your library. It will clearly show how to make each one of these ways work for you. I have listed them in the order by potential to bring in lots of money. Not all of the techniques will work in every library. They may have to be modified to work in a school or academic setting. If you are in a school or academic library, look for the heading *"For School and Academic Libraries"* in each of the 25 Proven Ways. The entire list includes the following:

1. Conduct Capital Campaign for a Building
2. Promote Deferred Giving
3. Open the Library, Say Thank You
4. Pass Bond Issue for Building Project
5. Pass a Referendum for Regular Funding
6. Appeal for More Regular Funding
7. Conduct Annual Campaign of Giving
8. Build Endowment
9. Solicit Funds Door-to-Door
10. Lobby for More State Aid
11. Write Foundation/Corporate Grant
12. Hold an Auction of Donated Goods
13. Organize Regular Annual Events
14. Set Up Retail Sales with Shop in the Library
15. Secure Matching Grants or Gifts
16. Use Recognition to Enhance Giving
17. Use Library's Web Page to Solicit Gifts
18. Have a New Book Fair

Everyone who reads this book will take away something different because our experiences are different. Our communities are different. Our libraries are different. Our funding partners are different. Yet somehow we are all the same in at least one way—we want more money for our libraries. I hope you find what you are looking for in this book.

I hope that *Fundraising for Libraries: 25 Proven Ways to Get More Money for Your Library* will fill many minds with all kinds of ideas that will help make money for our libraries. Some of the ideas will validate what you already know about fundraising. No doubt unique and personal ideas will pop into your head. I hope this book will motivate you to action.

Acknowledgments

I would like to thank everyone who gave me ideas and anecdotes to put in the book. I would like to thank Charles Harmon, Acquisitions Editor for Neal-Schuman Publishers, Inc., for encouraging me to do this book without being pushy. I would like to thank Michael Kelley for his encouragement during the writing of the book. I would like to thank my wife, Diana, for her support and for giving up her time on the computer so I could write.

Part I

Fundamentals of Fundraising

Chapter 1

Understanding Fundraising Fundamentals

Fundraising for Libraries is not a magic pill that if taken at the right time will solve all of your money problems. Almost every librarian I know struggles to have enough money to pay for essential programs and services. It doesn't seem to matter if the library gets by with $10.00 or less per capita, or basks in the relative luxury of $100 per capita. It is the job of every librarian and library board to advocate for the library and see that the library has the money it needs to do its job.

You have to be persistent to get the money you need for your library. If you have the determination to read this book and then muster the courage to implement some of its suggestions, *you will* have the power to improve funding for your library. You *can* make a difference. You *can* have more money for your library.

WHERE DOES THE MONEY COME FROM?

Essential to the business of asking for more money for your library, is knowing where the money will come from. It doesn't grow on trees, and it has to be somewhere before someone can decide to give it to you. Tax money that supports libraries comes from the taxpayers. Gifts from private individuals come from their regular income, from their invested assets, or from their estates. Grants awarded by state or federal agencies come from taxes. Grants awarded by corporations come from the profits of the corporation to be used for charitable giving. Grants from foundations usually come from interest income from the investment of donated funds.

This discussion may seem elemental but it is critical to understand if we need to find and get large chunks of money for big projects. (See

Principle-Centered Leadership

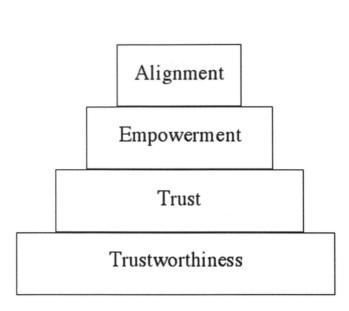

Figure I-1-1 Principle-Centered Leadership

Figure I-1-5.) Most taxpayers understand the need to provide public funding for a public good, but don't count on them to willingly give you more than they think you need. Individuals who feel they have benefited from the library or that others have benefited from the library are willing to give to the library from whatever pool of money they have that they do not need for some other purpose. The amount will vary greatly from individual to individual. Agencies that award grants usually employ individuals to administer grant awards and respond to questions from applicants. It is the job of the grant administrator to make sure that the project of the applicant is in alignment with the purposes of the granting agency and that the applicant can complete the activities of the project. When we understand where the money comes from, we will understand the importance of trust, empowerment, and alignment.

PROJECTING TRUST, BEING EMPOWERED, AND PRESENTING ALIGNMENT

Before we can ask for a quarter from anyone we have to be trustworthy. The people who give us money have to be able to trust us, and trust the organization we represent. Whether it is a fifty cent chance on a quilt or a million dollar bequest, people have to trust us before they will empower us to spend their money for the good of our library. Figure I-1-1 shows a pyramid that I adapted from Stephen Covey's book *Principle-Centered Leadership*. The critical message of this figure is that trustworthiness is the foundation of any fundraising effort. Donors need to feel that we are aligned with them, at least to the point that they want something good to come of their money. They need to trust us not to squander their money. Then they can empower us to spend their gift the way they would if they were running the library. When we understand this principle we can move on to the business of fundraising.

SOURCES OF PRIVATE GIVING

Successful fundraising from private sources is based on learning and using fundraising techniques that get results. But before we do that we have to understand where private donations come from. They have to come from the income of the individual or from his or her assets—usually in some form of interest-bearing investment. When we ask someone for a gift for the library and they give us $25, $50, or even $100, the money probably comes from his or her regular income. Few people carry a balance in their checking account large enough to cover a check to the library for $1,000. They have to dip into their savings. So, if you are looking for donations of a thousand dollars or more you are asking people to dip into their savings or investments. There is nothing wrong with this as long as people feel they can afford it.

The first reason people save is to have money for unexpected future expenses. The other reason for not spending their regular income is to invest it so that the earnings can be reinvested or used when their ability to earn money by working ends—they retire. Most people know they are going to retire someday. They save and invest while they are able to earn money from working so the income from their assets will be enough to support them after they retire. This brings us to an important concept connected with fundraising—the "coming transfer of wealth."

TRANSFER OF WEALTH

To understand this concept we need to understand the demographics of today's society. People born in 1930 or before, grew up during the Great Depression. They know what it is like not to have enough to eat or not have a job. They learned to be frugal and live within their means. Saving a dollar or two a week during the Depression was a great accomplishment.

After the Depression and World War II, anyone who wanted to work, including women, found jobs. They got married, had families, and bought homes and cars. They also started saving and investing their money. Some people have been more successful than others. Some have amassed great fortunes of millions and millions of dollars. Others have lived on the edge of poverty all of their lives. Most people in the United States live comfortably on investments of two, three, four, or five hundred thousand dollars, along with income from their pensions and Social Security.

A retired multimillionaire could drop $1 million on your library and probably not feel the financial impact enough to forego the purchase of a new Mercedes next year. The retired schoolteacher with $300,000 invested, however, needs every dollar of the income from his or her investment. A regular donation of $50 or $100 a year from this individual might be considered a sacrificial gift because it comes from his or her income. The multimillionaire can probably give the library $1 million from his or her income, too, but how many of us know a multimillionaire? So, most of us are left with the opportunity to solicit funds from people who have a modest income from the investments of a lifetime.

Starting today and for the next 20 years, libraries need to position themselves to receive a share of the wealth that will be transferred when the parents of "baby boomers" die. It would be nice to be thought of as members of the family. If a person has four children and an estate of $5 million, he or she could leave a million to each child and leave a million to the library.

This is not an unreasonable expectation. If a person has been visiting the library two or three times a week for the past 50 years why shouldn't the library be considered part of the family. In about 1950 Bernard Berelson and Lester Asheim did a study on the use of public libraries. They found that the predominant library user was a woman in her late 20s to early 30s who reads fiction. These same people are still using the library today, but now they are in their 80s, widowed and living on the income from their investments. Libraries are perfectly positioned to inherit at least a portion of this money. If these women had no children, libraries have even a better chance to get some of the money—provided these women know the library needs their money. That leads us to the section on deferred giving on page 155.

In general you can count on the parents of the "baby boomers" to have enough money to leave a bequest to the library. Their children, born between 1945 and 1960, the "baby boomers," probably have more debt than they have money to give away. That doesn't mean that we shouldn't ask them to donate to the library. We should ask them—every chance we get. They will tell us if they can give or not. Some of them can give large chunks of money.

Our job is to find the people with the willingness and the ability to give and ask them to give to the library.

DEVELOPING THE RIGHT ATTITUDES ABOUT FUNDRAISING

Since this book is about getting more money for your library, I think it is important to understand some necessary attitudes to raise money for libraries. Adopting these attitudes as part of the way you think will make the difference in your success as a fundraiser.

Attitude #1 Take Action—Do Something

Kris Adams Wendt of the Rhinelander (Wisconsin) District Library said, "If I had to select one truth to pass on to others it would be this: Stop sitting around at meetings wrisüing your hands at the enormity of your goal, wishing for the second coming of Andrew Carnegie and saying, 'Now is not the right time to do something like this.' Get up, get out and do something positive!"

You are the one reading this book. You are the one who will form ideas for action. As you read, let the ideas flow into your mind, then give them your own twist and write them down. Writing down an idea is the first step to creating a goal. If you can write out your goals you can achieve them. You don't have to do it all by yourself. In fact, the more people you involve in your goal the more successful you will be.

Before you decide to put this book down and move onto another task, take a minute and write down one idea you have already learned that you can implement next week. Then later on, pick the book up again and look for something else you can do. You will be on your way to successful fundraising.

Figure I-1-2 gives you a Fundraising Planning form. When you get an idea you want to try, make a copy of this form and fill it out. The questions will help clarify your thinking and get you started.

Attitude #2 Ask for the Money

Even though this book gives you 25 proven ways to get more money for your library, there is really only one way to do it. You have to ask for it. Whether you are trying to increase regular funding, writing a grant, or holding a used book sale, you are asking someone to give you some of the money they control. Whether you visit the wealthiest person in town

---

Fundraising Planning Form

What fundraising activity do you want to try? _____
_____

Why do you think it will be a good idea for your library? _____
_____

Who are the prospective donors? _____
How much money do you plan to raise? _____
What resources will you need? _____
How much money will you have to spend to get the project started?
_____

Where will you get the money if you cannot use library funds? _____
_____

How long will it take to recover your initial costs? _____
Can you accomplish the project on your own or, will you need some help?
_____
_____

Who will you get to help you? _____
_____

How many people will it take to make the project a success? _____
Can you count on the help of the people you plan to ask? _____
When do you plan to begin the project? _____
When will the project be completed? _____
What is the first step? _____
What steps follow? _____
_____

What additional information do you need to complete the project? _____
_____

What ideas from this book do you want to implement? _____
_____

How will you know the project has been a success? _____
_____

Figure I-1-2 Fundraising Planning Form

and ask him or her for $1,000,000, or put a jar on the circulation desk with a sign that says, "Please give us your loose change," you have to ask people to give you money.

You could write a letter or a grant proposal. You could have a bake sale or conduct a capital campaign. You are still asking people to give you money. Fundraising is no more complicated than that. But fundraising is not simple either. If you want more money for your library you have to ask for it. You have to overcome your fears and buck up your courage to ask for the money you need.

Attitude #3 Increase Tax Support

Most people believe that public libraries and libraries in public institutions should be supported with public funds. This is true, but if we never ask for gifts to the library we miss out on the benefits of the natural goodwill and kind feelings most people have towards libraries. Indeed, fundraising efforts may be a good precursor to asking for more tax money. M. P. Marchant, Ph.D., Professor of Library Science at Brigham Young University said, "Fundraising efforts are important because of their emotional impact in support of tax initiatives" (Swan, 1990:44). Library fundraising projects, by their nature, create a higher level of visibility for the library. People who will give $10.00 to a fundraising effort are more likely to vote in favor of a library bond issue or a mill levy increase. Fundraising itself is a powerful public relations endeavor. So, why not try a few fundraising activities before you push for a tax referendum.

If you have the choice between a really big fundraising effort and a tax referendum, go for increasing taxes. Both activities will be about the same work. Once you win the vote for more support for the library in the form of taxes, it will be there year after year with little or no effort on your part. Fundraising events have to be repeated year after year, and they never get easier.

If you need to build a new library, you may need to do both a bond election and a capital campaign. Both of these activities will help each other succeed.

Attitude #4 Boost the Library's Image

If you need more money you will do better to do a good job of making the best of what you have, rather than complaining about what you don't have. The image you send to the people when you complain speaks volumes. On the other hand if you project a helpful caring image you will have the support you need.

Try getting outside of your library and taking a critical look at your library. Ask yourself these questions to measure your library's effectiveness:

- Are the library hours convenient for most people?
- Is the staff helpful to customers?
- Do the services meet the needs of the community?
- Does the library have enough different services to meet the needs of all of the people?
- Are the materials in the library meeting the needs of the people?
- Are the materials up-to-date and of sufficient quality and quantity?
- Is the staff knowledgeable and well-trained?

- Are the materials they need available?
- Is the library conveniently located?
- Does the library contribute to the well-being of the community?
- Are people aware of the services of the library?
- Is the library being managed competently?

You may have to take a friend to lunch and invite him or her to help you see the library as others see it. Give your friend a tour. Afterwards ask him or her the questions listed above.

Attitude #5 Performance Precedes Funding

If you are asking people to give your library more money, they want to make sure that you are going to use it to improve services. Your reputation of giving the people what they want when they come to the library will serve you better than your promises to improve on current services.

LOOKING AT LIBRARY PERFORMANCE

How well is your library performing? How do people in the community perceive the library? Use the *Checklist for Library Image and Performance* on page 34 to see how well you are doing. If all of the answers are not 100 percent positive figure out what you can do to improve.

Attitude #6 Envision the Completed Goal

You have to be able to describe what success will look like when you achieve it. If you can't express it, your donors will not catch the vision and will not give you the money you need.

If you want to build a $5 million dollar library, your goal has to be the new library not the five million dollars. The money is only the means to the end. It becomes just one of the challenges you face along the way to achieving your goal. Goal setting requires creative thinking—the kind of thinking that can happen in a brainstorming session. In fact goals are often the product of brainstorming.

BRAINSTORMING

The key to a successful fundraising goal may depend on your ability to brainstorm. Brainstorming is a marvelous technique that can produce exciting, often unexpected results. You sit down with a group of seven to ten people who have the library's interest in common and think creatively. They need to be somewhat familiar with the problem, but it is not necessary that everyone know everything about the operation of the library. Set aside one hour of uninterrupted time. Assign two or more people to be note takers—one primary note taker and the rest are backups, in case the flow of ideas gets too fast for one person to write down all of the ideas. Select a leader whose job it is to direct the discussion. Select someone else to do the writing. The facilitator encourages participation by making positive statements about the process. For example: "We are going great. Let's keep it up. What else can we think of?" The leader reminds everyone of the rules, if that becomes necessary.

RULES FOR BRAINSTORMING

- *Appoint a timekeeper, and set a time limit.* Twenty minutes is usually an optimum amount for the creative phase of brainstorming.
- *Everyone contributes.* You can start by going around the table. If a person can't think of anything the first time around, move on to the next person. Maybe he or she will the next time. Soon everyone will respond spontaneously.
- *All ideas are written down as they are given.* The leader may repeat what has been said to give the contributor a chance to clarify the idea.
- *No evaluation of any kind is made at this time.* Negative comments are especially discouraged. Even negative body language or laughing at an idea is discouraged.

Brainstorming works best when the group focuses on a specific question: *"How can we raise $50,000 in the next six months to buy new carpet for the library?"* Write your focusing question on a blackboard, or separate chart where everyone can see it.

Once participants get into the process, ideas will flow like water. I heard of a group of seven secretaries one time that came up with 256 ideas in 20 minutes of brainstorming. It took five of them to write down all of the ideas. Restraining thoughts did not hamper their thinking. They did not worry about losing their jobs if they thought of ideas that might make their jobs more efficient. Not all of the ideas were used, but think of the power this method has for creating solutions. Think of the powerful goals that could come from a session like this in your organization.

Attitude #7 Never Doubt Success

Nothing succeeds like a positive attitude.

Right now you may be thinking,

"I can't ask people to give me money for the library."

"I don't know how."

"I don't want to."

"I am afraid."

What are you afraid of? Are you afraid that a friend will throw you out of his or her office? Are you afraid that you will be turned down?

Are you afraid you will lose something? Most of our fears are unfounded. As a rule people like to say yes to requests for help.

If you are afraid to ask for the money you need for your library, think of the Harry Potter story where the class is asked to think of the thing they feared the most. Then the class is told to imagine that thing looking ridiculous. If we can turn the thing we fear into something we can laugh at maybe it will be more approachable to us. At any rate we need to change how we feel about the person we are going to ask for a donation. It might be helpful to think of a prospective donor as a loving parent who is just waiting to help a child who needs nurturing.

If you knew someone was being paid $100,000 a year to give away money to libraries, would it be easier to ask for money from him or her? All you would have to do is convince him or her that your project is worth funding and then ask for what you needed.

Your job as a fundraiser is to find people who are waiting to give you money and then ask them for it. Your success depends on the conviction that you will not fail, no matter what.

Attitude #8 Seek and Accept Help

Fundraising is not something you do by yourself. Use all of the help you can get. In fact, fundraising by its nature is getting other people to give you money so that you can accomplish something you want to do. Before you take on a fundraising project, review some ways to find and use the help you need.

Buy a Book on the Topic and Read It

It is okay to borrow a book on grant writing through interlibrary loan to see if it is any good before you buy it. If you are serious about writing a grant you need to buy the book. You need it at hand before you start writing and every step through the process. You will need to refer to it often. The annotated bibliographies in *Fundraising for Libraries* will help you find books on various fundraising activities.

Reading a book could help you decide if you really want to write a grant or try direct mail as a fundraising technique. A book could help you assess your resources. It will help you estimate your potential for success. It is possible that the best decision you will make is to *not* do something because you lack key resources or the time is not right.

Reading a book will give you the basics of the fundraising activity you are thinking about. If you already know the basics, reading a book will reinforce what you already know. Look for the how-to-do-it sections for the really good stuff. Most of the books I have seen on fundraising focus on a single way to get more money. These books get down to specifics and give you examples and the nuts and bolts you need to flesh out your fundraising proposal or project. Reading one or more of the books listed in the bibliography at the end of each chapter will help you bring together the resources you need to be successful at the activity you select. It could be the roadmap you need to take you to your goal.

CHECK OUT THE INTERNET

The Internet is bursting with information. There is scarcely a fundraising term that cannot be found on the World Wide Web. Use the Web to find out what others are doing and get some tips from them. The Internet may not be as comprehensive or as accurate as a book or other information you find. Web pages often lack peer scrutiny that other publications enjoy. Anyone with a Web site and space on a hard drive can put up anything they write as though they were one of the world's top experts. Be cautious with the information you find on the Web, and evaluate it carefully. On the other hand, information on the Internet will be more up-to-date than anything you can read in a book or magazine. Use the Internet judiciously and it will help you hit your fundraising target.

USE THE CONSULTANTS AT THE STATE AND REGIONAL LEVEL

Consultants at the state library and the regional systems are usually experienced professionals with broad experience in a lot of areas. They can be of great assistance but they will not come into your area and solicit money for your project. You can count on them to help with grant writing, explaining the law regarding bond issues, referenda, and regular funding. They can do workshops on various fundraising activities, and they can put you in touch with other professionals with more expertise. Don't expect these consultants to do the work of a paid professional.

HIRE PROFESSIONAL CONSULTANTS IF YOUR PROJECT IS LARGE ENOUGH

Hiring an outside professional to tell you if what you want to do will be supported by the community could be some of the best money you will ever spend. Community leaders will tell a professional things they won't tell you, and the only way you can get their honest opinion is to have someone from the outside ask them. If you need $500,000 or more don't be faint-hearted, call someone and get the help you need. You may have to find someone outside the library to fund the initial cost of hiring a professional consultant.

Philosophy of Fundraising

1. Have a clear vision of what you want to do. Know what your finished product will look like when you get it.
2. Find out as much as you can about the persons or organizations that control the money you are asking for. The more you know, the better you will be able to align your project with their goals.
3. Select the fundraising activity that best matches your fundraising goal. A used book sale might bring in enough money to buy a new photocopier or a computer, but raising enough money to build a new library will take serious solicitations for large gifts.
4. Communicate the library's need clearly and precisely. *Clearly* means plainly, unmistakably, and without a doubt. *Precisely* means specifically, accurately, and in particular. These are the essential elements in your communications. Your own words can be your worst enemies or your best friends.
5. Explain to donors how their money will help you solve the library's problem. Everyone likes to think that his or her donation to the library will benefit someone.
6. Tell them how and why helping your library can help them. Help them see their gift to the library as an investment in the community.
7. Ask for the money. This is an essential part of every one of the 25 ways to get more money for your library.

Figure I-1-3 Philosophy of Fundraising

GET THE HELP OF THE FRIENDS OF THE LIBRARY

Enlist the help of your board members or Friends of the Library. If you are in a school setting, get the PTA to help. If you are in an academic setting try to mobilize the faculty and some students to help you. Whoever you find to help you, make sure they are committed to the cause and are not wishy-washy bystanders who got drafted to do something they never wanted to do in the first place. Nothing can kill a fundraising effort faster than a bunch of unwilling workers (volunteers) who didn't hire on as fundraisers, but got drafted later because they were on the library board or were members of the PTA.

Take advantage of the goodwill these people have for the library. When I was a Boy Scout leader I received a "He-Who Award"—He who enlists the help of ten men is greater than he who does the work of ten men. You cannot do everything yourself. You need all of the help you can line up. The fundraising activities that absolutely require the assistance of other people will have the greatest impact on your library. Your job will be to recruit and channel the work of others.

Library Needs for Funding and Fundraising

Fundraising Activities	Increase Salaries	Fund Operations	Buy More Materials	Add or Replace Computers	Fund Maintenance	Build or Remodel Library	Potential for Big Money
1. Conduct capital campaign for a building	NO	NO	NO	YES	NO	YES	Very High
2. Promote deferred giving	YES	YES	YES	YES	YES	YES	Very High
3. Open the library, say thank you	YES	YES	YES	YES	YES	YES	Very high
4. Pass bond issue for building project	NO	NO	NO	YES	NO	YES	Very High
5. Pass a referendum for regular funding	YES	YES	YES	YES	YES	NO	High
6. Appeal for more regular funding	YES	YES	YES	YES	YES	NO	High
7. Conduct annual campaign of giving	YES	YES	YES	YES	YES	YES	High
8. Build endowment	YES	YES	YES	YES	YES	YES	High
9. Solicit door-to-door for building	NO	NO	NO	YES	NO	YES	High
10. Lobby for more state aid	YES	YES	YES	YES	NO	NO	Medium
11. Write foundation/corporate grant	NO	NO	YES	YES	NO	YES	Medium
12. Hold an auction of donated goods	YES	YES	YES	YES	YES	YES	Medium
13. Organize regular annual events	YES	YES	YES	YES	YES	NO	Medium
14. Set up retail sales with shop in the library	NO	YES	YES	YES	NO	YES	Medium
15. Secure matching grants or gifts	NO	NO	YES	YES	NO	YES	Medium
16. Use recognition to enhance giving	YES	YES	YES	YES	YES	YES	Medium
17. Use library's Web page to solicit gifts	NO	NO	YES	YES	NO	YES	Medium
18. Have a new book fair	NO	NO	YES	YES	NO	NO	Low
19. Write an LSTA grant	NO	NO	YES	YES	NO	NO	Low
20. Hold a direct mail solicitation	YES	YES	YES	YES	YES	YES	Low
21. Sponsor special events	YES	YES	YES	YES	YES	YES	Low
22. Publish and sell a cookbook	NO	NO	YES	YES	NO	YES	Low
23. Organize a used book sale	NO	NO	YES	YES	NO	YES	Low
24. Hold food events	NC	YES	YES	YES	YES	YES	Low
25. Solicit memorial gifts	YES	YES	YES	YES	YES	YES	Low

Figure 1-1-4 Library Needs for Funding and Fundraising

PHILOSOPHY OF FUNDRAISING

Getting more money for your library may not be as big a task as you think if you understand the basic philosophy of fundraising (Figure I-1-3).

SELECTING THE RIGHT ACTIVITY

To help you select the right fundraising activity I have created two charts using the 25 ways to get more money for your library. The first one (Figure I-1-4) looks at Library Needs for Funding and Fundraising and suggests the appropriateness of each way to fund various library needs. If you ask the voters to pass a bond issue for a new library you can't spend the money on salaries. If you raise money for an endowment you can only spend the income derived from investing the money. If you pass a referendum to increase the library's tax revenue, you can spend the money for any reasonable library purpose.

The second chart (Figure I-1-5) considers the resources you need to make each of the 25 ways successful. If your analysis tells you that you don't have the votes on the city council to get more money by appealing to the governing body, you probably need to try another way. If you don't have a lot of volunteers to help with a door-to-door fund drive, you may want to try a direct mail solicitation. All of these considerations fit into the mix and you have to evaluate how they will work in your situation.

LIBRARY NEEDS FOR FUNDING AND FUNDRAISING

This chart lists the activities with the potential to produce large amounts of money first. Most library expenditures can be broken down into one of the six categories listed at the top of the chart. They appear to be self-explanatory, but maybe they need a brief explanation.

The heading "Salaries" means all personnel expenditures including employee benefits. It is difficult to ask people to donate the library money so you can give the staff a raise. The same goes for operations and maintenance. Donors will give, usually small amounts, to help the library buy books and other materials. New buildings require large chunks of money, and people will give more to build a new library than they will for any other library purpose. Generally speaking, if you need more money for normal library expenses like salaries, operations, materials, and maintenance, it is best to try to increase regular sources of funding first. When you need money to remodel an existing library or build a new one, use the ways that will bring in the big dollars. The last column tells you the potential for big money—very high to low.

Resources Required for Success

Fundraising Activities	Other's Help	Leadership Strong	Up Front Investment	Solicitors Must Give	Lots of Volunteers	Special Skills	Time Required
1. Conduct capital campaign for a building	YES Donors of big gifts	YES Committee chair	YES	YES Similar to gift solicited	YES	YES Selling	At least 2 years
2. Promote deferred giving	YES Attorney, accountant	NO	YES Publicity	NO	NO	YES Selling	Five years or more
3. Open the library, say thank you	YES Donors	NO	NO	NO	NO	NO	Effort never ends
4. Pass bond issue for building project	YES Voters	YES	YES Publicity	NO	YES To canvass residents	YES To prepare case	At least a year
5. Pass a referendum for regular funding	YES Voters	YES	YES Publicity	NO	YES To canvass residents	YES To prepare case	At least 2 years
6. Appeal for more regular funding	YES City Council	YES	NO	NO	NO	YES Speaking	At least 2 years
7. Conduct annual campaign of giving	YES Donors of big gifts	YES Committee chair	YES	YES Similar to gift solicited	YES	YES Selling 2 years	Initially, at least
8. Build endowment	YES Strong board	YES	NO	YES Similar to gift solicited	NO	NO	More than 5 years
9. Solicit door-to-door for building	NO	YES Committee chair	NO	YES Similar to gift solicited	YES	YES Selling	At least 6 months
10. Lobby for more state aid	YES Legislators	YES	NO	NO To lobby	YES Lobbying legislature	YES 5 years	At least
11. Write foundation/corporate grant	YES Grant readers	NO	NO	NO	NO	YES Writing	At least a year

Figure 1-1-5 Resources Required for Success

12. Hold an auction of donated goods	YES	YES Committee chair	YES Programs	NO	YES	YES	YES Auctioneer	At least a year
13. Organize regular annual events	YES	YES Committee chair	NO	NO	YES	YES	NO	At least a year
14. Set up retail sales with shop in the library	YES	NO	YES	NO	YES	YES	YES Retail sales	At least a year to set up
15. Secure matching grants or gifts	YES	YES	NO	NO	YES	YES	YES Writing	Three to six months
16. Use recognition to enhance giving	NO	NO	YES Plaques and engraving	NO	NO	NO	NO	Three months
17. Use library's Web page to solicit gifts	NO	NO	YES Online shopping cart	NO	NO	NO	YES HTML writing skills	One to three months
18. Have a new book fair	YES Good supplier	YES	NO	NO	NO	NO	NO	Six months
19. Write an LSTA grant	YES Grant readers	NO	NO	NO	NO	NO	YES Writing	Six months
20. Hold a direct mail solicitation	NO	YES	YES Cost of mailing	NO	NO	NO	YES Writing	As much as 5 years
21. Sponsor special events	YES	YES Committee chair	YES	NO	YES	YES	NO	At least a year
22. Publish and sell a cookbook	YES Recipes	YES Committee chair	NO	NO	YES To sell cookbooks	YES	NO	One year
23. Organize a used book sale	YES	YES	NO	NO	YES	NO	NO	One year
24. Hold food events	YES Donated supplies	YES	YES	NO	YES	NO	NO	Three months
25. Solicit memorial gifts	YES	NO	YES Publicity	NO	NO	YES	YES	One month

The 25 ways are more or less ranked in priority order according to their effectiveness at securing large amounts of money. Some of the ways may be impossible for some libraries because of their particular situation. If you do not have access to the ballot box to pass a referendum, figure out what you can do to get more regular funding and go for it. These two charts are designed to help you assess your situation and match it to the best fundraising opportunity. The heading for the second chart refers to the required resources for each of the 25 ways. Here is a brief discussion of these headings.

Others' Help

Can you do this one by yourself or do you need the help of others? "By yourself" means you can do it with the people in your organization and with the resources you have at your disposal. If you can't then you need the help of others. "Others' help" means getting taxpayers to vote for a bond issue, or persuading legislators to increase state aid. It also means using volunteers to solicit for donations or canvassing voters.

Strong Leadership

Can you find someone outside the library to lead the charge to make this effort a success? A strong leader has to have connections in the community and the ability to call in favors from other community leaders. This is critical if you conduct a capital campaign. Strong leadership is also necessary when you are working with lots of volunteers to succeed with a big moneymaking project like an annual event.

Up-front Investment

Do you need to spend some money in the beginning to make the fundraising activity a success? There are times when you will not be able to get everything donated. Most fundraising activities require some seed money. Publicity is one of the important ones. It would be ill advised to plan a special event and then not advertise to let people know about the event. You also need butter and syrup for a pancake feed or programs for an auction. The main concern here is to keep your upfront costs minimal in case your event flops.

Solicitors Must Give

We discuss this issue in more detail in other sections of this book. The principle is those who solicit gifts to the library are more effective when they make a significant gift to the cause before they do the asking. It is difficult to be a credible and successful fundraiser when you have not given to the fund drive yourself.

Many Volunteers

Some fundraising activities require lots of people to sell tickets, serve food, or solicit donations of cash or goods. Some fundraising activities could require the effort of more people than you have in your organization. Soliciting donations from other people is often on the bottom of the list of things volunteers like to do. If you don't have a lot of people waiting in the wings to help out, figure out a way to use the people you have.

Special Skills

Not everyone can write persuasively. Fewer people know how to be an auctioneer or a square dance caller. If you need people with specific skills you may have to pay someone if you can't find a volunteer. In most instances it is better to hire a skilled individual to do the job rather than let an amateur do it.

Time Required

Sometimes librarians need to raise money in a hurry. This column will help develop a sense of timing for fundraising activities. It is obvious that you wouldn't conduct a capital campaign to raise money for a photocopier if your old one just broke down. You need the money right away. This column will help you find a way you can finish in less than six months.

SETTING PRIORITIES

Successful fundraising requires us to set priorities. One way to do it is to set up a matrix using these two sets of questions:

Set I
1. Will the project result in a big difference?
2. Will the project result in a medium-sized difference?
3. Will the project result in little or no difference?

Set II
1. Can we accomplish the project ourselves?
2. Will the project absolutely require the help of others?
3. Will someone else have to do the project entirely?

Projects that won't make a difference and projects that have to be done by others get dropped immediately. Projects that will make a big difference and we can do ourselves have probably already been done. So, we focus on the project that will make a big to medium difference and require the help of others. This is our best chance for measurable success.

Fundraising Readiness Checklist

1. Assess the fundraising readiness of your organization
   - Do you have a brief statement describing the mission of your library?
   - Is your library succeeding at its mission?
   - Do you have a one-page description of the project you would like to fund but don't have the money for now?
   - Can you list the benefits of the project?
   - Does your library have strong internal leadership?
   - Does the public perceive your library as a relevant, successful, and a meaningful part of the community?

2. Conduct the necessary market research
   - Who will give to your cause?
   - Make a list right now of five people you can ask for a $1,000 donation.
   - Who cares about your service?
   - Make a list of five people who care about the library?
   - What groups benefit from your services?
   - Make a list of five groups that care about the library?

3. Project human resources
   - Are members of the staff knowledgeable and effective fund-raisers?
   - Are board members well-known, well-respected individuals in the area you serve?
   - Are board members willing to become involved in fundraising?
   - Are they willing to contribute to the cause?
   - Do you have a committed group of volunteers who will provide prospects and ask those prospects for money?
   - Will these volunteers give themselves?

Figure I-1-6 Fundraising Readiness Checklist

ARE YOU READY?

If someone in your fundraising group can't take a corporate president to lunch and ask for $50,000 or $100,000, you need some help.

- Are you ready for a fundraising project?
- You are not sure?
- If you aren't sure, you are probably not ready!

Complete the *Fundraising Readiness Checklist*, to see how ready you really are. Answering the questions honestly will help you isolate some shaky spots in your fundraising effort and you will be on your way toward overcoming these weaknesses.

Look for the green lights. When you see them, move ahead confidently. If you feel fuzzy or unsure about your answers to any of these questions, you may have identified some limiting forces. But don't let them stop you. Figure out how to resolve them and move on. You cannot give up every time something gets in your way. If you can deal with the limiting forces, you can be successful with a fundraising effort.

EVALUATE PROSPECTIVE DONORS

Appraise prospective donors on their capacity to give and their interest in your organization. You may know someone who has millions of dollars to give away, but may have little interest in your library. On the other hand you probably know lots of people who are very interested in the library, but have little, if any, money to give. Neither of these groups of prospective donors are very good prospects.

The job of the fundraiser is to find those people who have a high interest in the library and also have plenty of money to give. Most of the time they don't walk in off the street and write a check to the library. You usually have to find them, cultivate them, and win them over to the point of giving. This is the essence of fundraising.

ALL FUNDRAISING IS SELLING

Fundraising is basically selling. It is selling a product or an idea or just a good feeling. It is selling an investment in your cause. The secret is packaging the product in a way that will make the other person want to buy.

Jim Keller is one of the best sales people I know. He has been selling office products and equipment for at least 30 years. He uses what he calls "Conversational selling." He says, "You have it in your mind that you are selling something, but you convey the feeling that you are working for the customer. You are helping them solve their problems. To do that you have to understand exactly what the customer has in mind."

Jim says, "Five essentials must be in place before someone will buy something. Whether you are going to buy a pencil or a computer, every one of these has to be in place, but not in any specific order."

1. "Is it the right product?—If a farmer is looking for a pickup you don't try to sell him a sports car.
2. Need for the product—If the prospect is thirsty, don't try to sell him or her a car.
3. Price—Is the price within the prospect's ability and willingness to pay?

4. Time—Is this the right time?
5. Is it the right vendor? People do business with you because they like doing business with you."

Jim Keller says, "When I am not making progress, I stop and analyze where I am in the sales cycle. By asking these questions I can find out which of the five points I haven't met. The customer will often help you if the time is wrong or if he or she cannot afford it."

Every one of these points is just as critical in fundraising. When you find yourself floundering with a solicitation and you don't know what to say next, ask yourself these questions:

- Am I pushing the right benefit to this donor?
- Does the donor understand the need to give to my library?
- Am I asking for a larger donation than this donor is capable of giving?
- Is this the right time for me to ask for a donation from this person?
- Does this person care enough about my library to donate the amount I am requesting?

For the donor, the benefits of giving to the library can be elusive. On the surface you may be pushing the benefit of remembering a loved one and the donor may be interested in how his or her donation will benefit the children in the community. Your job is to discover the donor's need, and sell the benefit to children. In fundraising, your product has to be many things to many people.

Robert Hartsook, a professional fundraising consultant and former fundraising executive for Wichita State University said that people give for one of two reasons:

1. *Investment.* They want to invest in what you are selling. They believe that their contribution to the library building fund is an investment in the future of the town, the lives of children, the memory of their parents, etc. They value one or more of the following:

- Personal spirituality
- Humanity
- Personal gratitude
- Perpetuation of ideas
- Personal pride
- Assurance of meeting organizational goals

2. *Fear.* They are concerned for your organization, but they believe they won't see a return on their investment. Especially if you say, "We're

going to have to close our doors if you don't give something to us." Very few people will give because of fear. They may give if they feel strongly about:

- Preventing want.
- Assuring the continuation of service.

Your research will help you evaluate the prospect. You have to evaluate his or her capacity to give and his or her interest in your organization. Objections to price usually hinge on one of these two things. Does the prospect have the cash to give to you? And does he or she want to give it to you?

Learn the Importance of Asking

Sales people refer to this as "the close." Ken Watts, a car dealer friend of mine tells a story, which makes this point in a memorable way.

He said, "I went out to see this farmer at 8:00 in the morning. I knew he was going to buy the car. I pitched that car every way I knew how. We drove around the country in it. I let him drive it. I sold it from six positions. I bought him lunch. I knew he was going to buy the car. That is why I stayed with him. We must have walked around that car a hundred times. I must have gone over every feature at least twenty-five times. We went for another ride. When it was time for supper, I bought him supper. We were both getting tired, but I wasn't going to give up because I knew he was going to buy the car.

After 14 hours of selling the car every way I knew, I was all talked out. I sat down in his kitchen, exasperated. Finally and for the *first* time I said, 'Why don't you buy the car?' He said, 'O.K.,' and we signed the papers."

Everyone likes to be asked. It makes them feel important. You can do your best job of selling anything, but if you don't ask for it, you won't get the sale. In fundraising you have to *ask for the gift*.

Be Silent After the Ask

This is one of the most critical pieces of advice in this book. The words "Will you?" make the donor want to help you. For example, when you ask for the gift, say "Will you help us reach our goal by giving $10,000 to the library building fund?" Don't say another word until the donor has spoken. Researchers have learned that the average silence in any conversation is less than three seconds. Learn to be comfortable with the silence. Let your prospect speak next. If you speak next you will be letting the donor off the hook. You want him or her to feel the pressure to say yes. If your donor says "no," don't give up.

Listen!

He or she will probably tell you why he or she is turning you down. Try to find out why the answer is *no*. Agree with the donor and then point out another benefit of giving. He or she may feel that you are on his or her side. Sometimes you have to prove that you are seriously committed to your cause. Tell the donor you have already given $1,000. Now it is his or her turn.

Don't give up with the first "no." Keep on listening and talking. He or she may change his or her mind. If you don't get the gift you shouldn't be disappointed. You have still learned something. You probably failed to predict the donor's capacity to give (how much discretionary cash he or she has). Or you may have gauged his or her interest in the library wrongly.

Getting the donor to say "yes" may require several ploys, but it could be as simple as asking him or her, "What could I do to get you to say yes?" Maybe he or she will tell you a benefit that you haven't thought of, or maybe the library has the book drop in an inconvenient place. If you can fix it, you may be in line for a nice gift.

If the answer is still no, listen to him or her. Agree with him or her. Listen for clues that might give you a lead to a benefit that will make a difference. Chances are, he or she will give you several reasons for not giving. By listening carefully, you will learn what is important to the donor. Then you can connect a benefit of your project with something that is important to him or her. The connection between a benefit of your project and your prospect's "hot button" is the key to getting the gift.

SAY "THANK YOU" APPROPRIATELY

Saying "thank you" is the most obvious rule of all. The biggest question is how do I match my thank you with the size of the gift. Your thanks could range from a simple specific note to someone who gave you a hundred dollars to an elaborate reception honoring a gift large enough to build the entire new addition. The most important thing about saying thank you is to do it.

Saying thank you not only makes your donor feel good, but it also makes *you* feel good. It may be the only "return on investment" your donor will receive. Sometimes fundraising groups have a big bash at the end of the campaign for all the workers and the donors who gave $1,000 or more. It is a good opportunity to give public recognition to workers and donors alike.

On the other hand, how can you recognize a large gift from a donor who wishes to remain anonymous? A quiet meal in a fancy restaurant

---

Establishing a Gift Policy

Here are some topics you will want to cover:

- Procedures for processing gifts
- Types of gifts besides cash the library will accept
- Disposal of used books that will not be added to the collection
- Restrictions the library will accept
- Restrictions the library will not accept
- Acceptable types of memorial gifts
- Types of recognitions for memorial gifts
- Restrictions on gifts from the Friends of the Library
- Procedure for acknowledging memorial gifts and sending thank you notes
- Types of recognitions depending on the level of giving
- Standards for recognition plaques including materials and inscriptions
- Event sponsorship that includes discount coupons as rewards

---

Figure I-1-7 Establishing a Gift Policy

might work fine. Anyone who gives anything to your campaign deserves a thank you.

Give the Donor Something

Every donor who makes a gift to your library expects something in return, even if it is just a thank you note. They probably already feel good about the library. You can give them something that will help them feel good about themselves and their gift to the library. Here are a few ways I have found to say thank you. You may be able to think of several more. Mine are listed in descending order for the size of the gift. See Use Recognition to Enhance Giving on page 281.

Check with the donor before you try some of the more public forms of recognition. He or she may want to keep the donation quiet and avoid a lot of public praise. Some donors may not want the library to spend a lot of money to thank them for their gift. They would rather see their donations go to work quietly for the library. If you explain to the donor that his or her gift might be used to leverage comparable gifts from the community, he or she may be more willing to accept public recognition for the gift.

A frank and open conversation with each donor will help you gauge his or her comfort level with the various forms of recognition. Some of the items on the list do not require funds, others do.

Sample Gift Policy

The XYZ library accepts gifts from private individuals, businesses, and other groups and the basis that it can use the gift. The library reserves the right to reject any gift for any reason or for no reason. All gifts become the property of the library and may be used at the discretion of the library director. Donors may request that cash gifts be used for the purchase of books or other materials, but the donor may not specify the title of the book to be purchased with the gift.

All cash gifts will be acknowledged and receipted with a thank you note. Gifts of new books will be accepted if they fit within the library's book selection policy. Gifts of used books will be accepted only if the library has the authority to use the books or dispose of the books as it sees fit. Generally books that are not added to the library's collection will be offered to the public in the library's annual book sale. Otherwise books not included in the collection or the book sale will be recycled.

Figure I-1-8 Sample Gift Policy

ESTABLISH A GIFT POLICY AND PROCEDURE

Libraries should be able to accept gifts without strings, but without a gift policy in place you may not be able to. Your library's gift policy needs to be as well developed as your circulation or materials selection policies. Can you imagine defending a censorship challenge without a materials selection policy in place? You could be in just as big of a mess if someone wanted to give your library a million dollars, but with unacceptable strings. The only restriction on a gift I would accept would be to spend the money from the gift on extant library programs or projects. Try to create a policy that covers every contingency.

Sample Policy

Most policies on giving are much more elaborate than this one. This is just a beginning point for you. Your gift policy could include a statement similar to Figure I-1-8.

Other Examples

This sample policy is not comprehensive, but it gives you an idea of how a policy could be written. Check out the Internet to find other sample gift policies. The Pikes Peak Public Library has a well-developed policy on the Web. It is very detailed and worth checking out.

SUMMARY

Almost every library director works hard to have enough money to pay for essential programs and services. Most of the time it is a difficult task, but with the help of other people you *can* get more money for your library. The key to success is asking for the gift.

- Libraries have a built-in constituent base, and they provide a universally appealing service. Everybody, well almost everybody, loves libraries. They see themselves as constituents, with an obligation to help if they can.
- It is your job to determine if you are ready for a fundraising project. The Fundraising Readiness will help you decide.
- Getting more money for your library may not be as big a task as you think if you understand the principles of fundraising and apply them in the right places at the right time.
- You have to select the right fundraising activity to meet your fundraising goal. A used book sale might bring in enough money to buy a new photocopier, but trying to build a new library with money from used book sales is not very feasible.
- Fundraising is basically selling. It is selling an investment in your cause. Successful sales people base their sales approach on the following:

  1. Is it the right product?
  2. Does the customer need the product?
  3. Is this the right time?
  4. Is the price right for the customer?
  5. Is it the right vendor?

Fund-raisers need to relate their solicitation to these keys of selling:

- The key to getting to "yes" is saying, "Will you give $5,000 to the library building fund?" and then being silent until after the donor speaks.
- Donor recognition and saying thank you appropriately are the keys to additional giving and good public relations.
- You can avoid misunderstandings and hurt feelings by having a gift policy in place and broadly communicated.

BIBLIOGRAPHY

Aalto, Madeleine, and Trevor Knight. 1999. *Fundraising: Alternative Financial Support for Public Library Services.* Lanham, Md.: Scarecrow Press. Believing in the premise that public libraries cannot survive on tax funds alone, the authors have delivered a powerful little book on how to raise money from alternative funding.

Covey, Stephen R. 1991. *Principle-Centered Leadership.* New York: Summit Books. This book gives a no-frills way of becoming a trustworthy and competent leader, using certain basic principles of life and relationships. It teaches the relationship between trust, empowerment, and alignment.

Kelly, Kathleen S. 1998. *Effective Fundraising Management.* Mahwah, N.J.: Lawrence Erlbaum Associates. This book could be used as a textbook on fundraising. This easy-to-read book covers the history and basics of fundraising. It is unique to find a single book with so much information for the novice as well as the experienced fundraiser.

National/CASA Association. 2002. *28 Principles of Fund Raising* [Online]. Available: www.casanet.org/program-management/resource-dev/28.htm [2002, March 17]. This Web site suggests principles that can make a difference in the way you solicit money.

Stallings, Betty, and Donna McMillion. 1999. *How to Produce Fabulous Fundraising Events: Reap Remarkable Returns with Minimal Effort: Includes Step-By-Step Guide to the Perfect Fundraising Event.* Pleasanton, Calif.: Building Better Skills. This book stresses the significance of volunteers and the rules for volunteer guidance. This work should be required reading for everyone who is remotely connected with fundraising. The chapter "Choosing the Right Event" is right on target. Buy this book and read it before your next fundraiser.

Thornburg, David D. 1998. *Brainstorms and Lightning Bolts: Thinking Skills for the 21ˢᵗ Century.* Los Altos, Calif.: Starsong Publications. This is a good book for anyone who wants to expand the possibility thinking of a fundraising group.

You're in the MONEY!: Fundraising Fundamentals 1994. Videocassette. Towson, Md.: American Library Association Video/Library Video Network. This video will teach you how to tackle the duties of a fundraiser, organize a campaign, ask for money and get results and start a foundation.

Chapter 2

Increasing Regular Funding

ASKING FOR MORE MONEY

The best way to get more money for your library is to ask the people who already allocate money to the library to give you more. If you normally ask a city council or a county commission to approve your budget, this chapter will teach you how to ask for more money. If you have the option of going directly to the voters with a referendum to increase the mill levy, this chapter will give you the tools to make it happen. Of all the ideas in this book, these two options are the most efficient and most effective ways to get the most money over time for your library. Increased tax support is renewable year after year. You don't have to go out and raise the same amount of money next year. Look to the governing body or the voters before you try any of the other ideas in this book. The suggestions in this chapter apply to either of these efforts. You can also use some of the techniques we discussed in Chapter 1.

ASSESS YOUR PRESENT FUNDING

Every library in the world has a source of regular funding, and that is the first place to look if you need more money. Whether you are in a small public library with a few thousand titles or university library with millions of volumes, you know how regular funding comes to your library. You know the source of money to buy books and pay for upkeep of the library. Once you have decided that current income is not enough to meet present demands for service, you can use the help in this chapter to figure out how to get more money from regular sources.

It is perfectly legitimate to seek more money from the places that already fund your library. Public libraries are funded by taxes on local property; or some other form of taxes. School libraries are supported by taxes through the school district, and academic libraries receive an allocation from the university coffers.

You already *need* more money for your library or you would not be reading this book right now. You probably understand the budgeting process. Wouldn't you like a bigger share of the pie? Chances are you have to ask someone in a position of authority to change the current pattern of funding and do something more for the library. You may have to approach a dean, a school superintendent, or the city council. These are the places to start, depending on the type of library. You need to find out what it would take to get more money and then ask for it.

Ask yourself this question: "What three things does our library require the most?" If you can answer this question you are on your way to getting the money you need for your library. Your answers might be:

1. We need more books and materials.
2. We need more online databases.
3. We need more staff members.
4. We need to replace all of our computers.
5. We need to offer more classes on computer literacy.
6. We need more money to maintain the library.

And so on.

REINVENT LIBRARY SERVICES

In the past twenty years the role of the library in the community has changed dramatically. While people still come to the library to get a book to read, they are coming to libraries for a greater variety of services. Computers have all but taken over in many libraries. Audio books and videos are becoming the format of choice for some library users. Reference librarians are becoming computer tutors, and members of the circulation staff have become the gatekeepers for public access computers. Community information staff members are technology instructors because libraries are trying to fill the technology knowledge gap. Much of this shift away from traditional roles in libraries has occurred just in the past ten years. If we don't reinvent our libraries we will find ourselves serving a shrinking constituency. If we do reinvent our libraries we may find ourselves doing it without an increase in funding. How will we survive?

An interesting way to begin to find the answer to the question of reinventing the library is ask the library staff two questions: 1) If we had a 25 percent increase in funding, what services would we add, how would we spend the money? 2) Is their any service we are doing really well right now that could be eliminated altogether? The answers to these questions will give you a good start on reinventing your library and defining what is really important, because it will encourage the staff to think creatively about the future of the library. The answers will be different for every library. You cannot ask for more money just because you want more money; you have to have a plan to enhance services. The new money has to make a difference in library services.

DEVELOP A WINNING CASE STUDY

Whether you are using a referendum or making an appeal to the governing body you will need a case study. A case study is a document you prepare to explain the library's mission and vision. It includes a summary of your current situation and explains where you want to go in the future. It ends with a specific list of improvements you plan to make in the library and how much money you need to make it happen. Have it printed professionally and share it with the people you are asking to vote for more money.

Start with the mission statement of your library. A good mission statement is easy to remember and easy to quote and tells the public what they can expect at your library. Write it in 25 words or less—and put it in terms of benefits to the customer.

Make a list of three things you will do with the extra money when you got it. Set a goal. Write it down! There is tremendous power in creating a vision. If you can write it down you can have it.

Use the Power of Writing Goals

About five years ago my library board asked me to create a five-year budget. At the time increased revenue seemed impossible because we were under a statewide tax lid, but I went ahead and did the five-year budget. We needed a clear vision of our financial needs in five years. The board had the authority to exempt the library from the tax lid, but when it came to a vote, not enough board members were willing to vote to make it happen. Eventually the tax lid was removed by the state legislature, which resulted in a revenue increase for the library. Today, there is an uncanny resemblance between the five-year budget I developed, and what really happened.

Every good goal has to have a number and a date. Otherwise it is just a wish. I cannot overemphasize the importance of writing down your goals.

Checklist for Library Image and Performance

1. Is the name of your library clearly visible from the street?
2. Are library hours visible from the street?
3. Is library parking adequate?
4. Is library parking especially marked for short-term parking?
5. Is parking for patrons with disabilities clearly marked?
6. Does the library have a curbside book deposit for after-hours book-return?
7. Do library grounds and exterior appearance meet or exceed community standards?
8. Is the library accessible to the handicapped?
9. Are library hours adequate to meet community needs?
10. Is the library collection current and readily available?
11. Do the books look new and inviting to the reader?
12. Does the physical arrangement draw people in?
13. Is the staff friendly and courteous?
14. Is the staff knowledgeable and helpful?
15. Is the library a nice place to be?

Figure 1-2-1 Checklist for Library Image and Performance

ANALYZE YOUR LIBRARY'S IMAGE AND PERFORMANCE

We never get a second chance to make a first impression. Lots of people drive by your library every day, but few of them come in. Their image of the library will be based on what they see from the outside. They will notice the lawn, the parking, the exterior of the building, the landscaping, and the signage. If they feel positive about these things they will be more inclined to come in and see what is inside. Once they get there they should feel welcome and free to look around or ask questions. Tasteful, well-designed signs should direct them to important places in the library. The staff should be helpful and ready to answer questions.

Physical and emotional barriers can create a negative image and keep people from coming back. I remember my first visit to a small library in the Central Kansas Library System. It was a 1908 Carnegie building. After climbing eleven steps and turning sideways to get through a narrow door, I stood in the entrance of the library. The first thing I saw was a huge built-in oak circulation desk that was flanked by two large pillars. The desk was so close that I felt trapped. Behind the desk sat a stern-faced librarian. What an impression! I wanted to turn around and walk out.

Our job is to create a positive image in the minds of those who come

Two Lists

People Who Use the Library	People Who Control Library Funding

Figure I-2-2 Two Lists

to our library. It will be easier to get the money we need if we do.

Figure I-2-1 is a checklist to appraise your situation and develop a strategy to get more support for your library.

Sometimes perception is more important than reality. A poorly kept lawn or parking lot with weeds growing in it may have no connection to the quality of material or the service in the library, but many people form opinions about the library from what they see on the outside. A shabby inside could be just as damaging to the library's image. How people feel about the library makes a difference. If the answers to these questions suggest the need to fix something about the library's image, make the effort to do it before you ask for more money.

MAKE A LIST OF LIBRARY USERS AND LIBRARY FUNDERS

On one side of a page make a list of key individuals, special groups or audiences who use your library. Name names as well as organizations. On the other side of the page make a list of all those people who control funding for the library. How do the lists match? For example: Is the mayor on the list of library users? Are City Council members on the list of library users? Are members of the library board on the first list? If they are you probably already have good support for the library. If not, look for ways to get both lists to look similar.

You may not feel comfortable doing something as overt as taking the mayor to lunch, but you could make a photocopy of a magazine article about golfing or gardening, provided you know he or she likes to golf or garden, and send the photocopy to him or her. The subject of the article doesn't matter as long as you are reasonably sure the topic will be of interest to the mayor. You are not trying to establish a long-term personal connection with the mayor or members of the city council. You are trying to help them to become regular library users.

Do you send an information packet to your board members before regular board meetings? If you do, send copies of the same materials to the mayor, members of the city council, the city clerk, and the city manager. The packet might contain minutes of the last meeting, the agenda for the upcoming meeting, and a report from the library director to board members.

Have the library join the local chamber of commerce. Attend the meetings and invite other business people to visit the library. In my town the Chamber of Commerce has weekly coffees hosted by various members around town. The library hosts a coffee every year during National Library Week. This gives us a chance to show off new services and generally promote the library. It makes the members of the Chamber feel that the library belongs to them, too.

GETTING MORE TAX REVENUE

In public libraries there are basically two ways to get more tax money for the library. The first way is to get the residents to vote for the increase in general funding or a bond issue through a tax referendum. The second is to get the governing body to appropriate additional funding through their normal powers to levy taxes.

Gathering Statistics

You need to convince the residents or the city council to increase funding for the library. The first place to start is to gather statistics. They will help you make your case for additional funding. If circulation or other output measures have increased dramatically in the past five years and funding has remained constant you can make a case for more money. If the population has increased and the number of registered borrowers has doubled you can make a case for more money. As you gather and analyze the data you will develop points that will help make your case for more funding.

Most state libraries publish public library statistics. You should be able to find the answer to most of the questions below from the annual statistics report. You can get a sense for how your library compares to itself in previous years, how it compares with other libraries your size in the state, and with other agencies in the city. If the budget for another city agency has doubled in the last ten years, and the library's budget has only increased ten percent, you have a good argument for getting

Sample Questions for Gathering Budget Statistics

1. What is the city population?

2. How many registered borrowers does the library have?

3. What percent of city residents have library cards?

4. How many borrowers live outside the library district?

5. How many books does your library have?

6. How many books per capita?

7. How does this compare to other libraries of your size in the state?

8. How many hours per week is your library open?

9. How does this compare to other similar sized libraries?

10. What was last year's circulation?

11. What was the circulation total before that?

12. What was the circulation five years ago?

13. How many circulations per capita last year?

14. How does this compare with other libraries in your area?

15. What is your library's total budget?

16. What percent comes from the city?

17. What percent comes from the county?

18. What percent comes from the state?

19. What percent comes from other sources?

20. How do these figures compare with statewide averages?

21. How much money did you spend on books last year?

22. How much was spent on salaries?

23. How much was spent on operations?

24. How do these figures compare to other libraries in your area?

25. Was the expenditure for books and materials higher, lower, or the same?

Figure I-2-3 Sample Questions for Gathering Budget Statistics

Selecting the Right Budget Appeal	
Appeal	Example
Funding rule of state library:	"Local funding of public libraries must be the same level or higher each succeeding year to be eligible for state aid."
Rule of accrediting body:	"The North Central Accreditation Association says that our school library must have 10,000 more books to keep our accreditation."
Comparison to other libraries:	"Other libraries in towns the same size as ours receive $500,000 from the city—we only receive $350,000 from our city."
Comparison to a relevant standard:	"State public library standards for a library our size call for 100 periodical subscriptions. We have only 50 subscriptions."
Comparison of a particular measurement over time:	"In 1990 the library received 5.1 percent of the city's tax revenue. Today it receives 3.6 percent of the city revenue."
Identify a library service valued by members of the city commission:	If two or three members of the city commission have said they like what the library is doing for children, emphasize the value of the library's story hour.
Call on the knowledge of recognized experts:	Select libraries specialists that are far enough away to be recognized as authorities. "The State Librarian says that we should be spending 65 to 70 percent of our budget on salaries and benefits."
Show specific benefit to the city officials:	"The library is an information place for city officers, the Mayor, and council members." Or "Helping the library will make friends in the community."
Point out a sense of fairness over salaries:	"Is it right for city employees to earn $10.00 per hour, while comparable library workers earn only $8.00?"
Take advantage of community pride:	"The library is a source of satisfaction for the whole community. Let's keep it a place of beauty and a symbol of our city's dedication to progress."

Figure 1-2-4 Selecting the Right Budget Appeal

more money for the library. If the budget for a library in a town the same size as your town was the same as your budget 20 years ago, and is now double your budget, this would be a good argument for more money.

The most important questions in Figure I-2-3 are those that deal with comparing your library to itself over time, and the questions that compare your library to other libraries your size today.

Select the Right Appeal to Support Your Budget Request

Not every budget appeal will work for every library, but many of them will work for most libraries.

Whatever you decide to do, make sure you have the unanimous support of the library board. You don't want a dissenting board member showing up at the city council meeting to argue against your request for additional money.

APPEALING TO THE GOVERNING BODY

If a referendum is not an option, or if you think you will have a better chance of getting the increase through the city council, determine the best strategies and go for it.

Preparing Your Appeal to the Governing Body for Increased Funding

Use these questions to help clarify your thinking and give you some ideas on how to proceed:

1. What arguments (justifications) will you use?
2. What statistics will you use?
3. Do they support your argument?
4. What will be the format of your presentation? (Written only. Will you have a chance to speak?)
5. Is your written proposal clearly written and easy to understand?
6. Do your charts, graphs, etc., support your arguments? (Select only the best ones for your presentation.)
7. Is everything neatly done and easy to understand?
8. Who will make the presentation? (Who has the most clout with the City Council?)
9. How will you pre-test your presentation? (Try it on friends or co-workers?)
10. How will you handle questions? (Avoid answering a question by repeating parts of your presentation.)
11. Who do you have lined up to lobby the governing body in support of your budget?

Plan Well for the Library's Budget Request

If you are the one who will make the presentation to the governing body, here are a few suggestions that may help.

Prepare well prior to appearing before the governing body to make your budget request. Think of everything you can to help your cause.

Try to figure out everything someone might say to argue against your presentation. Try to think like the council members will think. Envision your presentation from their viewpoint. Then envision yourself standing up in front of the council and making a flawless speech. Mentally rehearse it over and over again in your mind. This will strengthen your position.

First, establish the library as a viable, valuable service organization. Try any or all of the following targets:

- Seventy-five percent of the people in our town have a library card.
- Last year we circulated (number) volumes.
- This is equal to (number) books circulated per capita.
- The president of the chamber of commerce said, "We have the best library in the state."
- No other agency in town does what the library does.
- In a survey we did last year, (number) percent of the people said they got what they wanted when they came to the library.
- The library meets the knowledge, information, and reading needs of the people.
- Interlibrary loan expands the resources for our patrons.
- We meet the special needs of shut-ins through our home delivery service.
- The library saves people money. For every book they can get at the library free and don't have to buy, they save about $30.00.

This is your time to brag on your library. Do it. You are showing confidence and commitment—not conceit. Think of as many positive things to say about your library as you can.

The next step is to use the budget and existing conditions to illustrate your library's need. Start by analyzing the budget and determine the library's priorities. Use only the data that will present the library's need. Be specific, yet brief in describing the situation. Know exactly what you want. Make a specific request. Ask for a dollar amount. Be silent. Wait for questions.

If you have a board member who has influence with the governing body and is willing to make the presentation, invite him or her to do it. If he or she is willing to use his or her influence to encourage increased support for the library so much the better. A librarian making the presentation may be perceived as being self-serving.

Use a PowerPoint presentation. If you can take the time to organize your thoughts and facts and present them in a colorful and graphic way you may increase your chances for success.

CREATE A WINNING STRATEGY TO PASS A REFERENDUM

Success in passing a referendum starts with public awareness of the need. If people think you have enough money for the library they won't vote to give you more. Inflation used to be the money-gobbling dragon we all pointed to. When double-digit inflation was prevalent and funding levels for the library remained the same, everyone understood the need. Inflation has leveled out and inflation isn't taking as big a bite out of our budgets today, but we still need valid arguments to get the money we need to run our libraries. We may need to be more creative now that we don't have a money-gobbling dragon to point at.

Learn from These Success Stories

In 1981 the Great Bend Public Library was struggling to survive. Revenue had remained the same for five years because mill levy limits for public libraries in Kansas had been fixed in state statute for the past 30 years. The economy was experiencing double-digit inflation and the tax base was not keeping pace. Since the city council was unwilling to increase our revenue, we went directly to the voters. We asked them to vote to increase the library's mill levy from three mills to four. Under the laws of Kansas a majority of voters can set aside the levy limit set by the legislature for their library and establish a new higher levy limit for the library. The issue in Great Bend passed by a 67 percent margin.

It didn't happen just because we asked the voters to vote for it. The referendum passed because we organized the citizens and they all worked together to make it happen. The library was perceived as an essential service in the community. It was already doing a good job and the people wanted to see it continue.

If the library has increased its share of the city budget over time, you must be doing something right. Figure out how it happened and keep it up. Who can argue with success?

Select Some Ideas from Key Strategies

- *Get help from the Friends of the Library.* In my town a few years ago we organized the Friends-of-the-Great Bend Public Library. Immediately we started a campaign to pass a tax referendum. Local leaders pitched in and donated money to finance the campaign. Everyone worked hard and felt good when we won passage by 62 percent of the vote.
- *Involve local leaders.* The mayor of Ida, Illinois, was a helpful member of the Friends. With his assistance, the Friends wrapped a crepe

paper "blue ribbon" around the entire library building to publicize the election. They also wrapped blue ribbons around trees on city property all around the town to remind people to support the library. Not all of this was exactly fundraising, but it was part of the overall program. Newspapers and television stations from neighboring Rockford, Illinois, covered the event. The referendum passed by 72 percent.

- *Publish your story in the newspaper.* Use the newspaper to let people know why the library needs more money. Publish a list of people who will let you use their name as being in favor of the tax referendum. If you have to pay for advertising in the newspaper determine beforehand if it is legal to use library funds to promote the passage of a referendum. If it is not legal you will need to use funds from other sources.

- *Tell your story on television.* You should be able to get some time on local television to provide factual information about the library's need and the cost of the tax increase to the taxpayers.

- *Use yard signs.* If possible find someone outside the library to pay for the signs. Use volunteers to assemble the signs and distribute them around town. The people who help you will vote for the tax increase. The people who let you put a sign in their yard will vote for the library. And if there are more signs for you than against you, you will probably win the referendum election.

DEVELOP OTHER STRATEGIES WHEN A TAX REFERENDUM IS NOT POSSIBLE

If raising taxes is not an option for you, either because of the laws in your state or because you are part of an educational institution, you need to find out what you can do to influence those who are in charge of allocating institutional resources. In most academic situations, going through channels first is the politically correct thing to do. If you are a school librarian, at least get the permission of the building principal before going directly to the district superintendent. To do otherwise would be like committing professional suicide.

There is a right way to present your request. Earlier in this chapter we talked about gathering statistics and selecting appropriate strategies. These guidelines are still appropriate, even though you may be making an appeal to your principal or dean. If you can convince him or her of the need for more money for your library, you may have done all you need to do. The various appeals under the heading "Select the right appeal to support your budget request" on page 191 will be just as valid for you as for someone in a public library.

My first choices to try would be to compare the growth rate of the district's budget to the growth rate of the library's budget. The authority of the accreditation standards is also a good argument. Comparing your library to the library in another institution may not work too well if their district budget is proportionally higher than your district. If you need more computers in the library, point to how busy the computers you have now are.

If your principal or dean isn't willing to carry your budget to the next level, ask for permission to carry it yourself. Don't do it without permission. You might even try asking your principal or dean to go with you to make the presentation. Remember this: superintendents and college presidents trust their principals and deans, and will look to them for recommendations about the library's budget. Going over their heads could backfire, so be careful.

If you have tried everything you can through customary routes and you still feel powerless maybe you need to find a "bigger bat." Find one big enough to change the thinking of the decision-makers to give more money to the library. A "bigger bat" is anyone outside the organization who has influence with the decision makers inside the organization. A "bigger bat" could be all of the teachers in the school or all of the professors on campus. As a body they have legitimate power. If you can gain their backing by supporting what they do in the classroom, you may be able to call upon them to use their combined influence to persuade those in power to stand up for the library.

A "bigger bat" might be the authority of the accreditation standards. These standards might compel someone in power to increase funding for the library. This is truly a "bigger bat" that you can use, but use it carefully. Those in authority may not care about accreditation for your library.

Learn How Districtwide Funding Works

In my first job as a school librarian I was a novice to the political intrigues of the school district. My predecessor had left some money in the book budget for her replacement to spend on new books. I was new to the job and wanted to get my feet on the ground before I spent any money. Then before the holidays, the principal came around and asked all of the teachers for their wish lists for end-of-the-year spending. The fiscal year was the calendar year and I didn't know it. I requested money for books in the amount I had left in the book budget, but the money that had been left in the library's budget went for mats for the gym. In the worst of all cases you may have to wait until the political climate changes.

SUMMARY

You can increase funding from regular sources if you will take the time to plan and develop strategies that will work. Keep these suggestions in mind:

- *The best place to get more money for your library is the same place you get it now.* Your right to receive funding from current sources has already been established. All you have to do is convince those that control the purse strings to give you more.
- *Start with your mission statement.* Clearly define what you want to do with the new money. Try to state it in terms of benefits to the public.
- *Develop the statistics you want to use to make your case.* Prepare your arguments and make the presentation to the people who will make the decision.
- *Get the word out.* Tell the public why they should vote to give more money to the library. Give them a few good reasons to vote for the library.
- *Give the governing body the same message.* If you have to appear before a governing body, follow the same plan, even though your appeals might be a little different.

Regardless of the venue for your presentation remember that the image of the library in the minds of the people has to be positive. A whining complaining appeal will not serve your case. The library should be a showplace in the community where people get what they want.

BIBLIOGRAPHY

Craft, Mary Anne. 1999. *The Funding Game: Rules for Public Library Advocacy*. Lanham, Md.; New York: Scarecrow Press; Neal-Schuman Publishers. When it comes to library advocacy *The Funding Game* tells it like it is. It discusses dealing with voter opposition, getting people to work together, and forming partnerships. Besides telling us how to do it, this book shows us how others have succeeded.

Governing and Funding Metropolitan Public Libraries. 1997. Evanston, Ill.: Urban Libraries Council. This book gives us a quick view of the various ways metropolitan libraries are funded across the country. It provides a good base of information for those who are responsible for promoting funding metropolitan libraries. It includes data on library boards, library governance, demographics, and funding trends.

Steele, Victoria, and Stephen D. Elder. 2000. *Becoming a Fundraiser: The Principles and Practice of Library Development*, 2d ed. Chicago: American Library Associations. This book gives us an honest view of fundraising from the inside. It tells how to select the right fundraising program based on the library, the administration, and individual skills of key participants.

Chapter 3

Exploring Funding Through Successful Grant Writing

TO WRITE OR NOT TO WRITE

Writing a grant is the first avenue some librarians want to explore when they are faced with a financial crisis. Maybe they think they won't have to ask someone for money. Maybe they think it will be easier because all they have to do is fill out an application form. The truth is grant writing is a highly specialized skill and requires more attention to detail than most people possess. Grant funding is often only available for special projects that are not part of the library's mainstream programs or services. Grant funding rarely pays for ongoing operations the way regular funding does. So, writing a successful grant and carrying out its objectives are often as much work as the grant is worth.

Before you decide to write a grant, answer these questions:

- What are you going to do?
- Why do you need to do it?
- Who is going to do it?
- How will they do it?
- How much money will the project cost?
- What do you plan to buy if you get the money?
- How will you evaluate the success of your project?

Your answers will give you the vision you need to write a successful grant. This chapter will help you weave your way through the maze of grant writing. Some directors think of grant funding as one segment of regular funding. If that is the case in your library and consistent successful grant funding is an integral part of your budget, hire a professional grant writer. At least have someone on staff whose job description includes writing grants. Make sure the person in that position has the experience and the skill to do the job.

When you write a grant you are still asking someone to give money to your library. The good thing about writing a grant is the grant readers are on your side. They *want* to give you the money you are asking for. The problem is there are a lot of other people asking for the same dollars you want. Your job is to convince the grant readers that your project will do a better job of accomplishing the objectives of the granting agency than the other proposals they see.

Grants are usually based on a specific project. You want to accomplish a specific goal like providing Internet access to a special population group or teaching computer literacy to senior citizens. You develop a project with goals, objectives, methodologies, evaluation, a budget, and plausible future funding. You believe this project will make a difference in the lives of the people you serve. You are asking someone with grant money to give to pay for your project.

Grant writing is like applying for a job. The employer advertises for applicants by outlining the essential elements of the job, describing the minimum qualifications for the applicant, and stating the amount of money the position will pay. Each applicant tries to convince the employer that his or her experience and qualifications make him or her the best person for the position. The employer looks for lack of experience or missing qualifications—anything to disqualify each potential employee. In the end the applicant that best matches the job requirements gets the job. With grant writing the applicant that does the best job of convincing the grant reviewers that his or her application best matches the grant requirement gets funded.

ALIGN YOUR GRANT WITH THE PURPOSES OF THE GRANT FUNDING AGENCY

The most important thing to remember about writing a grant is to align the purposes of your project to the purposes of the funding agency.

Permit me a short personal example. In the past 20 years we have shared our home with two house cats. Ginger got to sleep at the foot of our bed at night and Tiger did not. Ginger learned that she needed to align her body with our legs. Tiger insisted on sleeping with his body crossways across the foot of the bed. Tiger got kicked off the bed and had to find another place to sleep. The key to success for Ginger was to align herself with the people in the bed.

If we write a grant that is not aligned to the objectives of the granting agency, we will probably find ourselves looking for another source of funding. So, the first task in writing a grant is to find a grant source with objectives that match the project you want to accomplish. This strategy is preferable to developing a project and then trying to find a grant to match it.

Location disqualifies more grants than any other criteria. If you reside in Texas and a corporation wants to fund projects that will benefit its workers in California, there is no point to even applying. Once you clear that hurdle read the application materials carefully and determine if you have a chance of being funded. Some grant funders want their money to make a big difference for the projects they fund, so they make large grants to just a few, well-developed projects. Don't get suckered on a long shot, just because there is a lot of money involved. You could spend valuable time writing a grant that you have little or no chance of winning. I don't mean you shouldn't try. Just make sure your project fits the grant criteria exactly. Then take your time and give it your very best effort.

PLANNING FOR SUCCESS

Writing a successful grant proposal requires just as much planning as any other fundraising method. You start by figuring out what the community needs that the library can provide. There is not much you can do about child abuse or crime in the street, but there are some social ills you can address and if you had the money you might be able to do a good job.

Assess Community Needs

Critically assess the needs of your community and decide on a project that will make a big difference to the community. You are not in the business of childcare, but you could offer after-school programs for school-aged children. Technology training has not been a traditional library service, but you could teach people the basics of how to use a computer. Right now you can probably think of several projects that could help the people in your community. Pick a good one and go for it, even if it makes you stretch. Try something you can only do with the help of someone from outside your organization. It will have a greater impact on the community, and besides you will have a new partner. If you could have done the project on your own, you should have done it already.

A few years ago I observed a sharp increase in the number of people of Hispanic descent coming to our library. I knew we had only a few books written in Spanish. We needed many more books than we could afford. I wrote a series of grants to buy materials in Spanish. We now have an attractive collection for our Hispanic patrons. Entire families now come to the library. They use the computers, and they also check out books in Spanish and English. Children are teaching their parents to speak and read English using our bilingual books for children.

Size Up the Competition

It helps to review earlier grants that have already been funded by the granting agency. These grants will provide clues to writing a successful proposal. Call the applicants who had their grants funded and ask them to share a copy of their successful grant with you. If you can get access to the grants that were not funded, take a look at them. This will help you avoid the weaknesses of other grants.

Review your own grant. Compare it to a successful one, paragraph for paragraph. Then answer these questions:

- Does your grant measure up to previously funded proposals?
- Is there something in your grant that will cause grant readers to put it on the top of the pile?
- Do you have a unique approach to a serious problem?
- Is your plan easy to understand and conceptually doable?
- Does your application exude confidence that you can get the job done?

Funding Categories

Some funding agencies support only agencies dealing with the youth or the elderly or a specific ethnic group. Grant agencies that fund educational institutions may also award grants to public libraries. Check to see if any public libraries have been awarded grants in recent years. If not, you could be barking up the wrong tree.

Many funding agencies will specifically include what they will fund. If they specifically fund one or more of the objectives of your grant make sure you focus on what they will fund. Do not include elements you know they will not fund. It is all right to show local funds paying for the items the grant agency will not fund (see Figure I-3-1).

Nonfunding Categories

Certain foundations refuse to fund religious organizations or campaigns to eliminate or control specific diseases. Many foundations specifically state what they will not fund. They hope this will keep them from receiving a grant application that will not be considered. You might see a statement like this: "In order to make the best use of available funds, the foundation does not make grants for the following:" (Figure I-3-2)

Examples of Projects Granting Agencies Will Fund

- Construction projects up to a certain amount
- Engineering fees
- Fees for architectural drawings of a proposed facility
- Books and library materials
- Computers and electronic equipment
- Planning for a major project
- Salaries for the first three years of the project
- Travel for professional consultants
- Expenses connected with broadband connectivity to the Internet
- Murals or art displays that will be a permanent part of the facility.

Figure 1-3-1 Examples of Projects Granting Agencies Will Fund

---

Examples of Projects Granting Agencies May Not Fund

- Construction projects
- Capital campaigns
- Normal operating expenses
- Religious purposes
- Computer hardware equipment
- Advocacy purposes
- Political parties or campaigns
- Repayment of loans
- Multi-year funding

Figure 1-3-2 Examples of Projects Granting Agencies May Not Fund

Make sure that none of the objectives of your project fit any of these categories when a statement like this appears in the grant criteria.

FINDING GRANTS

Before you jump on the Internet to find grant funding for your next project, take a good look at home. What foundations and corporations offer grants right in your own backyard? If you have a Wal-Mart store go talk to the manager and find out how their grant program works. A local corporation may not have a giving program, but you might be able to get them to fund a project if you make a case that your project will benefit their employees.

Check with the State Library

Try your state library. Many states have programs to strengthen interlibrary loan or literacy. All state libraries administer LSTA (Library Service and Technology Act) funds. As part of their Five-year Plan, most states have a competitive grant program. If you have never written a grant before try writing an LSTA grant for a few thousand dollars, and see what you can learn from the experience. You will probably know the competition within the state, and you can count on feedback from the state library staff. LSTA competitive grants are awarded every year and you may have a better chance in the next round if your first grant is not funded.

Use the Internet

The Internet is the best place to go to find grant opportunities. Finding potential grant sources used to be a problem. Books were always out of date, and periodicals weren't much better. Now the Internet serves up a full plate of opportunities that boggle the mind. I went to a search engine on the Internet and typed in "grants for libraries." The search turned up 183 sites.

One of the first ones was The Council on Foundations Web site (www.cof.org). This is a nonprofit membership association of grant-making foundations and corporations. The Council exists to help grant writers connect with granting agencies.

Another site I found right away promotes the services of The Foundation Center (http://fdncenter.org/index.html). The Foundation Center has been in business for over 45 years with major centers in every state. Their Cooperating Collections are free funding information centers in libraries, community foundations, and other nonprofit resource centers that provide materials and services useful to grant seekers. They have vast print collections as well as a superb Web site.

Use This List of Internet Sites

Rather than give you a long list of grant opportunities for libraries you can find on the Internet, I am going to give you a short list and suggest that you do like I did. Go to a search engine like Altavista or Google and type in "grants for libraries" or some other phrase that will limit the number of sites you get and still give you the information you want.

List of Web Sites with Information on Grant Sources

These are a few of the many Web sites that highlight grant sources:

- Catalog of Federal Domestic Assistance—www.cfda.gov/public/faprs.htm.

- Institute for Museum and Library Services—www.imls.gov/grants/library/index.htm.
- Grant–Seekers Page—www1.surfsouth.com/~jperdew/grant.htm.
- The Grants for Libraries Hotline—www.grantshotline.com/lib/index.html.
- The University of Buffalo, Office of Sponsored Programs Administration—www.acsu.buffalo.edu/~edens/grants.html.
- The Body Heart and Soul of Grant Writing—www.friendcalib.org/newsstand/f3grant.htm>.
- University of Wisconsin Oshkosh, Office of Grants Proposal Writing Tips—www.uwosh.edu/departments/grants/tips.html.
- The Libri Foundation—www.teleport.com/~librifdn/index.html.

Books

The Big Book of Library Grant Money 1998-1999 presents state-by-state profiles of private and corporate foundations and direct corporate givers that are receptive to grant proposals from libraries. Most books including this one are usually obsolete by the time they are printed. I have not included a long list of books that have grant sources in them because other more reliable sources are available elsewhere. If you are inclined to find grant sources in books, go to one of the book-locating sources available to your library.

Newsletters

The online newsletter *Foundation News and Commentary* is a good place to find grant information. The Web site is http://intl.cof.org/foundationnews/index.html. *Grants for Libraries Hotline* is an excellent source to find out about grants, deadlines and profiles—www.grantshotline.com.

GRANT-WRITING TIPS

Before we get into the nitty-gritty of writing a grant, here are a few tips that have worked for others. They might help you avoid some problems.

- Read the grantor's guidelines and instructions carefully. Do not try to make the grantor's program fit what you want to do. Tailor your project to match the funding agency's priorities.
- Contact the secretary or executive director of the funding agency. Become acquainted with him or her. Try your project idea out on him or her. Most of the time the people who work for granting agencies are more than willing to answer questions as they come to you.

- Be innovative and creative! Knock their socks off with the newest greatest ideas they have ever seen. Grantors will rarely fund operating expenses. Who wants to pay for more of the same old stuff? Private foundations often seek creative solutions to problems they hope someone will solve.
- Propose a project that puts a fresh spin on an existing idea. If you can point to a previously funded grant that was successful, that will tell them you know how to make a grant work for you.
- Keep your goals realistic! It is important to have an evaluation plan. Grantors always want to know if the projects they fund are successful.
- Promote your proposal as a demonstration for other libraries. Explain how other libraries can replicate your project.
- Present a detailed reasonable budget. Know the cost of things before submitting your grant. Explain your budget even if you are not expected to do so.
- Find someone outside your organization to read and critique your draft application. He or she will discover holes in your presentation or lapses in the logic.
- Proofread the grant at least twice. Spelling and grammar errors do not convey a positive image and could make the difference between being funded and not.
- Follow the grantor's instructions precisely. Applications that do not exactly meet the funding agency's requirements will be turned away.
- Ask the grantor for reviewer comments if your grant is not funded. The comments often offer invaluable tips for future grant applications.
- Always write thank-you notes—even if your project is not funded initially.

WRITING THE GRANT

Write your grant so well that the grant readers will have to fund your grant. You don't have to write the grant all by yourself. Get whatever help you need to make your grant as good as you and others can make it. It is not like cheating in school if you get some help.

Howard Hillman and Karin Abarbanel in their book, *The Art of Winning Foundation Grants* (1975), give ten steps to success:

- Define your goal
- Assess your chances
- Organize your resources

- Identify your prospects
- Research your prospects in depth
- Make your initial contact
- Meet with the foundation
- Write your formal proposal
- Submit your formal proposal
- Follow up

Notice that writing the formal proposal is almost at the end of the list. Too often enthusiastic people jump to "action outbursts." They want to solve the problem immediately, without taking the time to assess the situation and plan appropriate actions.

Learn the Mechanics of Writing Well

If you feel that you need help with writing skills, read *The Elements of Style*, by William Strunk and E.B.White. It is one of the most clearly written books on the subject of writing. *Writing With Precision* (2000) by Jefferson D. Bates takes writing skill to the next step. Bates suggests preferring the active voice to the passive voice. This means the subject performs the action rather than being acted up. Note the difference in the following examples:

- The fundraising committee raised a million dollars. *Active voice.*
- A million dollars was raised by the fundraising committee. *Passive voice.*

(The grammar checker on my computer picked up the passive voice sentence right away.)

Get to the heart of things as soon as you can. Don't skip any points, but avoid spending too much time with any one point. You have to establish basic information about your library and its need, but don't overdo it.

Put yourself in the place of the grant proposal reader. Would you like to read a stack of 100 grants just like yours? Or would it make you tired after an hour? Would you want to read every last word of every proposal? Probably not! Do yourself and the grant reader a favor. Start by writing your grant proposal the way you normally write. Then cut it in half by taking out the words or sentences you don't need. Your writing will be better for it.

Keep the words that go together next to each other. Don't separate them. Take out the words that don't fit. Keep the adjectives next to the words they modify. Keep the verbs close to the nouns they act upon. Eliminate prepositional phrases at the end of sentences if the words that are left can carry your meaning without them. Use adverbs and adjectives sparingly.

Avoid weasel words. A weasel word is any word that weasels out of carrying its own weight in a sentence. A weasel word fails to convey a precise meaning. They are words that could be left out of a sentence and still leave the meaning intact.

Try using a semi-outline style. Separate your main points into paragraphs and use bullets or numbers for emphasis. This style is more open and accessible. Judge for yourself. Which of the following selections is easier to read?

> We need a literacy program in our community because thirty percent of the adult population read at or below the fourth grade level, ten percent of the people are foreigners whose first language is not English and forty percent of adults are not high school graduates.

Or this:

> We need a literacy program in our community because:
>
> - 30 percent of the adults can't read above fourth grade level.
> - 10 percent speak English as a second language.
> - 40 percent have not graduated from high school.

You are not writing masterful prose. You are writing a grant proposal and you want it to be funded. It won't be funded if your grant is not read. No one will read it if they have to hunt for your main points.

Get to the bottom line in the opening and repeat it again at the end. In the first paragraph or cover letter, state how much money you want and what you plan to do with it. The rest of your proposal will support and document your request. Don't make your reader wait till the end to discover the most important part.

It also helps to have a shtick—a special gimmick that makes you stand out above the rest. If you want to stand out in a crowd, you wear a red dress or wear a wild tie. Develop a style of writing that is easy to read, and filled with unique, graphic, even humorous, word pictures. Your grant proposal will look just like everyone else's unless you do something impressive to make it extraordinary.

The word image of a large man (Jim Swan) barely squeezing through a library door because it wouldn't open more than a few inches, created a vision that helped the McCracken (Kansas) Public Library secure a grant that guaranteed its completion. Truth was everyone who came to the library had to go through the doorway sideways. A large man squeezing through the door of the library created an effective vision.

COMPLETING THE GRANT APPLICATION

Grant applications vary from agency to agency, but they all serve the same purpose. They are the official document used by all grant seekers. A printed application form or a standardized format promotes uniformity among all proposals, and they permit grant reviewers to compare all of the grants on the same basis.

Follow the guidelines exactly. If they say two pages, then that's all you write. You might have a lot more to say, but don't. Write the grant in the order that is requested. Don't get creative because you think you know better.

Be realistic about what your staff can handle. Too many organizations submit projects that are far above their capability. The money may look good when you apply for the grant, but if you don't have the expertise or the staff to follow through, you could be embarrassed.

The first page is usually dedicated to identifying the agency requesting the funds—often referred to as "boilerplate." About the only thing you can do wrong on this page is to spell your own name wrong, fail to fill in an important blank, or make so many corrections that it looks sloppy.

The next section asks for names of your partner organizations and those you are working with to accomplish the project. Partnering has become a buzzword in recent years for grant givers and grant seekers. Make sure your partners do not weaken the overall proposal. It may seem that the more partners you can work with on a project the better the chances for funding, but that may not always be true. Don't introduce partners who have nothing to bring to the table. They may not contribute to the success of the project.

Stating the Need

The next step is to state the need you are going to alleviate if they fund your grant. You don't have to make it sound like starving children in Africa, but you need to present your case in a way that will make the grant reviewers care about the need. It could be as simple as the dramatic influx of an ethnic group in your community that needs reading material in their own language.

Numbers make a difference. Include authoritative statistics if you intend to target a particular segment of the population. Find some hard numbers gathered by the U.S. Census Bureau. You can't just pull the numbers out of thin air. Your project could focus on the specific needs of children under a certain age or adults over a certain age. Population numbers will document the number of people you intend to serve and quantify the depth of the need. You can get them from the U.S. Census Bureau (www.census.gov/). If you are applying to a corporation or the foundation of a corporation, identify the number of employees of the corporation who will benefit from the project.

Next describe the identifiable need common to this population group. For example "Ten percent of the Hispanic population in our town read English." or "Ten percent of the people over 65 are physically unable to get to the library." Or "Fifty percent of the people between the ages of 40 and 70 don't know how to access the Internet."

In the narrative include a list of the needs that will be addressed with your project. This will make it easier for the grant readers to learn what needs you intend to address. Don't make them hunt for the main points of your proposal. Put them right out where they can see them. Remember that you cannot alleviate all of the ills in the community with one project. You are just trying to solve one problem in your little corner of the world.

Expressing Goals

After defining the problems you are going to solve, discuss the solutions you plan to implement. At this point you are not providing minute details, but giving more of an overview of what you plan to do. Keep your statement simple and straightforward. Don't use flowery language or obscure the meaning with long sentences or jargon. Some grant writers think that they have to write differently than they speak. They use language they would never use in public because no one would understand them if they did. I have heard grant reviewers say, "I have read this grant twice and I still don't know what they want to do." Make it easy for them to figure it out. Say what you are going to do. Make a short list of the project goals. Don't leave anything out, but don't multiply words either.

Quantify Your Goals

A goal without a number and a date is only a wish. Reaching 100 percent of your target population is unrealistic, so carve out a reasonable segment and make that your goal, e.g. "In the next year we plan to provide computer and Internet training for 1,000 of the 10,000 people in our service area." Or "During the period of the grant we plan to identify 25 homebound individuals and provide home delivery library service to at least 75 percent of them." Create a vision in the mind of the grant reader of your library after the grant is implemented.

Explaining the Implementation Phase

This section is for telling the grant reviewers how you are going to make the project happen. This could be like a timeline with each step following the previous one in a logical progression. Include the essential element of completing the grant. Don't leave important steps out, but avoid filling up the page with nonessential detail. For example "We plan to buy six computers and connect them to our existing Internet network." You don't need to include the details of securing bids from vendors, placing the order, paying the invoice when it comes, and so on. The essential task is buying six computers and connecting them to the Internet network.

Each step has to be logical and doable. Don't leave the grant reviewer wondering how you plan to get from Step II to Step III. If technology you plan to use is new to your library, mention that you have researched the technology and know that it will work the way you expect it to, e.g. "The wireless network we plan to use works well in other installations and we are confident that it will work in our library."

Be sure to include the promotion or public relations aspect of the project, especially if a totally new service will be offered. For example, explain how you will tell the people that the library's catalog is now online.

Planning for Evaluation

Begin with the end in mind. Every grant application asks how you will evaluate the project after it has been implemented. The granting agency wants to know what you will do to measure the success of the project. Methods of evaluation include focus groups, questionnaires, interviewing, data collection, advisory groups, using existing data, and structured observations.

Think ahead before selecting an evaluation technique. You will be expected to do whatever you put down. You don't need a degree in statistical analysis to evaluate a project. If computer literacy is a goal, you could count the number of people who attended your classes. Then ask the participants to write down what they learned from the class.

The evaluation section of an adult education grant application I saw once said, "We will use quantitative and qualitative analysis to determine the success of the grant." It might have been better to say, "We will count the number of students who enroll in our program and measure their progress by monitoring their test scores."

Some grants require an evaluation by an outside consultant. Be sure to include the cost of their services in the budget. Other granting agencies have very specific guidelines for evaluating the project. Know what they are from day one and gather the data required as the project unfolds. Don't wait until the end of the grant period to face recreating the necessary information from thin air.

Providing Financial Data

This is the section where you explain how much money you want and how you are going to spend it.

PROVIDE THE PROPOSED BUDGET

Two schools of thought compete for presenting the budget for a grant. Some grant writers think you should ask for more money than you need. Then when the grant is cut you will have enough money to complete the project. The other school of thought is to carefully document what the project will cost and ask for exactly what you need. The documentation should include detailed price quotes from selected low bidders. It is all right to add a small percent to the total as a contingency because unexpected extras will always turn up. I do not advocate the first strategy because those who read the grants can spot a padded budget quicker than a three dollar bill.

Do your homework well and present what you honestly estimate the project will cost. I have written several successful small grants. Before I did the budget I checked with vendors to find out the cost of the books, videos, or computer components we planned to purchase, and cited my sources. I didn't just pick some numbers out of the air. Who knows, one of the grant readers may call a vendor to check the validity of the numbers you present. It is not a good idea to underestimate the cost of any project. You could have to find additional funds to make up the difference if the grant is awarded.

Present the budget in a way that is easy to understand. Not telling the grant reader how much money you want is just as bad as not telling him or her what you want to do with the money. Don't forget to include any indirect costs if applicable. It wouldn't hurt to set the total amount with an extra line space or bold letters. Make sure all of the numbers add up. To omit such an important detail could put your grant in the rejected pile.

SHOW DETAILS OF EQUIPMENT PURCHASES

If your grant includes the purchase of equipment make sure you include a detailed list of the equipment you plan to purchase, including brand names and model numbers. If the equipment includes leading edge technology you may want to have a footnote to explain how it works or why it is necessary for the project. Base the budget figures on actual bids you have requested from the vendors. Don't hold back because you think your project may be too ambitious. Grant readers like visionary plans that cause people to stretch.

In 1999 the Central Kansas Library System submitted a competitive LSTA grant for technology training. We asked for $18,000 to buy equipment for a portable computer laboratory for technology training. There was only $50,000 available for all of the libraries in Kansas. We referred to our grant application as a "modest proposal." In our view it was a simple proposal without an ounce of fluff or padding. In the end we received $13,000 for the project. Thirteen thousand dollars was more than one fourth of all the money available in the state for technology training. The project is still considered one of the most successful LSTA projects in the state. This project enabled our staff to travel to the 17 counties in our system and teach librarians and local citizens how to use computers. There was nothing super-fantastic about the project. It just worked the way we envisioned it. The grant readers were able to understand what we wanted to do and how much it would cost. They awarded us the money to do it.

Project Future Funding

Nobody wants to fund a grant and then see it die after the grant money is spent. Some grants require a commitment from the applicants to keep the project going after the grant period has ended. Even if future funding is not a component of the budget, it is a good idea to include a statement on how you plan to continue the project. Weasel words often dominate this section of the grant because grant writers seem to want to avoid making a commitment to use their own money to keep a project going.

For several years I served on the grant review committee of the Kansas Library Network Board. We awarded competitive grants to libraries in Kansas for interlibrary loan development projects. Librarians that did not include a number and a date in this section got marked down. Here is an example of a good answer: "We believe that books on kitchen collectibles are so important to our readers that we plan to spend $500 a year for the next five years on this topic." Whatever you say has to be believable. Grant readers want to know if you are committed enough to spend your library's money to keep the project going. Tell them how much money you plan to spend.

Evaluation of the project is often left out. Unless the grant guidelines specifically call for an evaluation process, grant writers could be tempted to skip mentioning how the project will be evaluated. Funding agencies want outcomes, measurements, and results. Make sure to have a solid evaluation plan as part of the grant.

PROOFREADING THE GRANT

Before you type the final draft of your grant look it over yourself. Check for spelling and grammar. Check for excess words or phrases that don't carry their own weight. Make sure the numbers add up correctly. Then give it to a friend to look over your grant. Have him or her read it to see if he or she understands it. Correct the problems and print it out for the final time.

Do a final check using the checklist at the end of this chapter. Make sure the address on the envelope is correct and get it in the mail on time.

AVOIDING COMMON MISTAKES

How many times have you heard someone say "It was just a simple mistake"? Sometimes we know better but we don't do better. Other times there is nothing we can do to improve our chances for being funded. Here are some common reasons that grants are not funded:

1. Available funding is limited.
2. Application is poorly written or appears to be sloppy.
3. Request exceeds limits for a single grant.
4. Budget numbers are inaccurate or lack detail.
5. Grant was not received on time.
6. Grant lacks evidence of participation of the target audience to be served.
7. Planning process is weak or sketchy.
8. Project lacks a logical plan of events.
9. Proposal lacks necessary detail.
10. Staffing appears to be inadequate or not specific enough.

You might submit a perfect grant application and still see it rejected. Most foundations and corporations have limited resources. The grant description will usually say how much money is available or state the maximum amount that will be awarded for a single grant. Do not get discouraged if your grant is rejected. Try again next year.

Checklist for Writing a Grant

1. Do the goals and objectives of your grant match the criteria established by the granting agency?
2. Is the community need clearly stated?
3. Does your grant appear perfect in every detail?
4. Did you tell the grant reviewer what you plan to do in one unambiguous sentence?
5. Is the proposed implementation clearly outlined in logical steps that follow each other?
6. Is the budget realistic and within the funding guidelines of the funding agency?
7. Do all of the numbers in the budget add up correctly?
8. Does the tone of the grant exude confidence?
9. Did someone outside the library proofread the grant?
10. Are all of the required signatures in order?

Figure I-3-3 Checklist for Writing a Grant

USE A CHECKLIST FOR WRITING A GRANT

Use the final checklist above (Figure I-3-3) to help you avoid some of the errors you could make.

GETTING OUTSIDE HELP

If you have never written a grant before and you think you want to write one now, get some help. Buy a book on grant writing and read it. Ask for help from the state library or regional library system. Hire a professional grant writer if the amount of the grant warrants the expense. All of these options are explained more fully in Chapter 8.

SUMMARY

Applying for a grant may seem to be an easier way to raise money for your project because you don't have to ask people for money face to face. True you don't actually walk into someone's office and sell someone on your project. You don't have to recruit a hundred volunteers to solicit donations from the community, but you are still asking someone to give you money. People give to people and your grant proposal has to be read by at least one real live person. He or she may not read more than the first paragraph, so make the first sentence unforgettable.

Don't hang all your hopes for fundraising on a single grant. Only one grant in ten is funded. The basics of research, planning, and organization still apply.

When you write a grant remember to:

- Keep it simple.
- Be brief.
- Don't use jargon.

Grant proposals are like resumes. You are trying to sell your idea to someone by proving that you can't wait to go to work for the funding agency, carrying out their goals and objectives in your hometown. The funder has the money and you are going to do the work.

If you are serious about grant writing as a fundraising activity, get some help. Don't try to do it all by yourself. Attend a workshop. Read some books. Pick the brains of other professionals. Check with the people at the state library.

BIBLIOGRAPHY

Annual Register of Grant Support 2001: A Directory of Funding Sources. 2001. New Providence, N.J.: R.R. Bowker.

Barber, Peggy, and Linda Crowe. 1993. *Getting Your Grant: A How-To-Do-It Manual for Librarians.* New York: Neal-Schuman. *Getting Your Grant* is a comprehensive guide to finding, researching, and writing grants. From determining whether an idea is fundable, to evaluating the project. How-to sections include approaching funding sources, doing the necessary research, creating a realistic timetable, and recruiting support for projects.

Bates, Jefferson D. 2000. *Writing With Precision: How to Write So That You Cannot Possibly Be Misunderstood.* New York: Penguin. Bates shares the benefit of his 40-plus years of experience writing. His ten principles and seven axioms of professional writers give us some powerful clues to effective writing.

Belcher, Jane C., and Julia M. Jacobsen. 1992. *From Idea to Funded Project: Grant Proposals that Work,* 4th ed. Phoenix, Ariz.: Oryx Press. Primarily written for members of colleges and universities who want to turn an idea into a grant proposal. It defines roles of departmental and administrative staff, specific parts of a proposal, and more. It covers presenting a proposal, its management, and evaluation. It has samples of forms and grant applications.

Brewer, Ernest W., Charles M. Achilles, and Jay R. Fuhriman. 1998. *Finding Funding: Grantwriting From Start to Finish, Including Project Management and Internet Use,* 3d ed. Thousand Oaks, Calif.:

Corwin Press. This book cites lots of successful funding efforts. It is replete with advice on locating funding, Internet options, project management, and examples of successful funding efforts.

Brewer, Ernest W., Charles M. Achilles, and Jay R. Fuhriman. 1995. *Finding Funding: Grantwriting and Project Management from Start to Finish*, 2d ed. Thousand Oaks, Calif.: Corwin Press. This is a powerful book on applying for federal funding. It explains the components of a proposal, how it is reviewed, and how it is implemented.

Geever, Jane C., and Patricia McNeill. 1997. *Foundation Center's Guide to Proposal Writing*. Rev. ed. New York: Foundation Center. Highlights proposal writing as part of planning. Emphasizes the partnership between the nonprofit organization and the donor. Details establishing funding priorities, writing the grant, and gathering needed information.

Hall, Mary. 1988. *Getting Funded: A Complete Guide to Proposal Writing*, 3d ed. Portland, Oreg.: Portland State University Continuing Education Publications. The author reviews more than 10,000 grant requests each year at the Weyerheauser Company Foundation. Dr. Hall is a frequent consultant to government and corporate funding organizations. This workbook-like text first covers how to do the planning and information gathering tasks prior to writing the grant. It leads the reader into the principles involved in the actual writing of a proposal. This book is a must-read for anyone who wants to write a grant proposal

Hall-Ellis, Sylvia D., and Frank W Hoffman. 1999. *Grantsmanship for Small Libraries and School Library Media Centers*. Englewood, Colo.: Libraries Unlimited. Almost every school librarian has faced the daunting task of writing a grant to get more money for his or her library. This book can lower the anxiety level for anyone who has to write a grant. The chapters take the grant right through the process one step at a time.

Norris, Dennis M. 1998. *Get a Grant, Yes You Can!* New York: Scholastic Professional Books. Primarily for teachers, this resource offers some good suggestions for teachers who want to apply for grants in the $100 to $5,000 range. It includes a list of 60 grant-giving organizations.

Orlich, Donald C. 1996. *Designing Successful Grant Proposals*. Alexandria, Va.: Association for Supervision and Curriculum Development. One of the best books on grant writing—most everything can be found on the Internet. All you have to do is spend the necessary time surfing the Web and put your program together.

Ramsey, Leslie A., and Phale D. Hale. 1999. *Winning Federal Grants: A Guide to the Government's Grant-Making Process*. Gaithersburg,

Md.: Aspen Publishers, Inc. This book reviews the federal legislative process, tells how to find out about federal grants, and how to avail yourself of your representative's help. It coaches grant seekers on the criteria used to assess a grant and suggests ways to score high on the point scale used by federal grant readers.

Ruskin, Karen B., and Charles M. Achilles. 1995. *Grantwriting, Fundraising, and Partnerships: Strategies That Work!* Thousand Oaks, Calif.: Corwin Press. This book is specifically for educators. It will help you identify granting agencies and harmonize your project with their goals. It will show you how to market your grant and cultivate partnerships with businesses in your community.

Ullman, Hannah. 2000. *Six Flawless Steps to a Winning Grant Pro*posal. Upper Fairmont, Md.: Barbara L. Dougherty. This is a clearly written monograph that fulfills what it promises. The six flawless steps are easy to read and understand. The reader cannot help but feel ready to tackle a grant proposal of any size. This book belongs in every development department.

Writing the Winning Grant Proposal: A Comprehensive Guide to Writing the Grant Proposal That Gets You Funded. 2000. Boston, Mass.: Quinlan Publishing Group. This book is for the first-time grant writer as well as the experienced professional. It is filled with lists of What To Do and What Not To Do. You won't go astray if you follow the advice of these lists.

Zinsser, William. *On Writing Well,* 3d ed. 1988. New York: Perennial Library, Harper and Row. This is my favorite book on writing. It cuts through the complicated rules of grammar and tells you how to write so people can understand you. Read it to learn how to write for clarity and understanding without being stuffy.

Chapter 4

Finding Funds for Capital Improvements

FINDING WAYS TO GET MONEY FOR A NEW BUILDING

The time will come when every library will need to build a new library or remodel the old one. These projects usually take more money than the library has in its entire budget for several years. Finding the necessary money in big enough chunks is daunting to say the least. It may seem totally impossible at the beginning. While every dollar from every moneymaking project will help, there are only a few ways to get the money you need to build a new library. They are:

1. Bond issues
2. Capital campaigns
3. Large gifts from individuals
4. Large grants

This chapter will help you figure out how to get the money you need to build or remodel your library. It may take a combination of all of the ways mentioned above. It may take every idea in this book. But if you will write down the amount of money you need for a new library and set a goal you will be able to have it.

USING OTHER ASSESSMENT TOOLS

Pull out the Checklist for Library Image and Performance from page 34 and use it to determine how well you are doing. Even if you score well on this test you need to prepare for some tough questions from the

voters. Here are some of the questions they might ask if you are planning to build a new library or remodel an existing building:

- What improvements in the library will be made if the issue passes?
- What will happen to library services if the bond issue doesn't pass?
- Will the appearance of the front of the building be changed?
- Will the parking lot be changed?
- Who will vote on the bond issue?
- What is the mill levy for the bond issue?
- How long will the taxes for the bond issue last?
- How much will the bond issue cost?
- Will any of the bond issue go towards operating expenses?
- Will passage of the bond issue increase staff wages?
- Is the library seeking grants and/or donations to assist with the cost
  of the construction?
- Does the public library have an operating mill levy?
- How is the library funded now?
- What is the library's annual operating budget?
- Who governs the library?
- How old is the main library building?
- How does the Chamber of Commerce feel about the bond issue?
- Why should I support the bond issue with extra tax dollars if no
  one in my family ever uses the library?

This last question probably deserves your careful attention. Some
people in the community will support the library bond issue no matter
what you do. Others will oppose it no matter what you do. The people
who will make or break the election for you often come from the segment of the population who never uses the library but believe that it is
good for the community.

Basically, the taxpayers want to know how much the proposed bond
issue will cost them and for how long. They also want to be assured that
not a penny of their hard-earned money will be wasted.

PUTTING IT ALL IN PERSPECTIVE

In 1989 I started working with the board of one of the libraries in the
Central Kansas Library System. They needed a new library in the worst
way. I presented four fundraising workshops in the community over a
period of years to help them see what they needed to do. To build
a new library they needed a capital campaign and some sort of
tax funding.

A woman in one of the workshops insisted that she would rather spend an hour crocheting a potholder and selling it at a bazaar for $1.25 than asking people for money. How many potholders would it take to raise the $500,000 they needed to build a new library? Unfortunately, making things and selling them will never produce the large amounts of money you need to build a new library—neither will chili suppers, bake sales, or car washes. These activities may supplement the big dollars that will have to come from gift solicitations.

At the end of a different workshop I told the participants that one of them would have to make a $50,000 donation to the library to guarantee the success of their $1,000,000 capital campaign. They all gulped and looked around the room and wondered who it would be.

Eventually, the people in these two communities were successful because they recognized the importance of a capital campaign and a bond election. Other library fundraising groups failed to meet their funding goals because they lacked the nerve to implement the suggestions in this chapter. It takes courageous actions to secure the big chunks of money needed to build a library.

Understanding a Bond Issue

In most communities a bond issue referendum is the best way to get enough money to build a new library. People understand that a bond issue means borrowing money and paying it back with an increase in future taxes for a certain time period, like ten years. The ability of a library to do this will vary from state to state. Usually the bonds will have to be issued by the city. If a library has autonomous taxing authority, the board can issue the bonds itself. It is also responsible for levying the tax and repaying the bonds.

Doing Your Homework

Before you decide you are going for a bond issue get someone outside the library to do a feasibility study. Like so many other issues in the political arena, don't ask people to vote on something if you don't already have a good idea that the issue will pass. If there is a lot of public support for the library then go for it. Don't hold back because the voters have recently turned down a bond issue for the schools, the jail, or the sewer plant. Libraries have survived an election when other issues were on the ballot at the same time. Never underestimate the community support that naturally accrues to the library.

Using a Telephone Survey

A telephone survey is a good way to assess your chances of getting a bond issue passed. With telemarketers flooding the telephone lines these days, it may be difficult to get people to talk to you. The effort is still worth the final result. Sampling may be difficult if you are trying to do it on your own. You could decide to call every 25th or every 100th number listed in the local telephone directory or use a random number generator and use it to select respondents. When you call a household and someone answers the telephone, that person could be a child, a teenager, or an adult. You really want to talk with and survey someone in the home who has the capability to vote in the bond election. Ask to speak with the adult that had the most recent birthday.

When you develop the questions make sure they get to the heart of the issue. You want to know if the respondent is aware of the possibility of a bond election for a library building, the need for a new library, and the likelihood that the respondent will vote in favor of the issue. Develop statements about the projects and then ask the respondent to answer with strongly agree, agree, not sure, disagree, and strongly disagree. Use a computer to help with recording and tabulating the results. As with other community assessment techniques you may want to get some professional help.

Several years ago the Great Bend (Kansas) school district secured the services of a television audience survey company doing business locally. The company used their regular staff and did it as a public service project. The school district obtained some accurate, valuable information. You might be able to tap into the resources of a telemarketing firm and get some much-needed information.

Using Focus Groups to Project the Mood of the People

A focus group is a gathering of few (seven to ten) people who have been selected because of their similar feelings on the issue being discussed. You may want to have several focus groups—each representing a different segment of the population. These people come together for an hour to an hour and a half to take part in a discussion led by a trained moderator (not someone connected with the library). The moderator uses the internal dynamics of the group to understand why people feel the way they do about a particular issue. For example, if a survey showed that the community was opposed to a new library, focus groups could be used to understand the reasons for the opposition. Specifically, how do people feel about building a new library? Maybe the old building has sentimental historic value. Or maybe they think the price tag for the new one is too high. Or maybe someone didn't like the way he or she was treated when a book was overdue. It would be very difficult to gather this type of in-depth information using conventional survey research. Focus groups can help you understand the complete picture.

Organizing Successful Focus Groups

If you follow a few easy suggestions you should increase the chances for success with focus groups. Specifically:

- Have specific objectives for the focus groups. You need to understand why you are using focus groups as part of your process. What do you want to accomplish by using focus groups?
- Select the right person to moderate your focus groups. One of the biggest issues of the focus group process is the reliance on the moderator as the leader of the process. Find someone who is highly trained as moderator. Make sure this person has experience with focus groups.
- Ensure that the moderator is an independent professional with no direct ties to your organization. This person must be completely objective about the research, and must avoid preconceived notions or partiality. This is essential if you expect unbiased analysis of the comments from members of the group.
- Encourage the active involvement of all people in the organization. People on the inside can feel threatened if they are not included in the process. There is a big difference between being at the sessions and watching them on tape.

Consider This Example

Our local school district struggled for years to put together a districtwide remodeling plan that the voters would approve. They finally resorted to focus groups and discovered a plan that was considered reasonable enough for people to vote for the bond issue. The focus groups told the school board that earlier "pie-in-the-sky" plans were too expensive. When all but the bare essentials were stripped from the remodeling plan the voters passed the bond issue. Focus groups can be an important part of assessing the community's response to a bond election.

Organizing the Bond Issue Campaign

Winning a bond issue is similar to winning a referendum to increase funding for operation, with two big exceptions:

1. The amount of money involved could be millions.
2. The taxpayers will get a new library they can drive by and see or go inside and enjoy the services.

There is something very much more exciting to having a brand new library than giving the library more money for operations. You can have a picture or a three-dimensional model of the new library. Hold them up and say this is what you will get if you vote for the library.

Foundations for a Capital Campaign

1. A specific plan for growth and improvement
2. Positive commitment from all key stakeholders (library staff, director, trustees, foundation and Friends board, donors)
3. Objectives based on carefully developed plans, goals, budgets, and needs
4. A feasibility study to evaluate readiness for a capital campaign
5. An unambiguous, succinct, and undeniable case for support
6. Leadership qualified and eager to solicit gifts
7. Key donors ready to make lead gifts

Figure 1-4-1 Foundations for a Capital Campaign

Other than these differences, conducting a campaign for a bond issue or a referendum are about the same. Review the information in Chapter 2 for details on how to encourage people to vote for a referendum. The same strategy applies to a bond issue.

ORGANIZING A CAPITAL CAMPAIGN

Even if you win a bond election you may still have to raise a lot of money to build a new library. A capital campaign is securing large donations for the purpose of building a new building. Of all the true fundraising activities you can be involved with, this can be the most work, the most exciting, and the most rewarding. People are more likely to give to a capital campaign than just about any other type of fundraising effort. They like to see their money go for something tangible—something they can see, something they can walk into and enjoy. Voters like to be part of a successful community effort. A capital campaign is the best way to raise a lot of money in a relatively short period of time.

Every successful capital campaign requires a foundation built on certain prerequisites. The pieces of the foundation are shown in Figure I-4-1.

Discovering the Positive Aspects of a Capital Campaign

There is a beginning and an end to a capital fund drive—usually close together. This is the best thing about a capital fund drive. Everyone working on it knows that it will end someday. You are asking people to give a considerable amount over a three to five year period. They know that you are not going to ask them again for the same project.

You recruit volunteers to ask for gifts. Among them, you recruit individuals with connections and influence—people who can bring other people into the group and together go out and get donations from their friends.

Start with a clear vision of your project. This can be an architectural drawing. A generous donor in Ellsworth, Kansas, thought so much of the library's project that he commissioned a scale model of the new library. It was easier to get people to give to the capital campaign when they could see a model of the new library.

CONSIDERING THE SERVICES OF A PROFESSIONAL

If you need more than $500,000 for a new building, seriously think about hiring a professional fundraising consultant. You will probably be able to get the first 25 percent of the money you need, but to get the last 75 percent you will need the help of a professional. Professionals do not go out to solicit donations for the library. They help local leaders organize and plan the capital campaign.

See Chapter 8 for more details on hiring a professional fundraiser.

Conducting a Feasibility Study

If you have a project that will cost $500,000 or more, have a professional fundraising consultant conduct a feasibility study before you announce the project to build a new library. Do not "pass go" without it. A feasibility study gets the process started. Some library board members become immobilized by the enormity of the fundraising goal. The feasibility study moves them from a passive role to an active one—nudging them into greater levels of involvement.

One of the greatest benefits of a feasibility study is to point out obstacles or misconceptions about the proposed project. This gives the project leaders a chance to see what must be done before a campaign is started. It gives them a chance to develop a public relations effort if one is needed, and how to word the proposals.

A feasibility study is a different process than using focus groups, though they both require hiring a professional. A feasibility study involves private conversations with influential individuals who have their finger on the pulse of the community. These individuals are often the people you will turn to for major gifts.

You can find more information about conducting a feasibility study in Chapter 8, page 125. Please read Chapter 8 before you begin work on a capital campaign.

It is possible to do your own feasibility study. But do not be too quick to jump into the task. The information gathered from visits with community leaders will not be as accurate if you do it yourself. They will tell you what they think you want to hear, and not always what they think is the truth.

ASKING THE HARD QUESTIONS

If you get a green light from the feasibility study, the capital campaign committee needs to ask these important questions:

- Do we have a clear vision of what we want to do and how we want to do it?
- Do members of our organization have the skills to assess the giving potential for our project in our community?
- Do we know who will lead us and are we confident that he or she can manage the campaign?
- Can we train our volunteers to be highly effective solicitors?
- Can we count on every member of the board to be committed to the project and give a sacrificial gift?
- Can we recruit people to help us sell our vision to others in a way that will raise money?
- Do we have the skills and resources within our organization to develop quality written materials to support our project?
- Can we write and produce a persuasive, polished case statement?

Asking and answering these questions begins the process of building ownership in the campaign.

Preparing a Case Statement

About the time you are conducting the feasibility study you begin preparing your case statement. A case statement is a brief summary of your library's purpose, the need for the fundraising project and how you plan to accomplish your objectives. Some professionals like to take a one-page draft of the case statement document with them when they visit with the community leaders.

Once you have developed your short mission statement, you need to make a brief statement about your project. John Naisbitt said, "Strategic planning is worthless unless there is first a strategic vision." You are creating a strategic vision when you say, "We want to build a new library." You flesh out the vision when you describe its shape and dimensions. It becomes more real when you draw a picture of it and give it a name.

Some libraries have given their project a name to generate more interest—even humanized it. NASA named the missions to the moon Apollo I, Apollo II, and so on. Everyone knew what Apollo stood for and everyone felt a part of lunar exploration.

One of the libraries in the survey I conducted had a "Pete the Penny" campaign as a fundraiser. Children collected 100 pennies and brought them to the library. The people in Rhinelander, Wisconsin, caught the vision of thousands of pennies marching into the library—going to work to remodel a Carnegie building.

After describing your project and giving it character, tell how you are going to accomplish the task. If you have a big project with many different fundraising activities, outline each project and the anticipated income from each.

If this is your first time to write a case statement, a professional's help may be worth every cent. Patricia Pawl paid $2,000 to have someone write the case statement for the Beaver Dam Public Library's campaign. The library spent another $1,000 to have it printed. The librarian considered the effort essential to the campaign. This is a critical document. Next to the people who carry it to potential donors, it represents your library. It has to look good. Depending on how you use it, your case statement can make a difference in the size and number of gifts. It can be a big factor in the total amount you raise.

Put the case statement up on the library's Web page. Libraries have to use their Web site more for marketing, promotion, and development activities. This is a perfect venue for informing people of the library's plans, but you can't just put it up on the Internet and think you are done. You also need to get people to visit the library's Web site and read the case statement. A promotional spot on television or an advertisement in the newspaper will enhance public awareness of the case statement on the Internet.

Selecting the Chair of the Capital Campaign

Part of the job of the professional consultant in conducting the feasibility study is to help select the chair of the capital campaign committee. There are no perfect formulas for doing this task. If you don't use a professional consultant, select someone who can make a major gift to the campaign, and then bring his or her peers to the table with comparable gifts. If the chair of the committee is not capable of making a gift of at least five percent of the total to be raised, other large gifts will not come in.

Someone in one of my workshops asked how important this point was. I said, "If you are going to raise a million dollars, $50,000 may be the price tag for the right to be chair of the fundraising committee." As it turned out $50,000 wasn't enough to be the chair of the fundraising committee. Even though a very dedicated library board member gave a home valued at $50,000 to the library, another donor who gave even more became the chair of the committee.

Campaign Goal = $1,000,000

	Number	Amount	Percent	Names
Major lead gift	1	$100,000	10%	_____
				_____
Lead gifts	2	$50,000	10%	_____
				_____
				_____
				_____
				_____
Major gifts	4	$25,000	10%	_____
				_____
				_____
				_____
				_____
				_____
				_____
Big gifts	10	$10,000	10%	_____
				_____
				_____
				_____
				_____
				_____
				_____
				_____
				_____

Figure 1-4-2 Chart of Giving

Developing the Chart of Giving

If you decide to use a fundraising professional (see Chapter 8), he or she will sit down with your group and complete this critical document. He or she will use it, without names, as part of the feasibility study. Eventually, you will have to have a name on every blank (three names for every gift you expect) and solicit them before you publicly announce the campaign.

The feasibility study will yield valuable information to help you develop your chart of giving. If your professional consultant asks 30 people how many gifts of $10,000, $5,000, and $1,000 can be expected in your community, the answers will cluster on a norm and provide a good target for your gift brackets. It will also help you predict how much money you can raise.

I recommend a chart of giving that looks like the one on page 76. It represents the top end of the giving scale. The goal is possible if the fundraising group can confidently write down three names for each gift sought. Some donors will not give at the anticipated level, but will give at a lower level.

Preparing Public Relations Materials

You will need news releases and brochures plus other materials to give to donors. The best is not too good to represent your library. Anyone can write a news release. Writing a release that will be run in the newspaper as you had written it will take a special skill. If you already write a lot for your library why not turn it over to the professionals? They may be able to give your project a slant you haven't thought of before.

My experience with public relations tells me that *cheap* can be very expensive when you are trying to influence those with power and money. People are not impressed with your poverty. Your publicity pieces don't have to be gold foiled. They just have to look good—printed on a good grade of paper.

Providing Guidance for Large Gift Cultivation

Forty percent of your money will come from 18 to 20 donors. The big donors take special cultivation. If your professional fundraiser can help you turn a $25,000 donation into a $50,000 donation, his or her fee will have been paid for in one gift. If your largest category of giving is $1,000 you may have gypped yourself out of $49,000 by not doing your homework or targeting a gift more suited to the donor's potential. It is difficult to go back to someone who has given a moderate amount and ask him or her to give more. Some professionals will accompany a volunteer to solicit a big gift, and if the volunteer fails to ask for the gift the professional will remind him or her of the main purpose of the visit.

Training Volunteers

It is easier to recruit volunteers than it is to train them to be effective solicitors. It may be a good idea to rely on someone who has done it several times before. One librarian said their fundraising consultant did three different training sessions: one for the big gifts committee; one for the medium gifts committee; and one for the telephone solicitation group. Each training session was specifically tailored to the needs of the volunteers and their targeted donors.

Formulating the Campaign Calendar

Most campaigns drag on too long. People get discouraged, not because they have failed, but because they have put off the task of asking for money. Fearing failure, volunteers lose their initial enthusiasm and what seemed exciting at first, has now become drudgery. Vance Associates like to set a 12-week maximum for making the initial contacts and follow-up. The whole fund drive, start to finish, is wrapped up in twelve weeks. That doesn't mean that all of the money is in, because some gifts are in the form of pledges. Collecting them may extend for up to five years. The key is setting a realistic, but tight calendar, generating enthusiasm among the volunteers, training them, and letting them go out to get the money. A member of the Vance team keeps the effort moving by staying with the project from beginning to end.

Most volunteer fundraisers have other responsibilities. They have jobs, social activities, and families who need them. They usually don't have the time to give full time to a major fundraising project. Since a professional is being paid to oversee the campaign, it becomes his or her job to keep people on schedule, to motivate them, and support them.

Managing the Campaign Office

Once volunteers are trained and have started bringing in money and pledges, someone has to be in the office to receive the gifts and provide backup for special situations. One library hired a part-time secretary to handle the extra paperwork generated by the campaign. The professional fundraiser provided technical assistance on matters that required more than clerical treatment. Most librarians are already burdened down with more than they can handle. Running a major fundraising campaign is like adding another full-time job. Unless you have some very dedicated volunteers with lots of time to give away, you may want to hire someone to run the campaign office and handle the extra paper work.

Developing Follow-Up Procedures

After the campaign is completed your money will still be coming in. Pledges will have to be collected. All of this takes more skills than a regular secretary may have. A professional can help you develop the forms you need to follow through on pledges and incoming donations. Regular well-worded form letters and reminders will keep the money coming in until it has all been collected.

Taking the Next Step

Now you have the board and the volunteer solicitors selected and everyone so far has given or made a pledge. What is the next step? You organize them into logical committees. In Ellis, Kansas, they organized the committee into the following: big gifts, city residents, and the rural residents.

The key to asking volunteer solicitors to give, is don't assume anything—even if you know how much they make. If they are willing to ask others for money to support your cause, they will probably give more than you think.

All along you should be developing your prospective donor list. This could be as easy or as hard as going through the local telephone directory and entering every name into a computer database. We are in the twenty-first century. Don't try to do this by hand. Use a computer. You can use a generic database management program and customize it to your needs or you can buy one of several good software programs that are specific for managing a fundraising effort. Don't forget to back up your data often and keep a spare backup file offsite. This is a job for staff if you have enough paid people to do it.

Every person who is assigned to solicit gifts should have a copy of the library's case statement and the chart of giving.

Giving Everyone a Chance to Donate

You want to give everyone in the community the opportunity to own a part of the new library. In a larger community going through the phone book would be impractical. So, a neighborhood approach might be more practical. Have members of the committee take a few of the streets in their neighborhood and develop a contact list.

Another way to get the names of prospects is to brainstorm. No suggestion is discounted. Every name mentioned is written down.

Here are a few other possibilities:

- Library users
- People who have given books to the library
- People who have made memorial gifts to the library in the past
- People who have volunteered service to the library
- Share lists with the community college
- Guest registers from special events at the library
- High school alumni lists
- Country club list
- Chamber of Commerce list
- Voter registration lists

Next look up the names and addresses and telephone numbers and make out a card for each prospect. If you are creating a long-term donor list you will want to keep more information on the card.

You will want to keep track of:

- Name
- Age
- Family
- Church
- Work
- Volunteer
- Where they live—census tract
- Political precinct

You may even want to create a full-page form to profile each donor. On the other hand, if this is a one-shot deal and you only need money for a new library, don't go to all that trouble. Filling out a form for every household in town could be a big job.

For additional ideas on training volunteers see Chapter 5.

Regular Reports

As the fund drive progresses, the committee meets weekly. Individual workers account to their team leader and turn in money and receipt copies on a daily basis. Team chairs stay close to their team members and report to their committee chairs, who in turn report to the chair of the whole committee.

End On Time

End on time and celebrate—even if you don't reach your goal by the time you said you would end. Dragging it out won't help your cause. Invite all the workers and the large gift donors to a big party to celebrate the success of your capital campaign. If you are short, who knows one of them may kick in another $10,000 if you ask for it.

TIMELINE

Figure I-4-3 is a timeline to help organize the work of the committee.

LARGE GIFTS FROM INDIVIDUALS

Large gifts from individuals are often a catalyst for building a new library. It usually starts with a person who has a great interest in the library and wants to help in a way that will make a difference. Sometimes it is a retired couple that wants to give some of their accumulated wealth to the library for a new building. They start by talking with the librarian or the president of the board to see how their gift might be used. Pre-

---

Time Line for a Capital Fund Drive

Six months before the campaign
Campaign committee in place.
Recruit a powerful person as chair.
Set up divisions.
Set up heads for each division (five divisions).
Each division head has five team leaders.
Each team has five members.

Five months before
All organizational work is done.

Four months before
Develop campaign materials
Brochure
Giving clubs
Pledge cards
Publicity
Radio
Newspaper
Plan events

Three months before
Create prospect list.
Rate prospect list.
Assign prospects to categories of giving.
Assign prospects to solicitors.

Two months before
Kick-off breakfast.

Last two months
Solicitors contact prospects and ask for gifts.

End of campaign
Victory dinner. Celebrate!

Figure 1-4-3 Time Line for Capital Fund Drive

liminary plans are made and the donors agree. The gift is made, sometimes with strings, but hopefully not. This large gift becomes the lead gift towards the construction of a new library or the remodeling of the old one. It could be large enough to cover the entire project or at least half of it. This becomes the lead gift and sets the stage for additional fundraising.

When the lead gift is not enough to complete the project, the people running the project can either go for a bond issue to raise additional funds or conduct a capital campaign. These details are usually worked out between governing body and the library board. I have seen all of these methods work. The result was a fine new library.

Seeking the Big Individual Gift

It is really nice when someone walks into the library and says, "I want to donate the money for a new library." If you need a new library don't hold your breath waiting for it to happen to you. But you might be able to spot an opportunity to ask for such a gift. When someone walks in and gives you a thousand dollars, two or three times a year, there is a good possibility that there is much more money where that came from. These donors are not strangers to your library. You probably visit with them several times a week. You don't have to know how much money they really have to approach them about making a large gift to the library. It may take some time to cultivate the donor, but with the help of a board member or two you should be able to find out how they feel about helping to build a new library.

Once you know that they are interested in making a gift towards a new library, set up a meeting. Take a board member or a friend of theirs with you—either to ask for the gift or to be there with you while you do the asking. Either way it is always good to have two people go together when asking for a large amount of money, just in case a misunderstanding arises or if the primary asker chickens out. If the person who is supposed to ask for the gift gets cold feet and wants to leave, the companion can either remind the person or make the donation request him or herself.

Once the commitment is made you can talk about recognition and other strings, though you might have to do this before securing the gift. Make sure the recognition is worth the gift. If someone wants his or her name on the new library or newly remodeled section like a children's room, make sure the gift is large enough to pay for the whole project. A portrait of the individual or couple displayed in a prominent place in the library is appropriate.

Some donors have other strings. A library in Kansas received a large donation if the library would build a new library according to the plans drawn by the donor. The community ended up with a beautiful large building that was structurally flawed. The people in charge should have had the plans reviewed by an architect or an engineer before construction started.

Seeking a Large Grant

Some foundations make large grants for construction projects. You have a better chance if the foundation only funds projects in your county or state. The library in Logan, Kansas, got a new home when a local family foundation made a gift to the city to pay for a new library. Nationally known foundation grants are more competitive (see the section on foundation grants).

These grants take a lot of planning and are difficult to find. If you are planning to restore an old building, you might try a foundation that likes to see historic preservation. Large manufacturing companies have foundations that may fund construction projects. Review all of the material in Chapter 3 and the section on foundation grants before you try to secure a construction grant from a foundation.

SUMMARY

In priority order the best ways to get money for a library building project are:

1. Bond issues
2. Capital campaigns
3. Large gifts from individuals
4. Large grants

When voters approve a bond issue the city or the library sells bonds to produce the capital necessary to build the library. Additional taxes are levied to repay the bonds. It pays to be positive about the natural community support for the library.

People in the library need to be prepared to answer questions like these:

- What improvements in the library will be made if the issue passes?
- What will happen to library services if the bond issue doesn't pass?
- How much will the bond issue cost individual taxpayers?
- Will passage of the bond issue increase staff wages?
- How is the library funded now?
- Who governs the library?
- Why should I support the bond issue with extra tax dollars if no one in my family ever uses the library?

Having a new library is more exciting than giving the library more money for operations, and people will be more likely to vote for a bond issue than they will for a mill levy increase to support the library.

Even if you win a bond election you may still have to raise a lot of money to build a new library. A capital campaign is securing large donations for the purpose of building a new building. It is easier to get people to give if they can see a model or a picture of the new library.

If you have a project that will cost $500,000 or more, you need to hire a professional fundraising consultant to conduct a feasibility study before you announce the project to build a new library.

Create a case statement, which is a brief summary of your library's purpose, the need for the fundraising project, and how you plan to accomplish your objectives. Part of the job of the professional consultant is to help select the chair of the capital campaign. Someone who can make a major gift and secure other major gifts must hold this crucial position. Committee members must also be able to make a sacrificing gift and secure others from the community.

Large gifts from individuals are often a catalyst for building a new library. These large gifts become the lead gift towards the construction of a new library or the remodeling of the old one. When the lead gift is not enough to complete the project, the people running the project can either go for a bond issue to raise additional funds or conduct a capital campaign.

Some foundations make large grants for construction projects. Large manufacturing companies have foundations that may fund construction projects. Their gift to the community blesses everyone when they do.

BIBLIOGRAPHY

Burlingame, Dwight F. 1997. *Developing Major Gifts*. San Francisco, Calif.: Jossey-Bass. Securing the big gift can make or break any capital campaign. This book tells you how to develop major gifts. It also tells you what to avoid.

Hartsook, Robert. 1999. *How to Get Million Dollar Gifts and Have Donors Thank You*. Wichita, Kans.: ASR Philanthropic Publishers. This is the bible on soliciting major gifts. This book belongs in every development office and needs to be read. Hartsook has distilled every essential element necessary to secure million dollar gifts.

Kihlstedt, Andrea. 1998. *Capital Campaigns: Realizing Their Power and Potential*. San Francisco: Jossey-Bass. Each chapter approaches a capital campaign from a different direction. Chapter titles are: Thinking Beyond The Dollar Goal: A Campaign As Organizational Transformation; Dynamics of The Challenge Grant; Achieving Leadership Gifts: The Investment Returns of Lasting Relationships; Campaign Goals: Taking Aim at a Moving Target; Information Systems: Managing The Database; Working From Strength: How Small Organizations Succeed With Big Campaigns.

Lansdowne, David. 2000. *Fund Raising Realities Every Board Member Must Face: A 1-Hour Crash Course on Raising Major Gifts*. Medfield, Mass.: Emerson and Church Publishers. Every board member of every nonprofit organization needs to read this book. Every library board member needs to read it, too. If they would they would understand the business and need for fundraising. They would also know how to do it.

Nichols, Judith. 2001. *Pinpointing Affluence: Increasing Your Share of Major Donor Dollars,* 2d ed. Chicago: Bonus Books. While fewer than 1,000 donors give a million dollars to nonprofit organizations every year, some 19 million people are capable of giving $1,000 to $100,000 every year. Judith Nichols tells us how to find them and how to ask them for a donation.

Prince, Russ Alan, and Karen Maru File. 1994. *The Seven Faces of Philanthropy: A New Approach to Cultivating Major Donors.* San Francisco, Calif.: Jossey-Bass. The authors define the seven types of donors: the Communitarian, the Devout, the Investor, the Socialite, the Altruist, the Repayer, and the Dynast. The book tells us how to approach each type of donor.

Sturtevant, William T. 1997. *The Artful Journey: Cultivating and Soliciting the Major Gift.* Chicago, Ill.: Bonus Books. Focused on getting the major gift, this book is the first really sensible book on the subject. It is a step-by-step guide to cinching a big gift. The book pledges a fail-proof roadmap, and it delivers.

Chapter 5

Soliciting Donations

The most effective way to raise money from private sources is to ask individuals for a donation. You don't have to bake a cake. You don't have to sell them anything. You just contact them and tell them why you need the money, and then say, "Will you give $100 to the library?" In this chapter you will learn how to find and evaluate prospective donors. You will learn how to ask them for money, and do it more effectively.

FINDING PROSPECTIVE DONORS

Finding donors who will give money to your library is somewhat like prospecting for gold. It is better to look where others have already found it than to take a shotgun approach and look everywhere. So, when it comes to finding people who will give money to a library project, your best bet will be to ask someone who has already given something to the library.

The best prospects can be ranked in the following order:

1. *Those who have already given major gifts to your library.* These donors have already demonstrated their interest in the library and their capacity and willingness to give. For them it is a matter of how much they will give.
2. *Those who have made regular donations to the library.* These donors have already demonstrated their interest in the library. Their capacity to give may be limited but they will still make a gift when asked to do so.
3. *Those who have given only once to the library.* The inclination to give is there but untested. Asking them for a larger gift may reveal their true interest and capacity to give.

4. *Individual members of the library board.* People offer to become library board members for a variety of reasons. Some have the capacity to give and are very interested in the library, but are unwilling to part with significant chunks of money. Others have limited capacity to give.

5. *Friends of the Library.* Some people join the Friends of the Library to help their library, more with their time and effort than their money. Their capacity to give may be limited.

6. *People who have paid to attend a special event at the library.* These people may consider themselves more of a customer of the library than a constituent. Nevertheless, they have supported the library in some way. Their capacity to give and their interest in the library may be untested until you ask them for a gift.

7. *Those who have donated books to the library.* These prospective donors may have been looking for a good home for their books rather than expressing an interest in the library. You will have to ask them to donate before you can know if they can or will make a gift.

8. *Regular library patrons.* People who come to the library on a regular basis and borrow materials are likely to feel obliged to help the library. Their capacity to give may be limited, but don't assume that it is so.

9. *Library volunteers.* People who volunteer to work at the library generally have more time than money, but they should not be overlooked as potential donors.

10. *Registered borrowers of the library.* Some registered borrowers rarely come to the library. Once the need that prompted them to get a library card has been met, they may not return until another need for the library arises. They have the same disposition to give to the library as the general public does.

11. *The general public—older people first.* Many people in your community do not have library cards and don't use the library. They will say, "I don't use the library myself, but I believe it is a good thing to have a good library." Researchers have found that older people tend to give more to charities than younger people.

Using this priority list tops opening the telephone and calling every listing. This list helps you focus your efforts and become more efficient. Somewhere in this process you will rediscover former donors who have been waiting for you to ask them for another gift. You will also find some new friends who are completely willing to make a donation, but have never been asked. Other people will take cultivation before they become donors. Remember that your goal is to find willing donors.

EVALUATING PROSPECTIVE DONORS

You can evaluate all prospective donors by asking these two questions:

1. What is this donor's capacity to give?
2. What is this donor's interest in your library?

These two questions will qualify every prospective donor. You may know someone who has a million dollars to give away, but if that person doesn't care about the library you are not going to get any of his or her money. At the same time you probably know lots of people who are very interested in the library, but have little, if any, money to give away. Your chances of raising lots of money from this group will be disappointing. You have to find people who like your library and have stacks of money to give away and then ask them for it. It is as simple as that!

When you ask someone to give you money for your library you assume that he or she is a constituent of the library. Members of a church are constituents. They are asked every week to donate to the church. People who consider themselves constituents of the library will give to the library when asked to do so, because they feel that the library is part of their lives. When library constituents feel it is to their advantage to give you money without being asked, so much the better.

EFFECTIVE WAYS TO ASK

When asking people for money the more personal you can get the better your chance for success. Friends respond to friends better than to strangers. We like to insulate ourselves from a face-to-face confrontation with others, including our friends. We would rather make a phone call than ask for a donation face to face. We would sooner write a letter than make a telephone call. We would rather sell them something than ask for a gift outright. Remember this. Asking someone we know face to face for a donation is the most effective way to solicit money. It is not as hard at you think once you get past the initial reluctance or fear of rejection. The friend will most likely be glad you asked and write a check. The gift may not be as large as you were expecting, but there is a good chance a friend will not turn you down flatly.

The following, in priority order, are the most effective methods to ask people to donate to your library:

1. *Friend to friend, face to face.* This is the most personal and the most direct. It is also the most effective.
2. *Peer to peer, face to face.* People who move in the same social

circles usually know each other even if they are not close friends. They can usually ask each other for favors. Soliciting at this level may require a favor in return from the solicitor.

3. *Non-peer to someone higher, face to face.* It would not be unusual for a customer of a bank to approach a bank president for a gift. But the solicitation might be more effective if it came from a golfing buddy.

4. *Stranger to stranger, face to face.* This could be difficult, but if the prospective donor has the capacity to give and is interested in the cause of the solicitor, it doesn't matter who does the asking. Face to face is always better than any other method of contact.

5. *Friend to friend, peer to peer, etc., on the telephone.* Telephone soliciting to people you know can be very effective, especially if you are calling people who live out of town. Telephone soliciting can also be less intimidating.

6. *Telephone call preceded by mail solicitation.* This could be the most effective and most efficient way of soliciting donations. Sending a letter before the telephone call explains the organization's need and gives the potential donor time to think about the request for money. The telephone call is used to answer questions and close the deal. This method is efficient because you can contact many more people in a short period of time.

7. *Personal handwritten letter, direct mail.* Writing to a friend is more personal and will probably elicit a response—maybe with a check.

8. *Telephone solicitation.* A cold call on the telephone will result in many more turndowns. You may never get the opportunity to explain the need or ask for the gift.

9. *Library's Web site.* Let your customers know you are a place for their charitable gifts. Give them the opportunity to participate online. It could be as simple as listing a wish list and having a printable form for them to print out and send in with a contribution.

10. *Personalized (Dear George and Laura) typed letter, direct mail.* Direct mail gives you the opportunity to explain the library's need and make a plea for money, but the recipient has to read it for the message to be conveyed. It may be read because it has the recipient's name on it.

11. *Impersonal (Dear Friend, Resident) direct mail.* The best reason to use this kind of approach is to locate new donors. Don't count on direct mail to bring in lots of money. Many fundraising letters end up in the trash unopened.

12. *Public Service Announcements.* Often radio and television stations will produce and air spots about fundraising efforts or projects.

Principles of Fundraising

1. *Know how much you need and the purpose of your project.* If you don't know the total cost of your project or why you need the money, your commitment will be weak. You don't have to share your goal with the donor, but you need to have it clearly in mind.
2. *Give before you ask.* Everyone who asks others for money must give to their cause themselves. They must give enough to make a difference in the cause or in their own lives.
3. *Ask for the gift.* If you don't ask, you won't get. Some libraries have been known to receive large gifts from unknown or unexpected sources. Don't count on it!
4. *Ask the right person for the right amount.* You don't pick one pound tomatoes from a cherry tomato plant, and you won't get a large gift from a homeless person who comes to the library every day. You have to do your research if you want to know who to ask for a big gift.
5. *Say thank you.* Say thank you as many ways as you can. Recognize everyone who helped. I believe that you have to say thank you seven times before you can ask for another gift.

Figure 1-5-1 Principles of Fundraising

These announcements will increase public awareness of the library's need for funds.

13. *Paid advertising on television.* This form of solicitation is not cost prohibitive, but its shotgun effect does not do a good job of targeting constituents. The best reason to use television is to make constituents aware of the library's need. Follow-up contacts will be easier to make if people are aware the fundraising effort.

14. *Paid advertising on radio.* Radio advertising is less expensive than television and more targeted to local constituents. Not everyone listens to the radio for more than a few minutes a day. Follow-up contacts are still recommended.

15. *Paid advertising in newspaper.* Not everyone gets or reads a local newspaper, but the print format gives you the opportunity to tell your story and make a pitch. Once we used a newspaper ad to supplement a direct mail campaign—only two of the more than 100 gifts came in with a coupon from the newspaper.

PRINCIPLES OF FUNDRAISING

While asking may be the most important step to fundraising, it is not quite that simple. If it were we wouldn't need books on the subject. Fundraisers have developed some techniques that help us organize our

efforts and refine our methods in ways that will help us raise more money
with less effort, and help us be successful most of the time.

Let's start with five tenets of fundraising through solicitation of gifts.
These five points (see Figure I-5-1) are essential to any successful soliciting effort.

Why Is Setting the Goal So Important?

If you don't know where you are headed you won't know it if you get
there. When you set a goal something happens in the subconscious to
bring people and opportunities together to help you reach your goal. I
don't know how else to explain it, but it happens. When I was still in
library school I made some projections/goals for the library I was going
to direct as soon as I graduated. Six years later I was gathering my things
to leave for a new job. In a file I had forgotten, I found the goals I had
set when I was in library school. The projections were uncannily accurate. I had correctly predicted the growth of the budget, circulation, book
stock, registered borrowers, etc. If you can envision what you want to
do and write it down, you can have it.

Why Do I Have to Give Before I Ask?

If you don't give yourself, you won't be convincing. Psychologists have
discovered that people who ask others for donations without having first
given something themselves are less effective than those who have given.
Their eyes drop when making the close. People who have given can say,
"I gave a thousand dollars to the project now it is your turn." They are
confident and committed. If your prospects don't feel that you are convinced to the point of giving yourself, they won't give either.

You might ask "How much should I give?" The answer is up to you,
but a lackluster donation will be perceived by others as a lack of commitment. The more you give the more you will feel empowered to ask
others to join you in a sacrificial effort.

A board member from Ellis, Kansas, said, "When I decided to give a
thousand dollars to the library, I was committed! I became a tiger at asking people for money." For this person who was living on her retirement
income a thousand dollars was truly a sacrificial gift.

Why Do I Have to Ask?

People won't know what you want if you don't ask for the gift. When
you meet with a prospect a normal opening might be to discuss the benefits of the library to the community. You might even discuss the merits
of your new building or your automated circulation system. If you have
never asked for a contribution, your donor may think you are there for
a friendly visit or to chat about the library.

How many times have you been in a situation where you had to communicate a difficult message? You thought you had said what you wanted the other person to do, but a friend who was with you confirmed later that you didn't come right out and say what you wanted. You need to say to the prospective donor, "We would like you to give five thousand dollars to the library building fund. Will you do it?"

Take someone with you or go with someone when contacting a major donor. If you fail to ask for the gift, your friend can remind you of the purpose of the visit. Together you can be sure to ask for the gift. That is why it is important to take someone with you.

Why Is It Important to Ask the Right Person for the Right Amount?

If a person is capable of giving $50,000 and you only ask for $5,000, you could insult him or her, but worse yet you could leave $45,000 on the table. In a small town, everyone knows everyone else. It won't take a twenty minute brainstorming session to learn the names of the richest people in town. But brainstorming is an effective technique for discovering the best people to ask in your community. You might also try these sources:

- *Proxy statements* for public held companies, available from the Securities Exchange Commission. You may uncover people who have large amounts of stock they may be willing to donate to the library.
- *Probate records.* Ask for will inventory. The survivors may be interested in making a sizable memorial contribution.
- *Divorce financial statements.* Someone may have a big chunk of money they don't want or need.
- *Country club list.* Those who belong to country clubs often have more discretionary income to give away.
- *Retirement centers.* People over 60 are some of the best givers—especially to libraries.

Trying one or more of these possibilities may uncover an untapped major source of benevolence.

What Does It Mean to Say "Thank You" Appropriately?

Saying thank you is the most obvious principle of all. The biggest question is how do I match my thank you with the size of the gift. Your thank you could range from a simple specific note to someone who gave you a hundred dollars to an elaborate reception honoring the donor of a gift large enough to build the entire new addition. The most important thing about saying thank you is to do it.

Be Attitudes of Fundraising:

- *Be committed.* If you aren't going to give it your full commitment, don't do it. When you eat, drink, and sleep fundraising for your library, everyone who talks to you will know it.
- *Be friendly.* Friends give to friends. Other people feel good about friendly people. They want be around friendly people more often.
- *Be positive.* Your attitude is infectious. If you never doubt success neither will the donors, who by their gifts are buying into your dream.
- *Be confident.* When you ask for a gift you can only win or break even. The only way you lose is by not asking at all.
- *Be bold and nice.* Boldness without being nice is "pushy." Twisting someone's arm until they give may get the gift, but what about the next time? Goodwill is an intangible asset.
- *Be firm.* Learn how to deal with objections. Most people have to get used to the idea of giving away money. It usually takes asking seven times to get the gift. Don't give up on the first time the donor says no.
- *Be knowledgeable.* Become an expert on the benefits of your organization. Tell the donor what you need and explain how their gift can help him or her.
- *Be considerate of your donor.* You donor has already given you a chunk of his or her time. Don't waste it. Make your pitch. Ask for the money. Get it. Say thank you and leave.

Figure 1-5-2 Be Attitudes of Fundraising

Saying thank you not only makes your donor feel good, but it also makes *you* feel good. It may be the only return on investment your donor will receive. Sometimes fundraising groups have a big bash at the end of the campaign for all the workers and the donors who gave $1,000 or more. It is a good opportunity to give public recognition to workers and donors alike. But how can you recognize a large gift from a donor who wishes to remain anonymous? A quiet meal in a nice restaurant might work fine. Anyone who gives anything to your campaign deserves a thank you.

SOLICITING WITH THE RIGHT ATTITUDE

Soliciting as a fundraiser is intimidating to almost everyone. We are afraid. We fear rejection. We fear change. The only reason we would even consider asking others for a donation is because we are firmly committed to the organization we support and the need is great. A positive attitude is the key to overcoming our fears. I would rather look forward to being thin than to think of being on a diet. It's just less stressful. Figure 1-5-2, a list of *Be Attitudes of Fundraising,* may give you a positive feeling about asking others for money.

GETTING TO YES

What do you say when asking for a gift? Ask for a specific amount. Be direct. Ask for the money with strong verbs such as: give, donate, contribute, or will you give. Don't say, *"We would appreciate if you would consider making a generous donation."* Your prospective donor can say "yes" to that question without giving a dime. He or she can consider the request and the answer is "no!"

Here are a few ways to ask for a gift.

Will you give . . .(an amount)?
Please give . . .(an amount).
Won't you please help?
You can make the difference.
This is your chance to help.
Help us reach our goal.

Be Silent After the Ask

This is one of the best pieces of advice in this book. After presenting your case say, "Will you give us $5,000 for the library building fund?"; don't say another word until the donor has spoken. Researchers have learned that the average silence in any conversation is less than three seconds. After three seconds people will begin to feel uncomfortable. They want to fill the silence by saying something. You hope your donor will fill the silence by saying yes to your request. Learn to be comfortable with the silence. Let your prospect speak next. If he or she says *no*, don't give up.

Listen!

He or she will probably give a reason for turning you down. Try to find out why the answer is "no." Agree with the donor, and then point out another benefit of giving. Sometimes you have to prove that you are seriously committed to your cause. Tell the donor you have already given $5,000. Now it is the donor's turn.

If the answer is still "no," keep listening and keep talking. Your prospective donor may change his or her mind. If you do not succeed don't give up or be disappointed. You have still learned something. You have probably underestimated the donor's capacity to give. Most likely you were unfamiliar with how much discretionary cash the donor had. Or you may have overestimated the donor's interest in the library.

Getting the donor to say "yes" may require several strategies, but it could be as simple as asking the donor, "What would it take to get you to say yes?" Maybe his or her response will let you know of a benefit that you haven't thought of. Or maybe the library is doing something that irritates the donor, such as having the book drop in an inconvenient place. If you can correct the problem the donor has with the library, you might get the gift.

What if the answer is still "no?"

Listen to the donor. Agree with him or her. Listen for clues that might give you a lead to a benefit that will make the donor want to give. Chances are, he or she will give you several reasons for not giving. By listening carefully, you will learn what is important to the donor. If you know what is important to your donor, you can connect a benefit of your project with something that is important to him or her. The connection between a benefit of your project and your prospect's "hot button" is the key to getting the gift.

Don't give up with the first visit. If you fail at the first try, try again or send someone else to try a few days later. On average, it takes seven requests to get to "yes." Your donor may change his or her mind after thinking about your request.

Earlier we learned five key points of selling from an experienced salesman, Jim Keller. He suggests that we ask these questions and use the answers to adjust our sales pitch.

Review in your mind these questions:

1. Is it the right product?
2. Does the prospect need this product?
3. Is the price within the prospect's ability and willingness to pay?
4. Is this the right time?
5. Is your library the right library?

If the donor is still reluctant to make a gift, chances are the hang-up can be found in one of these five points.

TRAINING VOLUNTEERS

You cannot send volunteers out to solicit donations without training. Hold a meeting with all of the volunteer solicitors. Teach them what the library does. Teach them how it is funded. Explain what the library needs and why. Come up with a list of eight to ten reasons why people should donate to your cause. Brainstorming works well for this part of the meeting (refer to page 10 in Chapter 1). Ask them why they think people will want to give to the library's project.

Develop two or three scenarios or dialogs for making the first approach. Have the volunteers learn the dialogs verbatim and practice giving them to members of the group. Then give the approach to someone outside the group—a friendly prospect. Make sure they follow the script and that the prospect follows the script, too. Include rehearsing objections. This gives the solicitors a security blanket. Everyone will be able to go out and deliver the dialog, but the highest achievers will probably use a combination of all the scripts.

Practice for Confidence

Confidence is a key to asking for money. Strive for a naturalness that exudes confidence. Training volunteers can make them more effective. With practice, their approach will become natural. You can create a positive experience for your solicitors. When you have volunteers who are willing, but a little hesitant, plan a contrived experience that will always allow them to win.

Start with training sessions followed by practice—lots of practice. Volunteers will become so drilled in the experience that their responses will become automatic. If a fundraising contact can become like a piano recital—so well practiced that the audience can't tell you are nervous—it will be a lot easier. Be careful to keep the presentation from sounding canned.

Win or Break Even

Teach your volunteers that they can only win or break even. I play a little game in my workshops. It is like "Odd Man," but I change the rules. I ask someone from the audience to come up and help me. I give the volunteer a quarter and I have a quarter in my hand and several more in my pocket. We each flip our quarters. If we match (both heads or both tails) we each keep our own quarters. If our quarters come up "odd" the volunteer gets my quarter. After play continues for a little while I ask, "How long would you like to play this game?" The answer is usually, "Until you run out of quarters." The only way the other person can lose is to not play at all.

Whenever we ask people for a gift to the library we are starting even. When the prospect says "yes," we win. If the answer is "no," we haven't lost a thing because we started with nothing. Fundraising is a win or break even game. We can never lose.

Empower to Succeed

Give your volunteers the power to succeed. Use these seven points to help them toward success:

1. Trust them to do the job they have been asked to do.
2. Make expectations clear.

3. Provide necessary resources.
4. Give them authority to act independently.
5. Give them feedback while the campaign is in progress.
6. Give them the tools to measure how well they did.
7. Give generous praise for work well done.

SUGGESTIONS TO HELP SOLICITORS

Here are a few ideas that may help the solicitor close more deals:

- *Break your categories of giving into segments.*
  $5,000 will buy one computer terminal for the public access catalog.
  $2,500 will buy a printer.
  $1,000 will buy a laser scanner to check out books.
  $500 will buy_____
  $100 will buy 10,000 bar code labels.
- *Offer to put the donor's name on a piece of equipment.* Long-term remembrance is a priceless commodity. You are not promising that they will live forever. You are just offering to place their name in public view for a long time. Everyone likes to be remembered.
- *Offer to memorialize a loved one who has died.* If they aren't vain enough to want their own name on a piece of equipment, maybe they have a loved one they would like to have the public remember.
- *Appeal to their sense of community pride.* We have one of the best libraries in the whole state. Your investment can make it a little better.
- *Appeal to their concern for children.* Children are the future of our community. Please give for them.
- *Ask the donor for the names of other prospective donors.* Sales people use this technique often. Whether your prospective donor has given or not, ask for the names of people who might be willing to give to your cause.
- *Ask for the prospect's help.* Say: "If there was one thing I could do to help you be inclined to give to our project what would it be?" You might get an unexpected answer. Such as: "Move the book drop to a more convenient place. Or plant some roses in front of the library." When you can comply with the request, do it. Then go back and ask for the gift.
- *Offer a premium.* Premiums are a good way to increase the number and size of gifts. If you offer a prospective donor a coffee mug

for a $50 donation or a tote bag for a $100 donation, you are offering the donor something for his or her contribution—an incentive to give if you will. Public television, radio stations, and alumni associations seem to do the best with premiums. Make sure your premiums are unusual and high quality. Who wants a cheap trinket to remind them that they gave $100 to your library?

DEALING WITH A SPECIAL OBJECTION

How do you deal with those who say the library is already funded with tax money? They say, "Why should I give to the library? I pay taxes. That should be enough." Chances are, your prospect is either not capable of making a donation or not interested in the library. Start by agreeing with him. He or she does pay taxes and taxes are the best form of support for libraries. Ask if he or she wants the library to be the best it can be. Point out that taxes aren't enough to provide the level of service the community requires. Everyone who benefits from the library should also support it with a gift.

SUMMARY

Anyone who lives within the library's service area is a constituent of the library and a prospective donor. Assessing a prospective donor's capacity to give and interest in the library is essential to soliciting donations.

The first people to contact for a gift are the people who will be most likely to give. Keep this prioritized list in mind as you look for donors:

1. Those who have already given major gifts to your library.
2. Those who have made regular donations to the library.
3. Those who have given only once to the library.
4. Individual members of the library board.
5. Friends of the library.
6. People who have paid to attend a special event at the library.
7. Those who have donated books to the library.
8. Regular library patrons.
9. Library volunteers.
10. Registered borrowers of the library.
11. The general public—older people first.

The five principles of fundraising are:

1. Know how much you need and the purpose of your project.
2. Give before you ask.
3. Ask for the gift.
4. Ask the right person for the right amount.
5. Say thank you.

The best closing technique I know is to be silent after you ask for the gift. A personal visit face to face and friend to friend is the most effective way to ask for a donation. It may not be the most efficient, but that depends on whether you count the contacts you make or the amount of money you take in.

Most of all never underestimate the generosity of good people. If they care about their library they will give you the money you need.

BIBLIOGRAPHY

Flanagan, Joan. 1999. *Successful Fundraising: A Complete Handbook for Volunteers and Professionals*. New York: McGraw-Hill – NTC. Joan Flanagan, an experienced fundraiser, shares her successful techniques that will give you the help you need to get more money from your fundraising efforts. The planning guidelines and sample worksheets, along with tips on using the Internet, will benefit any community-wide fundraising effort.

Nichols, Judith E. 1995. *Growing from Good to Great: Positioning Your Fund-Raising Efforts for Big Gains*. Chicago, Ill.: Bonus Books. In *Growing from Good to Great*, the author shows how the world of fundraising has changed, and how to dramatically increase the money we raise from fundraising, if we have the courage to change our methods.

Warwick, Mal. 2000. *The Five Strategies for Fundraising Success: A Mission-Based Guide to Achieving Your Goals*. San Francisco, New York: Jossey-Bass, Wiley. Building on the mission of the organization, the author shows us how to craft goals that can be turned into successful fundraising strategies. The book has plenty of samples to show us how to do it right.

Chapter 6

Selling Goods

The key to selling things to make money for your library is to keep your costs low and inflate the prices you charge. After all you are raising money for the library. In this chapter we discuss the fundamentals of moneymaking projects and how to make them work for you. There is more to having a successful ice cream social than setting a date and asking ten volunteers to bring a freezer full of homemade ice cream to the library.

Please keep in mind, however, that the only reason we sell things to raise money for the library is to get money from nonconstituents. One day at church I was asked to make a hundred loaves of bread to raise money for the missionary fund. I said no—not because I didn't want to support the missionary fund, but because I knew that the church members who would buy my bread for $3.00 a loaf, would probably give $25 to the missionary fund if they were asked to do so. It is also a lot of work to make 100 loaves of bread. When we deal with constituents like church members or club members there is an expectation that everyone will be expected to donate to support the causes of the organization.

GETTING MONEY FROM NONCONSTITUENTS

Churches hold all kinds of fundraisers that draw people from outside their faith to contribute to their building fund, missionary fund, relief fund, etc. You don't have to be a Mennonite to buy one of their beautiful quilts. You don't have to be a Buddhist to enjoy sukiyaki from a Buddhist temple. You just have to have enough money, which they are glad to exchange for their food or handiwork.

It seems easier for most people to sell something than solicit gifts or ask for donations. Somehow selling a tangible object is more appealing to the seller than asking for a contribution. The psychology of selling something at fair value is soothing to the seller's soul. Perhaps it harks back to our feelings of working for what we get. Do we feel that asking for a gift for the library is begging? I hope not. Do we feel that by offering people something in return for their money we have earned the money? Maybe so! Perhaps that is why we would rather sell something to earn money rather than solicit a gift outright.

Let's take an honest look at the ever-present moneymaking projects organizations get involved with. People will spend five or six dollars for the ingredients to make a cake, spend an hour or two making the cake and frosting it. Then they give it to the bake sale to be sold for $6.00. Wouldn't it be easier to donate the six dollars to begin with and not have the work of making the cake? Or worse yet, face the prospect of buying your own cake back for six dollars? Why not have a "bakeless bake sale"?

If you are going to sell something to make more money for your library, sell something you don't have to pay for. This insures a 100 percent profit on the activity. Otherwise you will be making money for someone else, too.

CHARGE ENOUGH TO MAKE MONEY

The biggest problem with moneymaking projects is not charging enough. We are trying to make money for our libraries not offer a bargain or even sell something at fair market value. A reasonable price is whatever a willing buyer and a willing seller agree upon. If no one complains about the price, you are probably not charging enough. If someone is going to buy something from you to help your organization, and you are selling something they want, any price under $10.00 will not deter them. Even $25 might not be too high. So, if you are selling a book bag that costs you $2.50 to produce, why not sell it for $10.00 or $12.00.

My pricing rule of thumb is charge four times the cost of the materials. If you can't make an item and sell it for at least four times the cost of the materials, don't bother. Find another activity. You will find that you are probably making in the range of $6.00 to $8.00 per hour. Your labor is worth more than that.

A few years ago two young women at church asked me to buy a cookbook their club was selling for a moneymaking project.

I asked them, "How much?

They said, "$6.00."

I said, "O.K." without asking to see one.

I asked how much they had to pay for them. They said, "About $3.00." The publisher had suggested selling them at $6.25. I suggested $7.00.

Hierarchy of Things to Sell

1. *Sell the opportunity to sell.* Others have products they want to sell. You create the forum and attract buyers. Turn a section of the library's parking lot into a flea market or arts and crafts fair.
2. *Sell donated items.* Donors give you items to sell rather than giving cash. All the money you make belongs to the library. Used book sales and auctions fit into this category.
3. *Sell something made with donated materials.* The ever-present bake sale leads this list. All you have to invest is your time and effort. You still get to take everything you make to the library.
4. *Sell something on commission.* In effect your fundraising group becomes a retail agent, earning a percentage of the price of each unit sold. If you can return unsold product, your only risk is your time and labor.
5. *Sell something you make with materials you buy.* With your labor, you convert raw materials into a saleable product. You are risking your up-front investment and your labor if things go south.
6. *Sell something you buy.* In essence you become a retail merchant for the producer. You have to buy everything you sell, and you could lose money if the product you buy doesn't sell. I would not try this one unless I could find products that are unique to the library and then sell them for exorbitant prices.

Figure I-6 I Hierarchy of Things to Sell

A dollar more for a cookbook does not sound like much, but if you are selling 1,000 cookbooks, you could earn another $1,000 just by charging a little more. Most people think of a cookbook deal like this one as a donation to the cause. So why not capitalize on their generosity. You are trying to raise money for your library. You are not trying to sell the lowest priced cookbook in town.

HIERARCHY OF SELLING PRODUCTS

If you have to sell a product to make money for your library, seriously consider the hierarchy of products shown in Figure I-6-1.

SELLING FOR A COMPANY

I don't recommend becoming retail agents for a wholesaler. Neither do I believe in exploiting children by making them solicit for the library.

When my oldest son was in junior high school, he became involved in a moneymaking project for the student council. Junior high school students went door-to-door selling summer sausages and specialty cheese products. The company offered inexpensive premiums to students who excelled at selling. When the merchandise arrived they delivered it and collected the money. The student council made a lot of money.

Sounds like a good deal for everyone, right? *Wrong.*

Guess who made the most money? *The people who sold the sausage to the school made the most money.*

Guess who did most of the work? *The students.*

Guess who got taken advantage of? *The customers.*

They were selling a $4.00 sausage for $6.00. I checked it out in the store. They were helping the manufacturer market his product at an inflated price and using children to do it.

If you are going to buy something and sell it as a moneymaking project, check it out carefully before you sign a contract or send money. First of all figure out what the product is selling for in the store. Then figure out what the manufacturer is charging you for the privilege of selling its product. If you are selling something for $6.00 and you get to keep 40 percent, you are paying $3.60 for the product. If you can buy it in the store for $3.75, chances are the merchant bought it for $2.50 or less. If you can't at least double your money and compete with the stores on price, don't sell the product. Find something else to sell.

SELLING TECHNIQUES

If you are selling a book get the person to read something from it. Cookbooks are popular fundraisers. More people buy cookbooks than ever use a recipe from them. But if they see one delicious recipe they think they might want to try, they will buy the book. If you are selling a community history book, they will look for their name. People identify with things that are familiar to them.

Try asking for a cash gift instead of selling a product. Some people would rather have a good feeling about giving to your organization than having a pound of fudge. If someone says, "I don't believe in buying raffle tickets," ask if they would like to donate $10.00.

Try not to compete with the stores at all. It's not nice to sell something they sell, and then go around asking them for a donation. Try to find something unique to sell or make it yourself. That way you can charge whatever you want.

The question then becomes what to sell. If you make something unique and sell it, everyone wins. A woman I know has developed the talent of making beautiful greeting cards. She gets card stock and envelopes from a local printer. She dries flower petals and leaves of all shapes, sizes, and colors. She places five or six dried petals or leaves on the cover of the card in a unique design and covers it with clear plastic adhesive. It costs her about 10 cents for the card and the envelope. She sells her unique gifts for 75 cents each and donates the money to her church.

Abiding by the Law

If you are going to engage in commerce your library is probably subject to the same laws as any other business. Become familiar with the laws regarding sales tax and sales permits. You cannot assume that just because the library is doing it that you are exempt from collecting sales tax and remitting it to the state. If sales permits are required for other businesses doing the same thing you are planning to do, get the sales permit and abide by the law.

Here is a word of caution about raffles, bingo, and gambling. Find out what the laws are and obey them. Some states have strict laws and stiff penalties for gambling and the like—even for charity. It is better to abide by the law than to be embarrassed by getting caught for trying to ignore it.

MONEYMAKING SAMPLER

Even though I have my reservations about moneymaking projects for libraries, they are often the only way libraries have to earn a little extra money. Let's take a look at some of the things they do to make money. Some of these ideas may be helpful to you.

Street Fair

Joan Duke of Sedona, Arizona, reported that $20,000 was made from a street fair organized by one of the board members. "It was a one-day event. Everything was donated for the fair. Twenty booths selling everything from plants, quilts, wood products, books, balloons, white elephant items, hand sewn, etc. A variety of entertainment occurred throughout the day, such as musical groups, gymnast, storyteller. No one charged for their services, time, or material" (Swan, 1990:157).

"The board member in charge had a committee of about a half dozen helpers. These people were all community members. But the Board of Trustees all worked on the fair, as did the library staff, and our 70-plus library volunteers. Community response was excellent."

Ice Cream Social

In Ellis, Kansas, on the second Sunday in August you can count on homemade ice cream, cake, iced tea, and live entertainment in the park. The men make the ice cream, almost competing with each other for best tasting batch of the day, though there is no judging or prizes. The women are almost the same about their cakes. They might spend five or six dollars and an entire afternoon on their favorite cake. Everything sells for a dollar a serving. They ask volunteers to donate cakes, ice cream, and tea. With a little advertising everything falls into place. A band, singing country and western music, volunteers its talents. Some feel it is a lot of work for the money they make, but everybody has a good time and they appreciate the live music.

Used Jewelry Sale

Another library has a used jewelry sale every year at the same time the downtown merchants have their annual sidewalk sales. About six months before the sale, the library advertises that it needs used necklaces, bracelets, earrings, and rings for the sale. People bring in items they don't want or need. Customers have found pieces made of solid silver with turquoise that probably sold for $50 or more. It's all donated to the library. The library puts these pieces in with the rest of the jewelry and sells them for 50 cents each. Bargain hunters love it and the library makes several hundred dollars.

Publish a Telephone Book and Sell It

In Prairie View, Kansas, library fundraisers discovered that the residents in three nearby towns could call each other toll-free, but they had no unified telephone directory. With a little help from others they published a directory and sold copies to the local residents in each of the towns. When a fundraising group is able to focus on a community need and make money by filling it, they are well on their way to success.

Hold an Auction

When you do it right, auctions are a great way to raise money for your library. Doing it right depends on your community and patterns of giving. Basically you get a retailer to give you new merchandise they haven't sold. You hold a silent auction for items valued under $100. Hold a live auction for items over $100. Be sure to get the services of a professional auctioneer. See the section on auctions on page 245 for more information.

Used Book Sale

Libraries are a natural for this one. I would not recommend used book sales for any other organization. Making big dollars from a book sale requires going into it in a big way and it means a lot of hard work. You will have to recruit plenty of volunteers and solicit tons of books from the community. If you expect to make money from a book sale by weeding your collection and selling your worn-out, dog-eared books, forget it. (See the section on used book sales on page 345 for more details.)

Flea Market

This is a good idea if you have the space. If you are serious about sponsoring a flea market check out the flea market in San Jose, California. Their Web site is www.sjfm.com/geninfo.html

These people have gone into the business in a big way. They have over 2,000 sellers offering a huge selection of collectibles, including arts, crafts, comic books, belt buckles, jewelry, clothing, furniture, tools, etc. The also have dozens of restaurants, food booths, and snack carts.

All of these vendors pay up to $20.00 a day for the privilege of setting up their booths and selling their wares. The people who run the flea market charge for parking—$5.00 on weekends and $1.00 on weekdays. They require all sellers to comply with state law regarding resale permits.

You could turn the library parking lot into a flea market once a week and make some good money. I would be sure to deal with these concerns:

- Do you have someone to be in charge?
- Do you have to get permission from the city to use the parking lot for a flea market?
- Do you plan to operate the flea market when the library is open?
- Do you have enough parking for customers if you rent spaces to vendors?
- Do you know the state law regarding the kind of selling that is done at flea markets?
- Will the community support such a venture?

Sell an Idea from Your Library to Other Libraries

You might have created a unique packet or publication to help you provide services to your patrons. Other librarians may be willing to pay to see a copy of it. In 1988 the Great Bend Public Library prepared "Assignment Alert Packets" for distribution to local teachers. The purpose of the packets was to encourage teachers to notify the public library when a library assignment was imminent. It was such a success that we offered copies to other libraries for $8.00. We sent copies to professional journals and asked them to feature it if they felt it was noteworthy. The library grossed over $3,500 in less than a year.

Author Luncheons

The Friends of the Willcox (Arizona) Public Library sponsor an annual author luncheon. They try to arrange for local authors to come and speak at a luncheon, which they arrange for with a restaurant. Advertising is low budget, using radio public service announcements and news releases. They sell tickets in advance and ask the authors to donate 30 percent of their profits from the books sold at the luncheon. They usually make less than $500 in a community of 3,800 people. It is a lot of work, but the visibility is worth as much as the money they raise. The next time they do it, they plan to step up promotion and have the food catered at the community center.

Local Trivia Game

A library group in Glasco, Kansas, teamed up with the local adult education group that needed money, too. Together they published a "Glasco Trivia Game." Townspeople submitted questions and answers. The library and the adult education group divided the work and split the profits.

Garden/Home Tour with Buffet

Diane Slater, librarian in Liberal, Kansas (population 16,000), raised $2,700 to help renovate and remodel their library by having a garden and home tour with a buffet dinner. They attracted a large number of donors.

They served 155 people with food costs of $3.70 per plate, but they made a comfortable profit. Diane suggests that it would be better to cater the food. She attributes their success to:

- Planning the meal carefully.
- Arranging to use the Petroleum Club kitchen and serving facility.
- Finding three or four volunteers to help prepare, cook, and serve the meal.
- Finding a social organization willing to act as servers and clean up afterwards.
- Buying all supplies through restaurant suppliers.

Recycle Junk Cars

Mark Cunningham, a local automobile dealer, was the chair of the fundraising committee for the Ellsworth, Kansas, library building fund. He made arrangements with a scrap metal recycling firm to come to Ellsworth to pick up junk cars and haul them off for scrap metal. They made about $50 per car. All of the proceeds went to the library's building fund.

Carnivals

Everyone has a good time at carnivals, especially children. Carnivals provide an opportunity for social activities for families, and they make money in a unique way. They require a lot of work for the money you make, but they are a lot of fun. If you do a raffle get the prizes donated.

When I was 16, my twin brother and I put together a 4-H carnival. We went all over town gathering refrigerator cartons to build the booths. We got various club members to be in charge of individual booths. Club members sold books of tickets with a chance on the door prize that had been donated. Everyone in the community came and the 4-H club made several hundred dollars.

Christmas and Greeting Card Sale

Every year the San Antonio (Texas) Parks and Recreation Department sells Christmas cards that feature winning art work from its annual art contest. Artists have portrayed Christmas scenes from around San Antonio. The Parks and Recreation Department has cards printed up as a fundraiser every year. They package cards and envelopes—15 to a box and sell them for $5.00 a box. Check out their Web site for more information: www.ci.sat.tx.us/card.htm.

With a little effort a library could replicate the project. If you have a famous building in your town you could create a greeting card based on a depiction or a photo of the building and sell the cards in the library. They make nice inexpensive gifts.

McCracken, Kansas, is the home of the hotel filmed in the movie *Paper Moon*. The library used a drawing of the hotel for the cover of a greeting card, which they sold in the library. This project has been going for 20 years. The library is still making money from selling the cards.

Final Moneymaking Suggestions

Here are a few last ideas you can offer in a brainstorming session. There might be a gem here you haven't thought of. Turn your brainstorming group loose on these. They might come up with a winner.

- Crafts boutique
- Dollhouse show
- Flower sales
- Swap meets
- Battle of the bands
- Card parties
- Celebrity baseball game
- Fishing tournaments

- Golf tournaments
- Horseshoe pitching tournaments
- Rodeos
- Street dances
- Talent shows
- Theater parties

Moneymaking Projects in the Big Picture

With moneymaking projects you are selling a product for its approximate value. Some people would rather sell candy or chances on a quilt than to just ask for money. Others prefer to simply ask for a cash gift. You have to be in tune with your volunteers and your community to make the right decision on this issue. But making things and selling them will never produce large amounts of money you need to build a new library. These activities may supplement the big dollars that will have to come from soliciting gifts.

USING VOLUNTEERS

Once you have sorted through all of the moneymaking projects and have selected the one you think will make the most money for your group, take some time before you jump into the pond and ask, "Who is going to do the work?"

If your organization is small you may find yourself looking around the room and calculating how many tickets or pounds of fudge you are going to have to sell. While getting the stuff to sell for free may be difficult but not impossible, finding enough people to do all of the work may be impractical. Check Figure I-1-5 Resources Required for Success in Chapter 1 to determine if the fundraising activity you want to try will require a lot of volunteers. Too often 20 percent of people do 80 percent of the work and the workers get burned out after a while.

If the people in your organization are already stressed to the max, you may want to opt for a "Bake-less Bake Sale." The alternative to a bake-less bake sale is a "non-event event"—you send everyone a tea bag and an invitation to stay at home and relax with a cup of tea. All they have to do to participate is send you $25.00.

SELLING SOMETHING VERSUS PREMIUMS

Don't confuse premiums with selling. Premiums never approximate the value of the gift, but you try to attach some emotional value or sense of loyalty by putting something on the premium like a logo or a symbol that means something to the donor. If you offer a prospective donor a coffee mug for a $50 donation or a tote bag for a $100 donation, you are not selling the mug for $50 or the bag for $100. If you are going to sell coffee mugs, price them at two or three times what you paid for them.

SUMMARY

The only reason we sell things to raise money is to get money from nonconstituents. It seems easier for most people to sell something than solicit gifts or ask for donations. I call these projects moneymaking projects—not fundraising!

Selling things to make money for your library is sometimes more work than it is worth. If you are going to sell something to make money for your library, the best thing to sell is something you don't have to pay for. The side benefits of increased visibility and adding to your donor base from nonconstituents may make the difference.

When it comes to fundraising, you have to start somewhere. Why not try selling something the people in your community will buy? We are trying to make money for our libraries not offer a bargain, so sell your products for as much as people will pay.

Try not to compete with the stores. Try to find something to sell that they don't stock. It's not nice to sell something they sell, and then go around asking them for a donation.

If you have a well-developed, generous constituency, solicit a donation rather than trying to sell something.

BIBLIOGRAPHY

Amos, Janell Shride. 1995. *Fundraising Ideas: Over 225 Money Making Events for Community Groups*, With a Resource Directory. Jefferson, N.C.: McFarland. If you are looking for some moneymaking ideas, this book has lots of them. They run the gamut from men-only beauty contests, to tearooms, to cakewalks, to kissing booths. Every event is described in detail along with the workers and tools needed.

Chapter 7

Understanding the Principles of Passive Fundraising

Passive fundraising is encouraging people to give money to your library without overtly asking for it. It is *not* doing *nothing*. It is doing something positive and letting people figure out that your library needs some of their money. Passive fundraising is letting what you do on a day-to-day basis speak for you. You are not getting in someone's face and putting the bite on him or her. You are doing a good job of running your library, and you are letting your actions speak for you.

People always want to be on a winning team. Think about it. Wouldn't you rather give money to a thriving organization that is doing good things for people than to give to a bedraggled homeless person with liquor on his or her breath? I would, even though I have given to both. I felt better about giving money to someone who was helping others. Your job is to convey the image that your library is thriving and doing good things for people. You just need the help of others to do even more good for more people.

WIN WITH QUALITY CUSTOMER SERVICE

The key to passive fundraising is absolute top-quality customer service. This means that customers get what they want when they come to the library. Here is how to make it happen (see Figure I-7-1).

Patrons will recognize your efforts to provide quality service, and they will look for ways to say thank you.

Essentials of Quality Customer Service

- Get to know your library users and find out what they want from your library.
- Create and communicate a mission for the library that focuses on your patrons.
- Treat your employees like you want them to treat your customers.
- Teach by precept and example that customers come first.
- Establish and reinforce positive behaviors that demonstrate quality service.
- Provide tangible and intangible reward systems as a form of staff recognition.
- Measure progress with numbers and positive anecdotes.
- Build a reputation of quality service at the library.

Figure 1-7-1 Essentials of Quality Customer Service

LEARN FROM A COMMUNITY NEEDS ASSESSMENT SURVEY

A needs assessment will let you know how well your library is meeting the needs of the community. It can point the way to the need for developing future resources and services. It will help you discover:

- What services and materials are being used and to what extent.
- Who is using the library.
- Ideas for reaching people who do not use the library.
- How well current services are meeting community needs.
- If library hours and staffing are adequate.
- If the space in the library is adequate to provide the services the community needs.
- Demographic and socioeconomic changes in the community.

If you have never assessed community needs for your library, doing a needs assessment can be a big job. You may even want to call in some outside help and pay a professional to do it. If you decide to do a community needs assessment you need to decide:

1. Who will carry out the research?
2. What kind of data should be gathered?
3. How will the information be collected?
4. How will the library use the facts and figures?

Your answers to these questions will determine the direction of the enquiry.

Who Will Carry Out the Research?

Whether you decide to use an outside consultant, the library staff, or library volunteers will depend on the resources you have available to conduct the study. My first choice would be to hire an expert from the outside if you have the money. He or she would have a better chance of obtaining accurate responses from members of the community. An experienced consultant can do the research quickly and produce a professionally prepared report. My next choice would be to use community volunteers. Their services are free and you can train them to gather the data you need. A serious drawback to using volunteers is their propensity to be biased. The respondents may tell them what they think the volunteers want to hear. My last choice would be to use the library staff. The information they gather could be inaccurate because people may not be willing to share critical comments about the library with the library staff members. Also the time they spend working on the needs assessment will be time spent away from working in the library.

You need to decide the most effective approach and then move ahead. You could use a combination of all three data-gathering groups. Use a consultant to help you design the study. Use volunteers to gather the data. Let the staff compile the raw data and then ask the consultant to help interpret the results and write the report.

What Kind of Data Should Be Gathered?

Don't gather the data if you don't plan to use it in the report. Ask questions that will provide answers that will assess the value of what you are doing now or the potential of planned future services. Here are a few broad areas you may want to explore:

- *Community background.* How did your community become what it is today? The answers will give you an insight into the kinds of resources the library needs to offer.
- *Geographical information.* How has community growth patterns affected transportation and population distribution? Answers could help assess the need for outreach services.
- *Demographic information.* How have age, ethnicity, and transience affected population distribution in the community? Data could help you provide materials and services based on ethnicity or primary language spoken in the home.
- *Income assessment.* What is the average family income by census tract? This information could help determine the need for different types of materials.

- *Economic assessment.* What is the economic base for the community? Having this information could lead to specific fundraising activities.
- *Social and cultural organizations.* What are the prominent social and cultural organizations? Working through these organizations could help the library meet the needs of a majority of the people in the community.

How Will the Information Be Collected?

Now you need to decide how to gather the information you have selected to use in your study. You can use:

- *Interviewing community gatekeepers.* These leaders have wide contact with many people in the community. Their opinions can be biased and skew the data you gather.
- *Holding neighborhood meetings.* When you hold a public meeting you hope all segments of the population will attend. Don't count on it. You may only attract the people who already love the library and think it is doing a wonderful job.
- *Using focus groups.* Focus groups are generally led by outside consultants and attended by different groups at different times—each group is made up of like-minded people.
- *Using public records to research demographic data.* Staff members can research public records, but it will take training to know what data to extract from these records.
- *Using census data to gather population statistics.* Just about any kind of demographic and population you want can be found at the Web site of the U.S. Census Bureau—www.census.gov/.
- *Using surveys.* This is a popular data-gathering technique. You can send out a questionnaire and ask people to fill it out and return it. You can call people on the telephone and ask them questions. You can hand out surveys to patrons when they come to the library. You can post a questionnaire on the library's Web site.

All of these methods of gathering information have their strengths and weaknesses. Don't discount a method because it has a weakness. Accept its drawback and figure out a way to compensate for the weakness.

How Will the Library Use the Facts and Figures?

The first step is to compile the data. The second is to interpret it through data analysis. Here are some of the conclusions that could come from the community needs assessment (see Figure I-7-2).

These are just a few of the perceptions or realities that could come

---

Examples of Needs Assessment Findings

- The general population is getting older.
- The number of children between the ages of one and six is shrinking.
- The number of residents of one or more ethnic groups has increased.
- The main businesses have moved to malls leaving the library in a blighted downtown.
- People are afraid to come to the main library after dark because of its location.
- People think the library looks shabby and unattractive.
- The materials in the library are outdated and irrelevant.
- All of the computers in the library have changed the way people get information.

Figure I-7-2 Examples of Needs Assessment Findings

from a needs assessment study. You can probably double the list, but you get the idea. Your job is to use the data to change the way your library does business and respond to the needs assessment. You may be able to use the results of the study as the basis for an appeal for additional tax revenue.

Once the data is analyzed you should be able to create a prioritized list that reflects the library needs of the community. Share the results with the people and tell them what the library plans to do to meet the needs of the community. Hold public meetings. Write articles for the newspaper. Post the results on the library's Web site. Do whatever it takes to spread the word.

You want to send a clear message to the people that the library is listening to them—you want them to get what they want when they come to the library.

PERFORMANCE PRECEDES FUNDING

Any kind of fundraising, passive or proactive, can only be effective if you have your act together first. Ask yourself, "How could we do better?" The results of your needs assessment will give you some ideas. If you need to fix some things, do whatever it takes to present a positive image to the public. Finally, toot your own horn long and loud and often.

When people give money to libraries they want their gift to make a difference. They don't want it to be used to make up for a lack of tax support or the neglect of a governing body. The job of all library managers is to make sure that their libraries perform well so that people get what they want when they go there.

If you are doing a good job people will walk in and give you money without your asking for it. They will name your library in their wills. They will respond to a plaque on the wall that doesn't include their name. I have seen it happen.

As the director of libraries for the past 30 years I have seen my share of unexpected gifts from people we didn't even know. We had done nothing special, except maybe treat the people kindly when they came in to the library, or take some books to people who were homebound.

WHAT CAN YOU DO?

Once you have done everything you can to improve library services it is time to do something to make people aware that your library will accept gifts from the public, and then letting that action ask for money in a passive way. You could put two or three donor recognition plaques on the wall—one for each level of giving.

For example, a woman walked into the library in Ellis, Kansas. She asked the librarian, "What do I have to do to get my name on that plaque over there?" She was pointing to a wooden plaque with names engraved on little brass rectangles. The plaque recognized those who had given $1,000 or more to the library's building fund.

The librarian said, "Give us a thousand dollars and we will put your name on the plaque."

The woman responded by saying, "Our wheat crop wasn't too good this year, but I will see what I can do."

About two weeks later she returned to the library and gave her check for a thousand dollars to the librarian and handed her a piece of paper saying how she wanted her name put on the little brass square.

The only thing anyone had ever done to ask the woman for money was to put up a plaque that recognized other $1,000 donors.

OTHER PASSIVE IDEAS

Here are a few of the ideas I have seen or heard about in the past several years (see Figure I-7-3).

What could *you* do to encourage people in your community to feel good about the library, perhaps to the point of giving money? Think about it for a minute or two. Discuss it with the library staff. You might even want to engage in a brainstorming activity.

TRY BRAINSTORMING

Brainstorming is a marvelous technique that can produce exciting, often unexpected results. In a brainstorming session of a library fundraising

---

Passive Fundraising Ideas

- Create a one-page flyer with a coupon to promote memorial giving for books. Patrons will take one and keep it until they need it to send with a donation to remember a friend who has passed away.
- Put a large jar on the circulation desk with a sign that says what the money will be used for, like the Summer Reading Program. People will often put pocket change in a donation jar to help a cause they feel good about.
- Put a flyer in funeral homes to suggest memorial giving to the library. Those who have to make funeral arrangements may want to give friends of the family alternative ways to honor their loved one.
- At Christmastime, decorate a Christmas tree with tags that suggest book titles that the library would like to have for Christmas. This is a little twist that gives people a chance to remember the library during the holidays.
- Write a letter to Santa Claus containing the library's wish list and have it published in the newspaper. You are just taking advantage of another opportunity to tell people what the library needs.
- Put a request for donations and the library's wish list on the library's Web site. Depending on how many people use the Internet to connect with the library, many people could find a giving opportunity.
- Offer magazines for adoption with a sign in the magazine area of the library, or by placing the names of other donors on the magazines that have been adopted. Once people discover that they can adopt a magazine they might be willing to pay for their favorite periodical.
- Write letters to attorneys to let them know of the library's planned giving program. Attorneys regularly draw up wills for people. If they know about the library's deferred giving program, they can help people make a bequest to the library in their wills.
- Place display advertisements occasionally in the local newspaper explaining one of the library's gift solicitation programs. This is just one way to maintain public awareness of the library's need for gifts.
- Make sure recognition plaques have room for the names of additional donors. If your recognition plaques have no room for more names people will think you don't need any more money.

Figure 1-7-3 Passive Fundraising Ideas

group in Ellsworth, Kansas, someone suggested writing a letter to Santa Claus. Maybe the situation seemed so hopeless that a letter to Santa seemed as good an idea as any. After the expected round of smiles and laughs, the note taker wrote it down and the group moved on.

Later on someone suggested that they go ahead and write a letter to Santa Claus. They did and saw it published in the local newspaper. They created a "wish list," naming several items the library needed. A bank bought a $600.00 set of encyclopedias. Others gave money. A simple letter to Santa brought in $2,500 for the library. This was a fairly passive activity—a general letter published in the newspaper for everyone to see.

What would have happened if someone had said, "What a stupid idea! That will never work?"

Brainstorming sessions are synergistic activities designed to create ideas that build on each other. The whole becomes greater than the sum of its parts. By now the sense of ownership of ideas is distanced by time and people are not as sensitive to critical comments about their suggestions.

You will be surprised at the power of allowing the subconscious mind to work on the problem. The time between the idea generation session and the evaluation and implementation session is "mulling-it-over-time." New thoughts will come to you and new twists on other suggestions enhance the process.

LEARN THE IMPORTANCE OF PUBLIC RELATIONS

All libraries have public relations. Whether they like it or not—whether it's good or bad, high powered or low-key—all libraries have it. Unfortunately, for some libraries it is often low profile and seldom pushed beyond the cloistered walls of the library itself.

When I first moved to South Carolina in 1971, I discovered that I needed to increase the visibility for the library. Before I could do that, I had to produce the programs people expected from a public library. It doesn't pay to advertise if you can't deliver the goods you advertise. I could have traveled all over the county inviting people to come to the library, and they might have come in once. But they would never have returned if we didn't have what they needed the first time they came to the library.

It was no surprise that the library needed money. We had less than $1.00 per capita for library services—barely enough to hire a few staff members and buy very few books, with no money for public relations. Fundraising was in order.

My first fundraising opportunity came because we needed money to promote the library. So I prepared a small project and asked a bank to underwrite it. I asked the bank president for $300 to pay for a library publicity booklet published by Channing-Bete. Information about the library and the bank's logo would be printed on the back. She agreed to the project and we were on our way.

With a booklet in hand for each student, I went to every elementary school in the county. I presented a program, passed out the booklets, and gave every child the opportunity to apply for a library card. We mailed library cards to the children with a letter encouraging them to use the library. At the same time we offered a card to their parents.

Borrower registration doubled overnight and circulation increased dramatically. When parents and children discovered their library, funding started to improve. When people believe you are doing something that will benefit them, they will see that you get the money you need to do even more for them.

Sometimes our problem is not our performance, but our image. We are doing a good job, but nobody knows it. That's why we have to take time to see ourselves as others see us. The clerk at the supermarket who said, "Oh, where is the library?" gave me an outsider's window through which I could see the library.

If the image of your library is inaccurate, you have to get outside the library to fix it. Changing public perception without getting out of the library is like taking a bath in a wet suit. You never get to the heart of the problem. You become so accustomed to the way you see your situation that you can't see it the way others do.

You could have all kinds of videos, CD's, and the latest best sellers, but if people think of your library as a warehouse of books, and the people inside don't care if you come or not, you will always have funding problems.

DO SOMETHING TO CHANGE THE LIBRARY'S IMAGE

Take a minute right now to assess your library's image. How do people see it? How do you see it? Make a list of three things you could do next week that would make a difference in how the public sees your library. Write one of the ideas on your "To Do List" for next Monday.

Then do it.

Did you have trouble thinking of some ideas to enhance your library's image? Here are a few you might try:

- Create a one-page, three-fold library brochure. Include library services, special programs for special groups, hours, address, telephone number, staff, and board members. You can do this with a typewriter. Use a photocopier to duplicate it. It doesn't take much money to do a nice looking brochure. If you want to get fancy, a desktop publisher can put it together in a few hours.
- Take a stack of your newly created brochures around to the business people in town. Tell them you are promoting the services of the library. Offer help to find information for their business. Ask for suggestions to make the library more visible in the community.
- Have business cards printed for the librarian and all board members, with individual names with the library's name, address, and telephone number on one side, and the library hours on the other.

- Take the head of the Chamber of Commerce to lunch. Ask him or her for ideas to improve the library's image with the business community.
- Obtain a list of local service groups and clubs. They are always looking for programs. Offer to do one for them.

Did you notice that all of these suggestions require that you get out of the library and do something besides check out books? Targeting public relations activities to those who already come to the library is like preaching to the choir. They already know and love the library. You want to reach those who don't know the good fortune of the library, but are ready to be converted.

LOOKING AT LIBRARY PERFORMANCE AND EFFECTIVENESS

Now take a look at your actual performance. Do your hours meet the needs of the community? Do you have the materials to give the people what they want when they come in? What about the staff? Are they friendly, helpful, and well trained? What do you do if the library doesn't have the material requested?

Thomas Childers and Nancy Van House in their book, *What's Good? Describing Your Public Library's Effectiveness* (1993), found that various groups considered the following to be important aspects of public library effectiveness:

- Convenience of hours
- Staff helpfulness
- Range of services
- Range of materials
- Services suited to community needs
- Materials quality
- Staff quality
- Materials availability
- Contribution to community well being
- Awareness of service

They surveyed community leaders, local officials, friends, trustees, users, library managers, and service librarians. The unusual finding of their survey was that all groups tended to respond alike.

You can gather statistics around these measurements and use the data to plan your appeal to the voters. If your library gets high marks on most of them you should have no difficulty passing a library referendum.

You can improve the performance of your library in other areas, if you will take the time to study what you are doing and make plans to enhance your service.

Robert Hartsook suggests establishing your identity by answering the question: "Who are we? Keep your image simple. Externalize your program. Describe it the way the donors see it. Be consistent and persistent. Do it the same over and over again. Be prepared to explain it one more time" (1989).

Performance does precede funding. They sustain each other. A library that does not give the people what they want cannot expect the support it needs. A poorly funded library cannot give the people what they want. If people perceive their library to be effective, funding will follow.

Passive fundraising can only be successful if the library is doing a good job of meeting customer needs and communicating the library's ongoing need for more money.

SUMMARY

Passive fundraising is encouraging people to give money to your library without overtly asking for it. It is doing something positive and letting people figure out that your library needs some of their money.

Your job is to convey the image that your library is thriving and doing good things for people, but it still needs their money and support to continue.

Do people get what they want when they come to your library? If so, you will probably have the support you need to get the funding you need. Sometimes we have to see ourselves through the eyes of others to become aware of our shortcomings.

When people give money to libraries they want their gift to make a difference. The job of all library managers is to make sure that their libraries perform well so that people get what they want when they go there.

All libraries have public relations. Unfortunately, for some libraries it is often low profile and seldom pushed beyond the cloistered walls of the library itself. You will have to get outside your library to truly assess its image and performance. Ask staff members and board members to help with the assessment. Ask for suggestions to make the library more visible in the community.

When people get what they want at the library they will help provide the funding it needs. Passive fundraising can only be successful if the library is doing a good job of meeting customer needs and communicating the library's ongoing need for more money.

Do people get what they want when they come to your library?

BIBLIOGRAPHY

Childers, Thomas A., and Nancy A. Van House. 1993. *What's Good? Describing Your Public Library's Effectiveness.* Chicago: American Library Association. This book is based on solid research that can help you assess your image and performance.

Field, Selma G., and Edwin M. Field. 2000. *Publicity Manual for Libraries: A Comprehensive Professional Guide to Communications: A Book That No Library Should Be Without.* Somerville, N.J.: Replica Books. This book tells you how to do press releases, write news stories, take and select photographs, use video clips, and write annual reports, brochures, and newsletters.

Short, Jack (John T.). 1998. *Library Fundraising Guidelines.* Avon, Conn.: Consultant Publications. Each chapter is a short essay on a fundraising topic. It has some nifty ideas for librarians and board members who also find themselves raising money for their library.

Walters, Suzanne. 1994. *Customer Service: A How-to-Do-It Manual for Librarians.* New York: Neal-Schuman. This book will help you refocus your goals and objectives on the needs of library customers. It will help you and the library staff become excited about serving the public.

Chapter 8

Enlisting Help from Other Sources

During westward movement days, pioneers would send scouts ahead of the main company to figure out the best route to follow. Usually mounted on fast horses, scouts looked for the best place to cross a river and good places to camp. Sometimes they would climb high peaks so they could see as far as possible into the distance. Sometimes they stopped and talked with other travelers. They were always on the lookout for hostile Indians, or other dangers. The job of the scout was to get the wagon train to its destination with the least difficulty.

LOOKING FOR HELP

According to Tom Vance of Kenneth M. Vance Associates (professional fundraising consultants), "A big advantage of hiring a professional is that he or she can provide a clearer assessment of your potential." A professional fundraiser can tell you if you need to build your image or sharpen your performance before you ask people to support a fundraising effort.

In this chapter you will learn where to go for help from experts and determine what level of help you need. Every fundraising effort needs a scout. You may need someone who has experience with fundraising to help you to avoid hostile people or lead you to the best watering places. If you don't think you have the expertise within your organization, get some help. You need knowledgeable people to help you make it all the way to your goal.

Consider these options:

- *Find a full-time fundraiser from another organization in your community.*

Most colleges have a development department. It may be called by a variety of names—foundation, scholarship fund, or development department. Their job is to raise money for the college—primarily for scholarships or building expansion. Sometimes they will be willing to meet with others and share their expertise—especially if they do not perceive your campaign as a threat to them. They realize that they cannot be the recipients of all local giving. They may even see your effort as augmenting their fundraising.

- *Approach the volunteer head of the United Way.*

Often these people have abundant experience in the area of fundraising. If they are convinced of the value of your cause, they can be very helpful. Local people already know your turf. It may be easier for them to understand your needs and help you develop a strategy for your community.

- *Use consultants from the state library or the regional library system.*

If you belong to a system that provides consulting services, you may be able to get some good help from them. Your state library may also offer consulting assistance. Either way, these consultants have a responsibility to help all libraries in the area. They can help you organize and get started. They will know your area better than someone from out-of-state. They can always be counted on to review or help write a grant.

- *Hire a professional fundraising consultant.*

Many librarians and board members are afraid of hiring a professional fundraiser because they believe that the community will react negatively toward them and they don't want to jeopardize their fundraising effort. It is important that the librarian, the board, and the community understand that professional consultants do no soliciting.

HIRING A PROFESSIONAL

A professional consulting firm will send experts into your area to help you organize and execute a fundraising campaign. They will move you through every step of the process and if you follow their guidance, you will raise money. Most of them work for a set fee. You contract with them for specific tasks for a fixed amount.

The Beaver Dam (Wisconsin) Library hired a professional fundraiser to do a feasibility study, write a campaign booklet, and find a volunteer chairman. In the leadership phase, they recruited 17 volunteers to solicit approximately 75 prospects. In the special phase they recruited 70 volunteers to solicit approximately 250 prospects. They also did a phone-a-thon using volunteers and city directory. The public response to the professional fundraiser was excellent.

Use the Associations of Professional Fundraising Consultants

Those who are members of the Association of Fundraising Professionals or the American Association of Fundraising Counsel, Inc. subscribe to a code of fair practice that prohibits them from charging a percentage of the funds raised. The purpose of the code is to set forth fundraising tenets that member firms are expected to follow.

You can learn more about the Association of Fundraising Professionals through their Web site: www.nsfre.org/. The Web address for the American Association of Fundraising Counsel, Inc. is www.aafrc.org/. Both of these Web sites offer suggestions about selecting a professional fundraiser.

Start with a Feasibility Study

Professional fundraising consultants conduct feasibility and planning studies, and offer campaign management, public relations, and other related services. Professional fundraising consultants believe that it is in the best interest of clients that volunteers solicit gifts.

The fees of fundraising consultants are mutually agreed upon in advance and are based on the services provided. Initial meetings with prospective clients are more of a sales visit—an opportunity for the professional and the client to get acquainted and to learn what is expected of each other. No payment is expected for these meetings.

A detailed agreement outlines the services of the professional consultant and the fee for each component. Costs vary, but usually run between six and fifteen percent of the total amount raised. Some professional fundraisers guarantee that their fees will not exceed ten percent of the money you raise. If you want to raise $500,000, count on spending between $30,000 and $50,000. The higher the goal, the lower the percentage.

Some consultants absolutely require a feasibility study before entering into a contract to assist with a fundraising effort. A feasibility study answers the following questions:

1. How much money can be raised?
2. Where are the funds coming from?
3. Who will be the most effective chairperson?
4. What is the best timetable?
5. What will be the budget for the campaign?
6. Do you have the volunteers to do the job?

Conducting the Feasibility Study

Most professionals like to interview at least 30 people. The first questions are: How do you feel about the library? Is it meeting your needs or the needs of the community? Could it do a better job? If so, what could it do to improve?

The professional takes two documents with him or her: 1) a list of library needs and their estimated costs; and 2) a scale of giving. After reviewing the list of needs with the person he or she is interviewing, the professional consultant explains that in order for the library to meet its needs, it has to raise so much money. Then the consultant shows the potential donor the scale of giving and asks how many gifts of a certain size he or she thinks can be raised in the community. A feasibility study pre-sells the need to prospective donors without asking them for money. Sometimes without asking, the prospective donor will volunteer to make the lead gift. What a nice surprise when that happens!

The professional begins with a short list of community leaders. As he or she interviews leading people, he or she will ask for the names of other prominent citizens. This gives the professional a sense of community attitudes toward the organization. The professional also gains an awareness of where the big money is. All the time he or she is looking for the best person to be the chair of the fundraising campaign. This is one of the best reasons to use a professional fundraiser. The library board may have handpicked someone for the task, yet the community may not perceive that person to be the most effective one for the job. Having an outsider help select the leader for the campaign can add credibility to the effort and help overcome the possibility of cronyism.

Within a few thousand dollars, most experienced fundraising professionals can tell you how much money can be raised. If they have doubts about the success of a fundraising effort, they discuss their reservations with the client before proceeding. They may suggest waiting a few months or a year to give you time to improve relations with the community or rebuild the library's credibility. This is an important reason to hire a professional to do a feasibility study.

Every community is different and you are the expert in your town. Whether you hire a professional or not is up to you. Taking this little quiz might help you decide whether or not to seek the assistance of a professional. If you can answer *yes* to most of these questions you may not need a professional fundraising consultant.

Professional Fundraiser Readiness Quiz

1. Do we want to raise less than $500,000?
2. Do we have a clear vision of what we want to do and how we want to do it?
3. Do members of our organization have the skills to assess the giving potential for our project in our community?
4. Do we know who will lead us and are we confident that he or she can manage the campaign?
5. Can we train our volunteers to be highly effective solicitors?
6. Can we count on every member of the board to be committed to the project?
7. Can we recruit people to help us sell our vision to others in a way that will raise money?
8. Do we have the skills and resources within our organization to develop quality written materials to support our project?
9. Can we write and produce a persuasive, polished case statement?

Figure 1-8-1 Professional Fundraiser Readiness Quiz

Use the Professional Fundraiser Readiness Quiz

The first question is critical. Raising less than $500,000 can probably be done on your own. Some professionals believe the return on the investment below this amount is open to discussion.

Whether you hire a professional or seek the advice of someone else, make sure they do or help you do the following:

- Conduct a feasibility or precampaign study.
- Review and refine your library's mission statement.
- Interview community leaders.
- Select campaign leader.
- Set a realistic goal for the project.
- Write and prepare a case statement.
- Formulate gift brackets to reach the goal.
- Train leaders to recruit volunteers.
- Train volunteers to solicit gifts.
- Kick off the campaign.
- Keep the campaign moving.
- Manage campaign office.
- Formulate total campaign calendar.
- Provide guidance for large gift cultivation.
- Write special proposals.
- Prepare public relations materials.
- Develop follow-up procedures.

Setting the Campaign Goal

Vance Associates use a precampaign questionnaire with library board members to help clarify their thinking and help them set the campaign goal. Here are the questions they ask:

1. Does the library board presently have a mission statement?
2. What are some past notable achievements of the library?
3. What are the library's physical plant needs?
4. What are the library's maintenance needs?
5. What are the library's endowment needs?
6. What are the library's staffing needs?
7. What are the library's program and service needs?
8. Are the architect's cost estimates complete?
9. Has a five-year financial forecast been completed?
10. Have the costs generated by contemplated goals been taken into account?
11. Are operating income projections realistic?
12. What are the board's capabilities?
13. Are they willing to work for the effort?
14. What level of goodwill for the library presently exists within the community?
15. What is the volunteer base?
16. What have been the results of past efforts?
17. What is the timetable for raising funds?

Assigning a dollar figure to each fiscal question is the basis for setting the fundraising goal. It is extremely important not to overlook any cost regardless of how obscure it is, or how insignificant it may seem. Architectural fees often run more than ten percent of the cost of the building. Yet they are often overlooked in the early planning stages.

Starting the Campaign

"Overcoming inertia is the most difficult part of any campaign," according to Tom Vance. Someone has to say, "*Ready, set, go!*" If you do it too soon or too late, you lose the continuity of a well-scheduled effort. You have to get off to a good start and keep moving until the goal is reached. You don't want your team to run out of gas before the end of the race. Neither do you want to get them all enthused and then make them wait two weeks for printed materials.

The person who chaired the volunteer committee in Beaver Dam, Wisconsin, agreed to the task only with the assistance of a professional fundraiser. He wanted someone to prepare the materials he needed and tell him when to send them out. He wanted someone to tell him what to do and when.

HIRING A FUNDRAISING CONSULTANT

When we hire someone to work in our libraries, we usually review our job requirements and look for the person that best matches those requirements. There is a good likelihood that you have never hired a fundraising consultant before, and you don't know where to start. You don't know enough about your fundraising job requirements to make a good decision. It is unlikely that you can pick up your telephone directory and find a professional fundraiser listed in the yellow pages. The best place to start is the Internet. Try the Association of Fundraising Professionals through their Web site: www.nsfre.org/ or the American Association of Fundraising Counsel, Inc. at www.aafrc.org/. Both of these Web sites offer suggestions about selecting a professional fundraiser.

You could go to a search engine and search on the phrase "professional fundraising" or "fundraising professionals."

Here is a list of questions you can ask yourself after you become acquainted with the consultant. They will help you clarify your feelings.

Questions for Selecting Professional Fundraising Consultant

Does the fundraising consultant . . .

1. Initiate proactive responses to change?
2. Focus on the goals of *your* library?
3. Try to understand your needs before trying to impress you with his skill?
4. Seek to organize and clarify needs?
5. Seek for a variety of solutions?
6. Initiate action by suggesting alternative solutions?
7. Consider the need in the context of the community?
8. Build on strengths rather than assess blame for a bad situation?
9. Encourage and support local efforts?
10. Challenge accepted thinking in a constructive way?
11. Possess relevant people skills?

If you and your board feel good about the prospective consultant, after having asked these questions and after having spent some time with him or her, go ahead with the contract. You have probably made a good choice. On the other hand if you have what I call "fuzzy" feelings, wait a while. If these feelings stay with you find another prospect.

In the end, whether you hire a professional fundraising consultant or not could make the difference in having enough money to build the new library you want and not having enough money. Tom Vance, professional fundraiser, says, "It is easy to raise the first 25 percent of any fundraising campaign. Anyone can do that. The professional will help you get the last 75 percent."

Paying for the Professional Consultant

We have discussed all of the great things a professional fundraising consultant can do to help move the campaign forward. This discussion begs the question how much will a professional cost? The answer is it all depends, but that is not a very good answer. Remember that fundraising consultants are professionals who are roughly in the same category with accountants and lawyers. You can expect to pay in the range of a thousand dollars or more per day plus expenses.

Here is a "ballpark" calculation. Suppose a fundraising consultant fee is $1,000 per day. Most professionals like to interview 30 community leaders. Suppose he or she can interview six people per day. Interviewing 30 people will take five days. Expenses can run $250 per day plus transportation, which can be all over the map. Writing the report will take another two or three days. Incidentals can run $250. We are looking at $11,500. Some professionals might charge more, others may be willing to do it for less—especially if your library is in a small town and cannot afford big city prices. Depending on the particulars of the situation, a feasibility study could cost between $8,000 and $15,000.

It is reasonable to ask a professional fundraiser to come to your community and discuss your needs and what services his or her firm can offer and the cost of each service, without paying for the visit.

The other "Catch 22" question is where do I find the money to pay for a consultant before I even begin the campaign? The answer could be as simple as the board personally donating for these costs to get the library going down the path of a successful campaign. Another option is to ask the Friends of the Library to fund the study. The cost should probably not come from regular library funds.

USING PROFESSIONAL GRANT WRITERS

Let's face it. Most librarians are amateurs when it comes to writing grants. Only a few librarians have experience at getting big bucks from government, business, or foundation sources. They are not sure what to say or how to put what they know into words. If they do possess these skills they often lack the time it takes to prepare a grant proposal. Unless you are an exception, you may want to explore the benefits of hiring a professional grant writer.

Functions of a Professional Grant Writer

- Provide a careful appraisal of the request for proposal and your proposal outline.
- Make an evaluation of earlier grant applications, if any.
- Gather information to support your proposal.
- Perform the research required by every good grant.
- Prepare the draft and final proposal.
- Edit grants to check for spelling, grammar, structure, flow of the narrative, and formatting.
- Review and critique proposals to make sure the RFP and your grant proposal are compatible.

Figure 1-8-2 Functions of a Professional Grant Writer

They know all the ins and outs of applying for grants and competing for large amounts of money. You usually have to do a lot of market research and provide demographics and other tools to prove that you are worthy of the grant. I would suggest going through a reputable firm or using someone that has applied for these grants before. They know the ropes and can show you how to be successful.

Above are some of the functions of a professional grant writer (see Figure 1-8-2).

Determining the Fees of a Professional Grant Writer

Most professional grant writers do not work on a contingency basis; that is they are not paid a percentage of the grant, if the grant is funded. There are three good reasons for receiving payment when the work is done.

1. Many very well done proposals do not get funded, and the proposal is only one of many factors that determine the decision to fund or not to fund.
2. Most grant funding agencies specifically prohibit the use of grant funds to pay for the services of a grant writer.
3. Reputable grant writers subscribe to a code of ethics that prohibits them from accepting work on a contingency basis.

Hiring a Professional Grant Writer

So, if you think you want to hire a professional grant writer, be prepared to pay him or her when the agreed upon work is done. How much you pay a professional grant writer will depend on the work he or she does. Most grant writers have a list of services they offer and a range of fees for each service. Similar to an attorney or an accountant they will charge by the hour. Their time and expertise are all they have to sell. Expect to pay from $500 to a few thousand dollars or more for the services of a professional grant writer. Of course the cost will depend on the work they do.

You can contact colleagues who have used a grant writer before to find one to work for you. You can also use the Internet to find a grant writer. Go to a search engine and search on the phrase "professional grant writer." If you find someone you feel might work in your situation, contact him or her and learn more about his or her services and charges. Professional grant writers are very much like professional fundraisers. You will need to use the same care and judgment when you hire either one. The big questions you have to ask are:

1. How much can we afford?
2. What is the potential return on the investment?
3. Is the potential gain worth the risk?

Those who have used the services of a professional grant writer say that they can pay their salary many times over with the additional money they bring in. If your organization is large enough, having a grant writer on staff may be the best investment you will make.

The Association of Fundraising Professionals is an excellent source for information on hiring a grant writer, what expectations and responsibilities should be, etc. Check out their Web site at www.nsfre.org/.

USING FRIENDS OF THE LIBRARY AS FUNDRAISERS

Friends of the Library are valuable as fundraisers. About half of the librarians I surveyed said that their Friends were responsible for all of the library fundraising in their community. If the library wants to pursue a major fund drive, Friends are a ready-made fundraising committee. Most Friends understand that fundraising will be part of the job when they join. Contrary to the attitudes of many library board members, they expect to give and they expect to get others to give. They like to work for the library because they enjoy the benefits of the library.

Benefits of a Friends of the Library Group

The benefits of organizing a Friends of the Library are not limited to fundraising. Here are a few other reasons you might want to organize a Friends group:

- Volunteer service
- Help with passage of a bond issue or tax referendum
- Lobbying the legislature or city government

- Public relations
- Programming for the library
- A focal point for community support of the library

Organizing a Friends Group

If you do not have a Friends of the Library organization right now and you would like to organize one, use this basic outline for starting a Friends group:

1. Invite a few regular patrons of the library to come to the library. Tell them you would like to organize a Friends group.
2. Develop a tentative agenda for the first meeting.
3. Brainstorm for a list of potential people to invite to the organizational meeting.
4. Set the date for the first meeting (about a month in advance).
5. Send invitation letters to those on the list and explain the purpose of the meeting.
6. At the meeting:
   - Ask the group if there is enough interest to organize.
   - Elect a temporary president.
   - Appoint a nominating committee.
   - Appoint a constitution and by-laws committee and give them a charge to bring proposed constitution and by-laws to the next meeting.
   - Set the next meeting date.
   - Adjourn.
7. Meet with committee to help draft by-laws. Have resource documents available.
8. At the organizational meeting, the temporary chair conducts.
9. Receives the report of the constitution and by-laws committee and distributes copies to everyone.
10. Business includes:
    - Discuss and approve constitution and by-laws.
    - Receive the report of nominating committee.
    - Elect officers.
    - Report from library director (plans and projects).
    - Appoint a membership committee.
    - Appoint projects committee.
    - Appoint a publicity committee.
    - Appoint committee to seek official recognition of the group from the state and to seek IRS 501 (c) (3) designation.
    - Adjournment.

This outline will help you get started.

You could also check with the state library to see if there is a state-wide Friends group. Contact them for help with starting your own Friends group.

GET HELP FROM FOLUSA

You can also contact Friends of Libraries USA at www.folusa.com. The membership of FOLUSA includes more than two thousand local Library Friends groups across the country. Their mission is "to motivate and support local Friends groups across the country in their efforts to preserve and strengthen libraries." They have lots of materials to help you start a Friends group.

If you are looking for help from the Friends for a fundraising campaign, organize, and put them to work, but don't be surprised if some Friends refuse to ask anyone for money. More on the subject can be found in: *Friends of the Library Handbook* by Jean A. Ashfield and *Friends of Libraries Sourcebook,* edited by Sandy Dolnick.

Revitalizing Your Friends Group

If you have a Friends group, but their interest is waning, try one or more of the ideas in Figure I-8-3.

Make sure you want a Friends group before you organize one. There is nothing more powerful for the benefit of your library than an active, well-directed Friends group. When the goals of the Friends coincide with the goals of the library, everything you set your hand to will succeed. The director, the board of trustees, and a Friends group need to have the same focus—to assist the library in serving the community. However, it is essential that Friends cooperate with both, but interfere with neither.

See sample by-laws in the appendix.

BENEFITING FROM A LIBRARY FOUNDATION

I like to think of the Friends of the Library as the group that sponsors fundraising and moneymaking projects for the ongoing needs of the library. I think of a library foundation, on the other hand, as being in the business of raising money to secure the long-term security of the library. Members of the foundation raise money to invest for the library. They would be the ones to create an endowment. If the library does not have a 501 (c) (3) designation to receive charitable gifts, the foundation could seek that designation. IRS Form 1023 must be used to apply for this

---

Ideas for Revitalizing a Friends Group

- Meet with those who are active and start a planning process to increase membership by a certain percentage.
- Meet with those who are active and ask them to help the library review its mission, goals, and objectives.
- Do a survey of all active Friends and ask them to list ideas for revitalizing the group.
- Ask them to help with a major public relations push.
- Start a literacy program and ask them to volunteer to be reading tutors.
- Develop a library "wish list" and encourage the Friends to raise the money to buy something from the list.
- Make plans for a colossal book sale and ask the Friends to be in charge.
- Brainstorm with them.
- Have someone there from outside the community (an expert) to talk about what Friends do, the benefits to the library of a Friends group, and the benefits to individuals.
- Have the library director outline two or three possible projects for the Friends and what might be expected of the Friends.

Figure 1-8-3 Ideas for Revitalizing a Friends Group

status. A copy of the form is available online at nccs.urban.org/irsforms/1023.pdf.

The purpose of a library foundation is to receive money, particularly large sums, charitable trusts, and bequests. The money is invested and a portion of the proceeds goes to the library each year. A foundation usually does not have a large membership, but everyone on the board should make regular contributions themselves and regularly seek gifts from contributors in the community.

If you are serious about organizing a foundation to support your library, check out the Council on Foundations' Web site www.cof.org/starting/index.htm. You could buy their book, *First Steps in Starting a Foundation, Fourth Edition,* by John Edie, published by the Council on Foundations, Washington, DC (1998).

Securing the IRS 501 (c) (3) Designation

One essential element of a foundation is the IRS 501 (c) (3) designation. Start by contacting your regional office of the Internal Revenue Service. Ask them for Application for Recognition of Exemption under Section 501 (c) (3) of the Internal Revenue Code. Your foundation must have been in operation for 15 months before you can have this designation. Don't be intimidated by the process of filling out the forms. Just take everything one step at a time. Ask for help if you need it. Some corporate donors absolutely require a copy of the letter designating your foundation as a 501 (c) (3) agency.

Get the help and advice of a lawyer when you organize a foundation. Everyone I know who has done it says, "Get a lawyer." Organization of a foundation follows much the same outline as a Friends of the Library group, except you will not have as many members. Make sure the people you recruit for the foundation know up front that they will be expected to give to the foundation and they will be expected to ask others for donations.

See sample by-laws for a foundation in the Appendix.

GETTING HELP FROM THE FUNDRAISING AND FINANCIAL DEVELOPMENT SECTION OF LAMA/ALA

Some of the best help and advice I have received about fundraising has come from fellow librarians in the Fundraising and Financial Development Section of LAMA/ALA. This is an active group and they do things that help members of the profession. If you are already a member of ALA consider joining FRFDS and volunteer to be on a committee. Check out their Web page at the ALA site, www.ala.org/lama/committees/frfds/index.html. Join their mailing list. Go to www.ala.org/lama/committees/frfds/resources.html LAMA FRFDS Resources and Activities and click on Subscribe to FRFDS-L. I have queried this group several times and the results were always helpful.

FRFDS has an online bibliography for *Choosing and Using a Fund-Raising Consultant* at www.ala.org/lama/committees/frfds/frfdsbibl.html. They also have *Selected World Wide Web Sites for Library Grants and Fund-Raising* at www.ala.org/lama/committees/frfds/grants.html.

SUMMARY

When it comes to getting help with fundraising, librarians have lots of places to go. From books to Web sites, to consultants, to organizations, to individuals, help for fundraising abounds. Some of the help is free and some you have to pay for. My best advice is to take advantage of all the free help you can get and pay for professional help if your project is really big. As a profession, librarians could be much better fundraisers than they are. They just need help.

Every fundraising effort needs someone to scope out the landscape. You can use:

• State library staff members

- Consultants from your regional system
- Specialists on your own staff
- Professional consultants

These are the main points of this chapter:

- A professional consulting firm will send experts with loads of experience into your area to help you organize and execute a fundraising campaign, conduct a feasibility study, offer campaign management, public relations, and related services.
- Check the Web sites of the Association of Fundraising Professionals and the American Association of Fundraising Counsel, Inc. for a list of qualified professionals.
- Friends of the Library are valuable as fundraisers. Most Friends understand that fundraising will be part of the job when they join.
- Friends of Libraries USA can help you organize a new Friends group.
- A library foundation can help secure the long-term security of the library.
- The Fundraising and Financial Development Section of LAMA/ ALA can help you.

The decision to hire a professional fundraising consultant depends on how much money you want to raise. Don't hire a professional to make up for a lack of community support or a shortage of willing volunteers. Remember a professional won't do the work for you. He or she will just help you organize your efforts and teach you how to be more effective.

BIBLIOGRAPHY

Ashfield, Jean A. 1980. *Friends of the Library Handbook: A Guide for Volunteers, Trustees, Library Directors, and Administrators of Nonprofit Support Groups.* Hampton, N.H.: Ashfield. This book deals with the organization and administration of Friends groups and outlines the public relations and fundraising activities for Friends.

Dolnick, Sandy, ed. 1996. *Friends of Libraries Sourcebook,* 3d ed. Chicago: ALA. Dolnick, the executive director of Friends of Libraries USA, covers a broad range of issues on how to organize and manage a Friends Group.

Rich, Elizabeth H., and Joan Seabourne. 1999. *Guide to U.S. Foundations, Their Trustees, Officers, and Donors.* New York: The Center. This book is the most complete source for active philanthropic organizations in the United States. While this work is not intended expressly for librarians, it still provides the library grant seeker with needed information on who's giving and how much they gave.

Staying Friends: Revitalizing and Maintaining the Momentum; Friends in Need; "Fun"draising Ideas, Felicia Cogley, 112 min., Nebraska Library Commission, 1999, videocassette. Felicia Cogley, Coordinator for the Friends of the Hastings Public Library, presents two sessions at the "Friends Indeed" workshop sponsored by the Nebraska Regional Library Systems and the Nebraska Library Commission. This video discusses a variety of issues related to Friends groups and provides examples of creative library fundraising projects.

Part II

25 Proven Fundraising Techniques

Chapter 1

Conduct a Capital Campaign for a Building

DESCRIPTION

A capital campaign is the best way to raise a lot of money in a relatively short period of time. A capital campaign is an intensive fundraising effort on the part of a nonprofit organization to secure extraordinary gifts for a specific purpose like building a new library. People are more likely to give to a capital campaign than just about any other type of fundraising effort. They like to be part of a successful community effort that gives them something they can see. The campaign starts with a lead gift of approximately ten percent of the goal amount. The lead gift is followed by two major gifts of five percent each, and so on. A capital campaign can also be the most work, the most exciting, and the most rewarding.

PURPOSE

Capital campaigns are used to secure large donations to build a new library or remodel an existing one. The funds raised in a capital campaign are also used for equipment including computers. They are often used to supplement a bond issue or to leverage the passage of a bond issue.

BENEFITS

Capital fund drives have a beginning and an end, usually close together. Everyone working on it knows that it will end someday very soon. You are asking people to make a sacrificial gift over a three to five year period. Donors will dig deeper because they know that you are not going to ask again for the same project. The entire community becomes galvanized on helping the library reach its goal. The end result is a beautiful new library everyone can be proud of.

EXAMPLE

In 1990 I had the opportunity to consult with the board of the Chanute (Kansas) Public Library. They had invited me to advise them on their million-dollar project to build a new library. When I returned for the final dedication of the library and a museum in August of 1993, I saw a magnificently restored Santa Fe Railroad depot. The original idea was a straightforward plan to expand the library, but it ended up being part of a multiphase downtown redevelopment project that provided a new home for the library and the museum. The library board had looked at the depot early in the planning, but had rejected it because it was too large and would be too costly for the library to handle on its own.

Larry Hudson from the Larry D. Hudson Family Foundation made a lead gift of $500,000, which guaranteed the success of the project. The foundation later made a challenge grant of $250,000, which gave added incentive to community fundraising.

The combined fundraising effort was unique because its multifaceted approach broadened the constituent base and made soliciting for donations easier. Those who wanted to support the library could see their dollars going for a new library. Lawyers could buy into the project because of the new District Court and Judicial Center. Museum supporters could help their favorite institution by giving to the project. Downtown merchants could invest in their own future by giving to the project. And some people gave because they just wanted to see the depot saved. It was truly a win-win situation for everyone.

Successful elements of the project included:

- They hired a professional fundraiser to do a feasibility study and helped them find the major lead gift. (For more detailed information about a feasibility study see page 125-140 in Chapter 8.)
- The professional consultant helped organize the campaign.
- The major lead gift equaled 37.5 percent of the total cost of the project.
- All of those who solicited gifts gave to the project themselves.
- They broadened the constituent base to include everyone in the community.

They said thank you to everyone with a gala opening night celebration. They were overwhelmed to see the transformation of the old depot into a new library and museum. The Chanute project was successful primarily because the lead gift was 37.5 percent of the goal. In all, nineteen contributors donated over 80 percent of the money.

HOW TO DO IT

Before you jump into a fund drive for a new building you may want to do a thorough building needs analysis. Use this list to help you discover the deficiencies in your building.

- Exterior inviting/appealing
- Building meets fire codes
- Roof in good condition
- Ceiling insulated
- Walls insulated
- Windows efficient
- Doors accessible to disabled
- Foundation structurally sound
- Entrances/exits easy to open/close
- Adequate parking
- Handicapped parking
- Well lit at night
- Effective signage
- Hours visible from street
- Name in four inch letters
- Heating and cooling in good condition
- Flooring, walls, and ceiling in good condition
- Basic layout aids traffic flow
- All areas controllable from main desk
- Elevator for multilevels
- Restrooms handicapped accessible
- Electrical and lighting adequate
- Computer support adequate
- Phone and modem support adequate
- Suitable lighting in all areas
- 100 ft. candle lighting in study areas
- Public space adequate
- Display areas adequate
- Computer area adequate
- Book stack areas adequate
- Reading areas adequate
- Children's area adequate

- Storytelling area
- Small conference rooms
- Staff areas and office space adequate
- Storage area adequate
- Break area adequate
- Book sorting area adequate

This analysis will help you develop a clear vision of your needs. The next step is to create an image of the new building. This can be an architectural drawing or a scale model of the new library. It is easier to get people to give to the capital campaign when they can see what the new library is going to look like.

You create a strategic vision when you say: "We will build a new library by the end of next year." You flesh out the vision when you describe its shape and dimensions. It becomes more real when you draw a picture of it and give it a name.

The public library in Rhinelander, Wisconsin, had "Pete the Penny" campaign as a fundraiser. Children collected 100 pennies and brought them to the library. The people in the community caught the vision of thousands of pennies marching into the library—going to work to remodel a Carnegie building.

Tell how you are going to accomplish the task. If you have a big project with many different fundraising activities, outline each project and the anticipated income from each.

Recruit volunteers to ask for gifts. Among them, recruit individuals with connections and influence—people who can bring others into the group and go out and get donations from their friends and associates.

Preparing the Chart of Giving

I recommend a chart of giving that looks like Figure II-1-1. It is included here in case you missed the chart in Chapter 4. It represents the top end of the giving scale. The goal is reachable if the fundraising group can confidently write down three names for each gift sought.

Some donors will not give at the expected level, but will give at a lower level.

The success of a capital campaign depends on securing at least 40 percent of the needed funds using the chart of giving.

Chart of Giving
Campaign Goal = $1,000,000

	Number	Amount	Percent	Names
Major lead gift	1	$100,000	10%	_____
				_____
Lead gifts	2	$50,000	10%	_____
				_____
				_____
				_____
				_____
Major gifts	4	$25,000	10%	_____
				_____
				_____
				_____
				_____
				_____
Big gifts	10	$10,000	10%	_____
				_____
				_____
				_____
				_____
				_____
				_____
				_____
				_____
				_____

Figure II-1-1 Chart of Giving

SELECTING THE CHAIR OF THE CAMPAIGN COMMITTEE

Fill out a worksheet like this for each person to be considered for the position of Chair of the Capital Campaign.

Chair Selection Worksheet

Name _____

1. Is this person capable of making a major gift to our project?
2. Does this person appreciate and use the library on a regular basis?
3. Will this person make a big gift to our project?
4. Does this person have the personal connections and clout to get the big bucks for the project?
5. Can this person secure a lead gift of 10 percent of our goal?
6. Can this person recruit others who will give themselves and then solicit the money we need?
7. Can this person train and motivate others to solicit?
8. Can this person delegate and follow through?
9. What is this person's track record for other fundraising projects?
10. Will this person's name associated with our fund drive help us?

Interview Prospective Chairs

The professional fundraising consultant will want to interview everyone you are considering for committee chair. These interviews could double as a preliminary search for a lead gift. If the chair of the committee is expected to make a major gift, secure the gift before inviting him or her to chair the committee.

The best scenario is for the library leader to accompany the professional consultant in the visits to the top candidates to chair the committee. Once the lead gift is secured the person might be asked to chair the committee. If this is not possible because of age or health, the person might be asked to be the honorary chair.

Write out a job description for the committee chair. Write across it draft copy. Take this document with you when you visit the few people you have selected as possible candidates for the job. Ask each one what they think of the draft document. Ask them if they can think of anything else you should have included. Their reactions to the questions will be very revealing. The people you visit will begin to internalize the purpose of your visit. They will see themselves in the role of committee chair, without your asking. They will begin to think of their own contribution to the fund drive. You will be surprised at the answers you get.

Chairing the Fundraising Committee

The Chair of the Capital Fund Drive Committee will be expected to:

- Be absolutely committed to the project.
- Make a significant (sacrificial) gift.

- Ask for the lead gift—the single largest gift, or help someone else do it.
- Attract and recruit and solicit five team leaders.
- Be enthusiastic about raising money for the library.
- Generate that same enthusiasm in others.
- Know everything about your library's fundraising project.
- Be friendly to everyone in town.
- Use his or her personal influence for the good of the library.
- Know the committee system and delegate effectively.
- Work with the people who may express differing opinions
- Never doubt victory.

Recruiting Committee Members

The next step is to recruit committee workers. This is the rank and file who will go out, knock on doors, and ask people for money, face to face. The key to recruiting them is selling them on the worth of the library's project and putting them to work. Nothing succeeds like people who have been given clear instructions and the latitude to do the job as they see fit.

- Be honest with them.
- Give them lots of support.
- Recruit enough people so the faithful don't get exhausted.

You need one volunteer for every five people to be contacted. Ask and expect these volunteers to give to the campaign. People who ask others for donations without having given something themselves are less effective than those who have given. Giving time does not count like giving money. Fundraisers who do not give money to the campaign are at a psychological disadvantage when they ask others to give. Their eyes drop and their voices lack conviction when asking for a gift.

Imagine the power of someone who gives $1,000 to the capital campaign asking a friend to do the same. He or she could say, "I gave a thousand dollars to the new library and now it is your turn to ante up."

Communicating with Committee Members

Set up a discussion group or mailing list using e-mail to facilitate communicating with and between members of the committee. E-mail is a powerful tool and can be used very effectively to expedite communications. Some of the Internet search engines like Yahoo provide the opportunity to set up a mailing list and make it easy to do. You set up the list and subscribe each member of the committee to the list, using his or her e-mail address.

RESOURCES

The best resource you can have for a capital campaign is well-connected people in high places who are willing to support the campaign with their money and their hard work. A good professional consultant comes in a close second. Let's face it. Most of us are amateurs at fundraising. Our confidence soars when we have someone who does fundraising for a living at our side. The next best tool is a long list of volunteers who will make a gift and get their friends to give, too. It may seem funny to think of people as resources in a capital campaign, but good people that are motivated are the key to success of any fundraising effort.

SPECIAL CONSIDERATIONS

Broaden your constituent base by appealing to many facets of the community, if you can do it without giving up more than you are willing to.

Since a capital campaign is going to fund a building that will serve the community for 20 years or more, ask donors to make a three-year sacrificial pledge. Some families may be able to afford $1,000 per year, but a three-year pledge of that amount would be $3,000 instead of $1,000 for a one-time gift.

PITFALLS

Don't leave money on the table by asking too little from a prospective donor. A donor willing to give $10,000 could receive a direct mail solicitation asking for the maximum of $1,000.

The chair of the capital campaign committee is so important that you cannot have someone in that position because he or she is popular in the community. This person has to give a big chunk of money and get others to make comparable gifts.

End the campaign on time. Prolonging the campaign beyond the advertised deadline will serve no useful purpose. You might follow up on some pledges that haven't been collected or contact a few people who were out of town during the fund drive, but publicly end the campaign when you said you would.

For Schools and Academic Libraries

If a school needs a new library it will usually be part of a bond issue for the entire district. I have never heard of a capital campaign for a new school library. Academic libraries will have to work through their organizations. Working through the alumni association is a good idea and has worked remarkably well for many colleges and universities.

CHECKLIST

Here is a short checklist to help jog your thinking as you plan a capital campaign.

1. Do you have clear vision of what you want to do?
2. Do you have a drawing or three-dimensional model of the new facility?
3. Do you know how much money you need to raise through a capital campaign?
4. Are you going to hire a professional fundraising consultant?
5. Have you conducted a feasibility study to determine if the project has sufficient community support?
6. What have you included in the project to broaden the appeal to more segments of the community?
7. Is the person you have selected to be the chair of the committee able to make a lead gift of at least five percent of the amount needed?
8. Does the chair have the clout to get the necessary gifts from the movers and shakers in the community?
9. Do you have lots of volunteers who are eager to give and get their friends to give, too?
10. Do you have someone who will keep his or her eyes on the details?

GETTING RESULTS

Leading the community through a capital campaign to build a new library will be one of the best things you will ever do. It will require the support of most of the people with money to give away and almost everyone else in the community. Everyone who participates will make a big difference in the library for many years to come.

What Do I Do Next?

Once the library board decides to use a capital campaign to fund the construction of a new library or remodel the old one, get all of the help you can find. If you are a librarian don't try to do the work yourself. If you are going for $500,000 or more, you gather information on hiring a professional fundraiser and present it to the board. They may decide against it, but you will have made the effort. See Chapter 8, page 129.

The librarian's role in a capital campaign is to provide support services to the leaders and volunteers. The best things a librarian can do are to help recruit good leaders and back them up. Unless you have $100,000 to donate to the library, let the people who do lead the campaign.

What Are the Policies and Procedures Needed?

Chapter 4 and the "How to do it" section of this chapter give you enough detail to help you get started. The resources listed in the bibliography give you the step-by-step details you need to succeed with a capital campaign.

How Much Time Should This Method Take?

Don't let a capital campaign drag on—even if you don't reach your goal. Organization and planning will take about six months. The precampaign activities including selecting the campaign chair and securing the lead gifts and major gifts could take up to another six months. The public part of the campaign should take no more than six months—preferably three months. In all, the capital campaign should take between 12 and 18 months.

When Can I Expect Results?

Many of the donations will come in the form of pledges over a period of three to five years. Many donors will commit to a large gift when it is needed—for example, after construction begins on the new library. It could take as long as two or three years to get all of the funding lined up, hire an architect, and begin construction. The finished building could take five years or more to complete.

What Can I Realistically Expect the Costs to Be?

You will need some seed money up front to be successful with a capital campaign. If you decide to hire a professional fundraiser to do a feasibility study, help find the lead gift, and help organize a campaign, you could be looking at an expenditure of $25,000 or more. This could be some of the best money you will spend if you need to raise enough for a big new library. Other costs could run from $5,000 to $10,000.

SUMMARY

Capital campaigns can be the most successful type of fundraising you can do. People are more likely to give to a capital campaign than just about any other type of fundraising effort.

- Capital campaigns make it possible to secure large donations to build a new library and equip it.

- The library staff and the board need to work together to communicate the needs of the library to the community.
- Professional fundraising consultants are an invaluable resource when conducting a feasibility study or finding the lead gift.
- The case statement briefly summarizes the need for the project and the benefit to the public.
- The chart of giving is an essential planning document, and becomes the solicitation blueprint to success.
- Everyone involved in the campaign needs to make a significant (to them) gift to the cause.

BIBLIOGRAPHY

Bancel, Marilyn. 2000. *Preparing Your Capital Campaign: An Excellence in Fund Raising Workbook Series Publication*. New York: John Wiley and Sons. This is a good book for the novice fundraiser. Its step-by-step approach to getting ready for a capital campaign make it an indispensable tool.

Burlingame, Dwight, ed. 1995. *Library Fundraising: Models for Success*. Chicago: ALA. This is a book with less than 100 pages, but packed with successful fundraising stories. Each of the seven chapters comes from the experience of the author. This book has solid how-to advice.

Dove, Kent E. 1999. *Conducting a Successful Capital Campaign: The New, Revised and Expanded Edition of the Leading Guide to Planning and Implementing a Capital Campaign*. San Francisco: Jossey-Bass. This book is filled with helpful resources and advice for planning and managing a capital campaign. It breaks a campaign into bite-size elements and gives plenty of successful examples and samples. Every library needs this book.

Kihlstedt, Andrea, and Catherine Schwartz. 1997. *Capital Campaigns: Strategies That Work*. Gaitherburg, Md.: Aspen Publishers. This book is the one-stop shop for comprehensive information on conducting a capital campaign. Don't try a capital campaign without this book at your side.

Schmacher, Edward C. 2000. *The Capital Campaign Survival Guide: An Easy-To-Use Guide to Conducting a Capital Campaign*. Seattle, Wash.: Elton-Wolf Publishers. In this book, Ed Schumacher shares his more than 35 years of experience as a fundraiser. He covers the entire gamut of planning and executing a capital campaign and tells us how to survive the experience. This is an exceptional reference tool for anyone who is facing a capital campaign.

Chapter 2

Promote Deferred Giving

DESCRIPTION

Deferred giving is postponing the realization of the gift until a later time, usually until after the death of the donor. In the next 10 to 20 years the people who lived through the depression will die and their wealth will be transferred to others. This is not a small thing. We are talking about trillions and trillions of dollars. Hence the "great transfer of wealth." Who will this wealth be transferred to? Most of it will go to family members. A small percentage will go to the financial advisors who help the individuals amass and manage their investments. The rest, about 17 percent, will go to charity. The challenge for those whose job it is to raise funds for libraries is to get their library on the list of charities destined to inherit this wealth.

Bequests in Wills

Almost all deferred giving will be in the form of a bequest in a will. Bequests can be cash, stocks, bonds, or real estate. In fact I know of several libraries that own wheat farms as the result of a bequest. Another library owns an oil well. All of which produce income for the library. The key to deferred giving is asking to be included in a person's will or whatever instrument of giving they wish to use. From a donor's standpoint deferred giving makes perfect sense.

Insurance Policies

An individual usually buys life insurance to protect the security of his or her family. Once the family is reared, life insurance is almost worthless to a widowed spouse. He or she may have a paid-up life insurance policy just gathering dust in a file drawer. It would be an easy, no-cost thing to make the library the beneficiary of the policy and let it ride.

Someone may want to buy a policy to give to the library as a means of making a large donation. Using a life insurance policy the donor could make a larger gift than might otherwise be possible with cash or a bequest. This option also allows the donor to offer the gift without restrictions. Check with an insurance agent if you have someone interested in this method of giving.

Trusts

A revocable living trust permits the donor to have complete flexibility to administer his or her assets while he or she is alive. At the death of the donor, the outcome is a generous gift to the library. The trust distributes the remaining assets according to the donor's wishes.

There are significant tax advantages to setting up a trust and your donor may be looking for some tax write-offs now. A charitable remainder trust allows the donor to make a large gift to the library and receives a sizable tax deduction. If someone offers to set up a trust for your library, thank the person and put him or her in touch with an attorney.

A charitable lead trust works the opposite of a charitable remainder trust. The income from investment the donor places in the trust is directed to the library at the beginning rather than at the end of the trust term. Using this option, the donor determines a definite number of years for the income to be given to the library. At the end of the trust term, the asset reverts to the donor or the named beneficiary.

Gift Annuity

The gift annuity allows the donor to make a meaningful gift to the library, but at the same time provide for his or her own future well-being. A gift annuity makes it possible to transfer cash, marketable securities such as stocks, bonds, and mutual funds to the organization. In exchange the donor or someone designated by the donor will receive fixed payments for life.

Deeds

A remainder interest deed on a home or property that is mortgage-free can allow the donor to continue to use the property during his or her lifetime and at the same time make it a gift to the library. At the donor's death, the property passes on to the library. This type of deed provides an instant tax write-off when the property is turned over to the library.

PURPOSES

From the view of the librarian whose library receives the deferred gift, it is not a good idea to count on deferred giving to pay next month's light bill. A deferred gift, if it is large enough, could be the catalyst for a building program or establishing an endowment.

BENEFITS

Libraries benefit from deferred giving because it helps them develop a stable future, based on larger gifts that will produce income for years to come. Deferred gifts tend to be larger than ordinary gifts and are sometimes easier to secure. A well-publicized deferred gift can be used to attract other large gifts.

Deferred giving gives those, whose assets are tied up in their home and other belongings, an opportunity to leave a larger gift to their favorite charity, which you hope is your library.

EXAMPLES

A family of modest income wanted to memorialize a child who had been killed in an auto accident. They continued a life insurance policy, which was originally taken out to provide cash for the child's college education. The family gave the paid-up policy to the library for an endowment to fund the summer reading program at the local library.

In 1999 the Lincoln (Nebraska) City Library Foundation received $1.2 million from the estate of Raymond L. Nestle. The gift was added to the Lincoln City Library Foundation Endowment Fund, which was established to provide funds to supplement tax support for the library. Income from the gift will be used to develop the endowment and funds for books and technology. Mr. Nestle was an avid reader and enjoyed the services of the library throughout his life.

HOW TO DO IT

Large bequests have been the catalyst of many library construction programs. If you are not actively seeking bequests, you are missing out on one of the great fundraising opportunities open to you. Being written into someone's will usually requires a nurturing relationship that has been cultivated over a period of several years, but it starts with general awareness, and can end with a vision-changing gift.

Sometimes a librarian doesn't know the library is included in someone's will until the donor dies. In the past 30 years the libraries I have been in charge of have received nice bequests—all of them were unexpected gifts. Nice surprises, yes, but think of the increased potential of someone from the library cultivating the prospect and working with him or her to maximize the gift. Every library ought to be actively engaged in cultivating and soliciting deferred gifts.

Hold Estate-Planning Workshops

Try holding an estate-planning clinic. Invite a lawyer, an accountant, or a trust officer from a local bank to sit on a panel to discuss wills and estate planning. Hold the program in the library. People who come to the library for an estate-planning program may already have good feelings about the library. You will be providing a valuable service, even if you don't receive a gift from any of the participants. As you close the discussion, mention that the library is seeking deferred gifts. Send letters to all participants and thank them for coming to the program. Send your deferred giving brochure and remind them of the investment opportunity through deferred giving to the library.

Don't try to tackle the legal complication of deferred giving, wills, estates, and insurance yourself. Unless you have someone on your board that can handle it, get good professional help. Leave it to the bankers, attorneys, and insurance agents.

Locating Potential Donors

Most people don't wait until they are ready to die to write their wills. They often write their wills when they are young parents and then revise their wills after their children leave home. There is never a perfect time to contact people to make a deferred gift. The important thing to do is to create a general awareness in the community that the library actively seeks deferred gifts.

The next step is to target prospective donors of deferred gifts. Take a look at your list of current contributors. Who among them are over 50 years old? They are good prospects to include the library in their wills. Many of them have friends who have died and they may be thinking about how they want their assets used when they don't need them any more.

Contacting Prospects

Once you have peaked someone's interest, don't put off contacting him or her. You may lose the opportunity forever if you wait for a better time. The prospect may get sick, forget, or die before making a gift. If possible have a board member or some other third party make the initial contact. Your role throughout should be a helpful supporting one. Be knowledgeable, perceptive, and low-key. If a prospective donor gets the idea that you are after his or her money, they may balk at the whole idea of a deferred gift. Your job is to point out that their gift to the library will be a long-lasting investment.

RESOURCES

The resources for deferred giving are not just the documents you create, but the people you choose to help you and the connections they use.

Use Current Soliciting Tools

People often write their wills after someone that they know passes away. They might notice a little check-off box on your memorial-giving coupon that offers more information about the library's deferred giving program. Board members can be extremely helpful when approaching a potential donor. The best thing you can do is to make your board members aware of the program. Give them information to share with friends if an opportunity arises to discuss a deferred gift. Potential donors need to see the library as a logical beneficiary of their estate.

Develop a Brochure

Develop a brochure that explains your deferred giving program. This is not an easy task and takes coordination with the library's financial officer, bank officer, or whoever is going to handle these funds. Lots of policies and procedures need to be developed and approved by the library board before you can start advertising that you seek deferred gifts. Get legal assistance with the creation of these materials.

The brochure is a logical extension of your memorial-giving program. Send copies of the brochure with a letter to local attorneys. Let them know that the library has a deferred giving program. They may be willing to suggest the library as a possibility. Most people want to be remembered after they die. You need to be sensitive to their feelings, but bold enough to suggest the library as a possible investment that will last beyond their lifetime.

Use the Library's Web Site

If your library has a Web site include a page that encourages deferred giving. It will create awareness that should not offend anyone. Figure II-2-1 is an example of a page we created for the Great Bend Public Library's Web site.

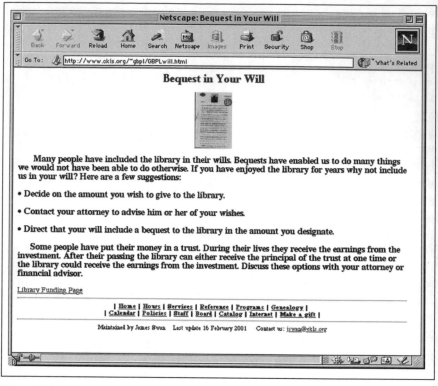

Figure II-2-1 Example of Web Page Solicitation for a Bequest

SPECIAL CONSIDERATIONS

Be careful not to offend the donors when you solicit deferred gifts. You are treading in very personal territory—the donor's money and the donor's eventual death. Everyone knows they are going to die someday, but they don't usually like to talk about it with strangers. That is why it is good to enlist the service of someone who is a friend of the prospective donor and a friend of the library. If the donor cares enough about the library these issues will not get in the way of including the library in his or her will or some other instrument that will benefit the library.

On the other hand don't let your timidity keep you from asking someone to include the library in the final disposition of his or her assets. I know of several opportunities that were lost forever because someone on the development team was hesitant to contact a prospective donor before he or she died.

Make sure you have a giving policy in place. Suppose a rich patron came to you and said, "I will name the library in my will to the tune of $10 million if you will name the new library after my mother." What would you do? All of these contingencies should be spelled out in your policies *before* the opportunity presents itself.

PITFALLS

Don't try to tackle a complicated legal system yourself. Get the help of a professional when it comes to trust, wills, and deferred giving. It is possible to ask a donor to include the library in his or her will without developing a personal relationship or bond of trust, but the request may not be answered positively. Be sure to take the time to build a relationship with the person before asking for the gift. Remember, you are competing with the person's family members and other people he or she has known for a long time. The library has to be pretty important to a donor before he or she will include it in his or her will ahead of family and friends.

FOR SCHOOLS AND ACADEMIC LIBRARIES

Deferred giving is the bread and butter fundraising for many colleges and universities. Librarians in these institutions need to make sure they get their share of gifts to the institution. Indeed, an academic library may have its own development officer, whose job it is to seek deferred gifts.

For school librarians, deferred giving is more difficult though not impossible. The same principles and activities apply as for other libraries. The problem is overcoming the bias in favor of academic and public libraries.

CHECKLIST

Use this checklist to evaluate your program of deferred giving or potential for one.

1. Does your library have patrons or alumni who have sizeable assets and have fond memories of their time in the library?
2. Does your library have a development officer or someone on staff that can devote more than a casual effort to discover the potential for deferred gifts and ask for them?
3. Does your library have the necessary mechanisms in place to receive large gifts and provide a tax benefit to the donor?
4. Do you have a working relationship with attorneys, bankers, and other professionals that can help donors make the legal arrangements to make a deferred gift?

5. Does your library have a visible project that will be benefited by the gift?
6. Does your library have in place a recognition policy that will cover a wide range of gifts and individual preferences?

GETTING RESULTS

Fundraising through deferred giving is largely untapped by libraries. Sometimes getting a deferred gift is just a matter of asking.

What Do I Do Next?

Many deferred gifts come in without being solicited. Read some books on deferred giving and try some of the suggestions if you want to be more proactive. Begin to develop relationships with potential donors. You can't just walk up to someone you know in the supermarket and ask him or her to include the library in his or her will. Start with the people who come into your library every day. Create a brochure on deferred giving and give a copy to everyone who comes to the library.

What Are the Policies and Procedures Needed?

Follow the library's policy on giving. You may have to establish procedures for soliciting and handling deferred gifts. Become aware of the tax laws and/or benefits of deferred giving. The estates of most people who die today are exempt from federal estate taxes because the estate is not large enough. Leave the technicalities to the attorneys and financial advisors.

How Much Time Should This Method Take?

It will take years to build a relationship of trust sufficiently strong to be included in a person's will. It could take 20 years for the gift to be transferred to the library.

When Can I Expect Results?

You will be lucky to see the results of your efforts in your lifetime, though you may benefit from the efforts of someone 25 years ago. Deferred giving has to be part of the library's long-term goals.

What Can I Realistically Expect the Costs to Be?

You could spend $500 to $1,000 on a nice looking brochure. Budget $100 or more a year to take prospects to lunch. If you know that Daisy Smith is declining in health and she has included the library in her will, pick a day and call it Daisy Smith Day at the library. Spend $100 to $200 on a reception in her honor.

SUMMARY

From a donor's standpoint deferred giving makes perfect sense. Deferred gifts are primarily bequests in a will. You need to be aware of life insurance and a variety of other trust instruments, but don't spend too much time on them because about 90 percent of all deferred gifts are bequests.

- A life insurance policy lets the donor make a larger gift than might otherwise be possible with cash or a bequest because the premium is invested.
- A trust gives the donor the income from investments and then distributes the remaining assets according to the donor's wishes.
- A charitable remainder trust allows the donor to make a large gift to the library and receives a sizable tax deduction.
- The gift annuity allows the donor to make a meaningful gift to the library, but at the same time provide for his or her own future well-being.

Libraries benefit from deferred giving because it helps them develop a stable future based on larger gifts that will produce income for years to come. Large bequests have also been the catalyst of many library construction programs. A well-publicized deferred gift can be used to attract other large gifts.

Soliciting deferred gifts requires tact and skill. A prospective donor's death and money are very personal discussion points. Make sure you respect his or her privacy.

BIBLIOGRAPHY

Barrett, Richard D., and Molly E. Ware. 2001. *Planned Giving Essentials: A Step-By-Step Guide to Success*, 2d ed. Gaithersburg, Md.: Aspen Publishers. If planned giving is one of your fundraising strategies, you must have this book. This 166-page work is a gem. It is easy to read, well organized, and on target.

Moerschbaecher, Lynda S. 1998. *Start at Square One: Starting and Managing the Planned Gift Program.* Chicago: Bonus Books. Of the few books that focus on planned giving for nonprofit organizations, this is one of the best. This superior guide starts with a preassessment checklist and then furnishes each of the steps toward building a successful planned giving program. The Sample Detailed Chronology gives you specific examples of steps to take to realize your goal.

Prince, Russ Alan, Gary L. Rathbun, and Chris E. Steiner. 1997. *The Charitable Giving Handbook*. Cincinnati, Ohio: National Underwriter. Russ Prince is one of the best-informed market researchers on private wealth in the world. He knows where the money is and shares expertise in this book.

Schmeling, David G. 2000. *Planned Giving for the One-Person Development Office: Taking the First Steps*, 2d ed. [rev.]. Wheaton, Ill.: Deferred Giving Services. This book was written for the fundraiser who wears many hats. It tells the average fundraiser what he or she needs to do to let donors know that his or her organization would appreciate a bequest. A must read for anyone who wants to use planned giving as a resource for the library.

Schoenhals, G. Roger. 1997. *Getting Going in Planned Giving: Launch Your Program with Powerful Ideas From the Pages of Planned Giving Today*, Seattle, Wash.: Planned Giving Today. This is a banner resource for the beginning planned giving program. It suggests specific first steps for initiating planned giving. It discusses instruments for planned giving and offers insights on ethical issues.

Schoenhals, G. Roger. 1999. *First Steps in Planned Giving: Practical Ideas From the Pages of Planned Giving Today*. Edmonds, Wash.: Planned Giving Today. Learn how to inaugurate a thriving planned giving program. Discover about some pitfalls to dodge. This book is filled with practical ideas on how to venture confidently into the world of planned giving.

Sharpe, Robert F., and Robert F. Sharpe, Sr. 1999. *Planned Giving Simplified: The Gift, the Giver and the Gift Planner*. New York: John Wiley & Sons. The examples in this book clarify planned giving options and explain the benefits of each. It emphasizes planned giving as a gift to charitable institutions rather than a tax shelter. The author focuses on the human side of planned giving, and emphasizes the importance of developing a relationship with donors.

Sharpe, Robert F. 2001. *Participating in the Coming Wealth Transfer: Surprising Advantages for the Nation's Libraries*. Chicago, Ill.: American Library Association (Produced and distributed by Teach'em Continuing Education, 2001). 2 sound cassettes. This is a recording of a program presented at the 2001 ALA Conference in San Francisco, California. Get this program and listen to it several times. It will give you some solid information about planned giving.

Smith, Amy Sherman, and Matthew D. Lehrer. 2000. *Legacies for Libraries: A Practical Guide to Planned Giving*. Chicago: American Library Association. If you want to start a planned giving program for your library, start with this book. It is easy to read, easy to understand,

and practical to use. It explains the benefits of establishing a program of planned giving, and then it takes you step-by-step through the process of implementing a program.

Chapter 3

Open the Library, Say Thank You

DESCRIPTION

The idea of passive fundraising is to be so good at providing library services that people will give you money without your asking for it. Librarians everywhere have stories to tell about unsolicited gifts and bequests from rich people and people who they assumed had no money to give away. People who use libraries, like libraries and appreciate the service they receive and recognize the value of the service, and since it is usually free, they often feel inclined to pay something for it. For many library users the only friendly contact they have in a day is a greeting from their friends at the library.

PURPOSES

This is the most passive technique on the list of 25, yet it has great potential for large unexpected gifts, and it makes soliciting other gifts much easier. Don't count on this method to provide money for a capital campaign or some other project that is on the front burner. This is the kind of money you are grateful to get, because you really didn't ask for it. After you get it you figure out how to spend it. The most important thing you have to do is say, "Thank you."

BENEFITS

The benefits of this kind of giving is that it is unexpected, and often unencumbered with strings on how to spend it. You can often leverage an unexpected gift to encourage other giving in the community. A large unexpected gift could be the catalysts for a building project. If you have half the money you need for a new library it will be easier to raise the rest than if you are starting from scratch.

Benefits of Saying "Thank You"

People feel good about themselves when they give to others. They feel even better if they are thanked for their gift. So if people give money to your library say "thank you." Say thank you as appropriately as you can. The least might be a handwritten card expressing your thanks with the promise of an invitation to the library to show the giver what you have purchased with the money. If the gift is a large one, an invitation to lunch or dinner with a companion or friend might be an appropriate way to say thank you. Sometimes you might even want to hold a public reception for someone who has made a very large gift to the library. Just make sure the person is willing to participate in the program and will appreciate the attention.

EXAMPLES

On December 30th of every year, as regular as clock work, Milton Boyd brought a check to the Great Bend Public Library. Some years it was a few thousand dollars. Other years it was a little less. As far as I know no one ever asked him to make a gift to the library. He just did it every year. I never did ask him why he did it. He might have given the money to the library to avoid giving it to the IRS. Mostly, he just enjoyed the library. He took great delight in making his annual gift. Once in a while we took him to lunch, but mostly the staff just treated him nicely. In his will he left 20 percent of his undivided estate to the library.

HOW TO DO IT

There is an old saying that "performance precedes funding." When people give money to libraries they want their gift to make a difference. They don't want it to be used to make up for slipshod management or the benign neglect of a governing body. The job of all library managers is to make sure that their libraries perform well—that people get what they want when they go there. When you enhance the image and the performance of your library you enhance your chances of receiving unexpected gifts.

You could have all kinds of computers, videos, and the latest best sellers, but if people think of your library as a warehouse of books, and the librarian as their babysitter, you will always have funding problems. On the other hand if the people in your community see the library as a vital helpful part of the community you will always have enough money.

Take a minute right now to assess your library's image. How do people see it? How do you see it? Make a list of three things you could do next week that would make a difference in how the public sees your library. Write one of the ideas on your "To Do List" for next Monday.

SPECIAL CONSIDERATIONS

Remember that people are the most important elements of good library service. Most of the stories of unexpected donations to a library lead back to someone helping the donor in a significant way. Would the way your staff treat the customers of your library qualify for a million dollar gift?

Staff members respond positively to expressions of appreciation, being in on what is happening, having control over their own jobs and responsibilities, and having their thoughts and ideas heard by managers.

PITFALLS

Complacency is the biggest pitfall for those who wait for unexpected gifts. It is pure folly to think that you can keep on doing the same old things day after day, week after week. You have to keep your finger on the pulse of the community and what is going on in the library world. You can't always be out on the point with new things, but you need to try.

FOR SCHOOLS AND ACADEMIC LIBRARIES

It is possible for someone who has graduated from your school or university to go away and get rich and come back with a wheelbarrow full of money for your library. Being nice to people never goes out of style—even if they are obnoxious students. If you cast your bread upon the water it may come back as chocolate cake. This technique is a good springboard for other more proactive ways to raise money. In fact good library service is the basis for funding requests of all types.

CHECKLIST

Use this checklist to help you be in line for more unexpected gifts.

1. Does your library pass the checklist for image and performance?
2. What could you do to enhance your library's image or performance?

3. Are staff members aware that the way they treat patrons could affect donations to the library?
4. Does your plan for recognition and saying thank you encourage additional giving?
5. Do library policies discourage goodwill and alienate people?

GETTING RESULTS

The way people are treated when they come to the library often determines whether or not they will make a gift to the library. Focusing on quality customer service will improve your chances for fundraising success no matter what technique you use.

What Do I Do next?

Decide if you need to spruce up your library's image. If you do, get some help from someone outside the library because your eyes are clouded over from being too close to the situation

What Are the Policies and Procedures Needed?

Once you have a reasonable outside assessment, present the findings to the staff. Ask for ideas they can do among themselves. Use the priority-setting matrix mentioned in Chapter 1 to help decide what to do. Some image issues fall outside our ability to fix. If you are in a Carnegie building it will be nearly impossible for you to overcome the eleven steps it takes to get into the building.

How Much Time Should This Method Take?

This method will take vigilance every day the library is open for as long as you as you are connected with the library. It will be the same for every library you work in. This method of fundraising takes a career commitment for everyone who works in the library.

When Can I Expect Results?

You are probably seeing the results of the work of your predecessors right now. About the time you think what you are doing isn't working something will happen to tell you that it is. Results can come every day. They may not be in the form of a donation.

What Can I Realistically Expect the Costs to Be?

How much does it cost to run your library? That amount plus a little more is what it will cost to make this method a success.

SUMMARY

Opening the doors of the library, being nice to people, and saying thank you when they give you money is a good way to start your fundraising effort. It will build confidence and lead to other ways of getting the money you need for your library.

Librarians everywhere have stories to tell about unsolicited gifts from rich people and people who they assumed had no money to give away. Here are the main points to encourage unexpected or unsolicited gifts.

- People use libraries, like libraries, and appreciate the service they receive.
- For many library users the only friendly contact they have in a day is a greeting from their friends at the library.
- A large unexpected gift could be the catalyst for a building project.
- Saying thank you appropriately could be the catalyst for a major gift.
- The job of all library managers is to make sure that their libraries perform well.
- People should always get what they want when they go to the library.
- When you enhance the image and the performance of your library you enhance your chances of receiving unexpected gifts.
- If the people in your community see the library as a vital helpful part of the community you will always have enough money.
- Make sure the physical arrangement of the library draws people in.
- Do everything you can to guarantee that your library is a nice, friendly place to be.
- The way your staff treats every customer could be worth a million dollar gift to your library.

BIBLIOGRAPHY

Karp, Rashelle. 2002. *Powerful Public Relations: A How-to-Guide for Libraries*. Chicago: American Library Association. Forthcoming book.

Steele, Victoria, and Stephen D. Elder. 2000. *Becoming a Fundraiser: The Principles and Practice of Library Development*, 2d ed. Chicago: American Library Association. The first edition of this book won the Highsmith Award in 1995. It is a basic text that covers all of the bases in library fundraising.

Chapter 4

Pass Bond Issue for Building Project

DESCRIPTION

A bond issue is usually voted on by the people to provide the money necessary to build a new library or some other capital project. Issuing bonds is a legal way for public entities to borrow money for large projects. The money is paid back, with interest, over a period of years. Sometimes taxes have to be raised to retire the bonds. The city or the county has the authority to levy for bonds, but if the library has autonomous taxing authority it issues the bonds itself. This is a legal maneuver with many technicalities. Secure the help of a qualified attorney before you initiate a bond issue. Turn the legal part of the bond issue over to him or her. The legal department of the city or county may be the best source of legal help.

PURPOSE

About the only purpose for a bond issue is to secure funds for a new building, a remodeling project, or for land. Bond funds may also be used to purchase equipment and furnishing for the new facility.

BENEFITS

The main benefit of a bond issue is getting the money to build a new library sooner rather than later. It is just like a family buying a new home. If they tried to save until they have enough money they might never have a new home. By issuing bonds the people can enjoy a new facility while they are paying for it.

EXAMPLES

In 1998 the residents of Port Washington, New York, passed a bond issue worth almost $6 million to expand and renovate the 30-year-old building. The vote passed by a 63 percent margin thanks to a lot of work on the part of the library staff, Friends of the Library, and the library board. The yes vote was encouraged by the early announcement of the Port Washington Library Foundation to donate $420,000 to the library if the bond vote passed.

The people in Broward County, Florida, passed a $139.9 million bond issue in April of 1998 to fund improvements and expansion of library facilities. The vote passed by a 72 percent margin.

In 1997 the voters in Provo, Utah, approved a $16.8 million bond issue by 58 percent of the vote to build a new library on the site of the old Brigham Young Academy. The Brigham Young Academy Foundation raised $5.4 million to pay for the reconstruction and renewal of the 100-year-plus building. The new 96,000 square-foot structure replaced a 29,000 square-foot-library.

HOW TO DO IT

Show the people what they will get if they vote for the bond issue. Start with an architectural drawing or a three-dimensional model.

Winning a bond issue uses the same strategies as winning a referendum; except you will have a new building when the project is complete. Review the information in Chapter 2 for details on how to encourage people to vote for a referendum. Make sure you abide by any state or local laws that restrict the use of tax dollars to promote the passage of a bond issue.

If the public has a negative perception about the library, passing a bond issue will be that much more difficult. So before you try to pass a bond issue for a new library, find out how the people feel about the library. The Checklist for Library Image and Performance from page 34 is a good tool to assess how well you are doing. Here are a few suggestions to help you get the job done.

Get the Issue on the Ballot Correctly

Most municipalities hire an attorney whose job it is to assure the bond approval process meets the legal requirements to sell the bonds. The librarian doesn't need to be an authority on all the details associated with bonds, but he or she should have a working knowledge of the principles and procedures.

Ideas to Encourage Voters to Pass a Bond Issue

- Develop a flyer or brochure that you can give to *everyone.*
- Use volunteers to canvass every neighborhood inviting people to vote for the library.
- Put advertisements in the newspaper, on the radio, and on television.
- Get people to write "Letters to the Editor."
- Use highway billboards.
- Put up yard signs.
- Make public appearances.
- Give talks at service clubs.
- Call voters on the telephone.
- Mail flyers to everyone.
- Put information about the bond issue on the library's Web site.
- Get friends to use their e-mail connections to promote the bond issue.
- Create a public service announcement for television and radio and ask local stations to air it as a public service.

Figure II-4-1 Ideas to Encourage Voters to Pass a Bond Issue

You need to find out how much your municipality can borrow and determine if your new library fits within those limits. You need to know the legislative requirements to get a bond approved. Find out how many public hearings need to be held. Learn the proper notifications and the timing requirements.

Organize a Campaign Committee

Getting a bond issue passed by a community takes a tremendous amount of coordination. This task falls to the head of the campaign committee. This person is every bit as important as the chair of the capital campaign committee. The chair of the committee has to have strong leadership skills and give great attention to detail. The campaign committee chair is much like a conductor of an orchestra—insuring that everyone on the committee works in harmony with each other. The job of the committee is to decide on what will be done to encourage voters to vote for the bond issue on Election Day. Here are a few activities others have done to get out the vote in favor of the library (see Figure II-4-1).

This is not an exhaustive list, but I hope it gets the creative juices flowing. A good brainstorming session with members of the community should come up with some real zingers for your community.

Market Your Library

More than anything you have to market your library. In spite of what you as the librarian believe about the need for a new library and the merits of the bond issue are, you will not get a new library unless you can convince the requisite number of people to think the way that you do. Marketing your library can play a major role in getting the bond issue approved. You have to sell your library to everyone you talk with. So does everyone on the campaign committee.

Take Care of Media Coverage

In an effort to present all sides of the issue the news media may present the arguments of the opposition. Do your best to win the endorsement of the news media. A positive editorial in the newspaper, on the radio, or on television can give your cause a real boost.

Try to get as much free publicity as you can, but don't be afraid to pay for a few well-placed advertisements.

If the people at the newspaper do not support your bond issue, don't try to overcome their objections. It is not wise to get into a war of words with people who buy ink by the barrel.

Compare Tax Increases in Everyday Terms

When you ask people to make a commitment to spend their money for the next several years, they need to understand why. They also need to know what their options are. If you are going to win their support and their votes, you need to explain the bond issue in terms they can understand. If you can, put a dollar value on the various services of the library. Explain the benefits of the new library and the new taxes in terms they can understand. Tell them how much it will cost them each year based on the value of their home.

Deal with Organized Opposition

Some people honestly oppose any and all taxes regardless of the benefits they derive from the services they receive from places like the library. You can't do much to change their attitude. You can, however, present your case with well-founded facts and persuasive arguments. The best way to deal with the opposition is to present your case in a factual forthright manner. People will understand the truth.

Some people may believe the town needs a new library but not the "Taj Mahal" you have planned. They might oppose the library because they think you can get by with one that is a lot less expensive. That is why it is good to use focus groups or telephone surveys.

Regardless of the opposition you need to keep your cool and deal with all objections in a matter of fact way, and not leave incorrect comments without a positive response.

Never Give Up

Many bond issues take more than one try to gain approval. If you lose the first time around, find out what the people who voted against the bond issue didn't like and try to answer their concerns. Keep the faith with the voters. Never lose sight of what you promised once the election is won. After five years you have to be able to say, "Your tax dollars were spent exactly as we promised."

RESOURCES

The best tool you can have for getting a bond issue passed is a good working knowledge of the process and procedures for doing it. Next to that find a friend who has a good working knowledge of these things and let him or her help you. Winning a bond election takes a lot more specialized skill and knowledge than running a library. Get some help. Borrow the best minds you can find and get them to help you with the campaign after you get the issue on the ballot.

SPECIAL CONSIDERATIONS

Don't back down or be faint-hearted if other capital projects are going to be on the same ballot with the library bond issue. I have seen schools, jails, swimming pools, and sewer systems fail when the library issue succeeded. The library offers something good for everyone in the community, and stands apart from other agencies.

PITFALLS

The most difficult thing to judge when proposing a bond issue for a new library is how much to ask for. If you ask for too much money in a bond issue, people will think you are building a larger, fancier library than the community needs. If you ask for too little and the bond issue passes, the building you can afford may be scaled down. You have to be accurate and realistic with your estimates and then convince the voters that you are sensitive to their concerns.

Remember that many segments of the population will be voting on the bond issue, and you need to make sure that as many constituents as possible are satisfied.

FOR SCHOOLS AND ACADEMIC LIBRARIES

Schools and academic libraries may not have access to passing a bond issue to get a new library, except through the institution. The library could be a part of a larger project for the entire school district or university. School and academic librarians need to support institutional initiatives that include enhancement to the library.

CHECKLIST

Use this checklist to determine if you are ready to put a bond issue before the voters to build a new library.

1. Do you have the unanimous support of all library board members?
2. Have you conducted a feasibility study to determine if the community will support a bond issue?
3. Can you document a need for a new library?
4. Do you have an architectural rendering of the new library? Do you have realistic cost estimates for the new library?
5. Can you tell homeowners how much their taxes go up if they vote for the bond issue?
6. Do you know what actions are necessary to get the issue on the ballot?
7. Can you count on leaders in the community to support the bond issue?
8. Do you have the support of the general public?
9. Does the library have a Friends group or other support organization with many volunteers to campaign for the bond issue?
10. Does the Friends group have the resources to aggressively promote the bond issue?
11. Once you have arranged to have the issue on the ballot, what appeals will you use to encourage the voters to approve the tax increase for the library?
12. What activities do you intend to use to promote the vote?

GETTING RESULTS

Passing a bond issue to build a new library can produce some powerful and long-lasting results. You will need some powerful allies to make it happen.

What Do I Do Next?

Once the library board has decided to push for a bond issue to build or remodel the library, seek out and recruit the best leaders you can find. If you are a librarian don't try to do the work yourself. Turn it over to a board member or someone in the Friends group. Try to build a coalition of groups or people who will work within their own circles to make people aware of the need and promote the passage of the bond issue.

Create a support role for the library staff and follow through with every assignment as promptly as you can. Share the "How to do it" section of this chapter with members of the bond issue committee. Empower them to carry the issue to the voters.

What Are the Policies and Procedures Needed?

If this is the first time your library has tried for a bond issue get help from the people in other agencies who have tried it before. They will know the law and will have some good suggestions for you. Be very careful to conduct the effort within the law. You could alienate an otherwise positive group if you skirt around the law. Call the city legal department and ask for clarification about the law or anything else you do not know about getting the bond issue on the ballot. Confer with others to refine your application.

How Much Time Should This Method Take?

From the day the library board decides to move forward with the bond issue until the vote should take between six months to a year. If you try to do it in less than six months, you could miss some steps or fail to build the constituent support you need to win the election. It takes time to conduct the voter surveys and evaluate your potential for success. If the issue passes, getting the money could take another six months to a year depending on how long it takes to issue the bonds and sell them. Don't worry about the amount of time this phase will take. The architect will need all of it to design the building and help secure bids.

If the bond doesn't pass the first time, you may be looking at several years before it finally does pass. Try to find out why the bond issue failed and overcome the objection in the next try. Sometimes it is all demographics and there is nothing you can do.

When Can I Expect Results?

It could take as long as two or three years to witness the dedication of the new library or even longer if the project is large. Celebrate success as often as you can. You will be so busy that you could overlook natural opportunities to recognize those who have been part of the success and celebrate the milestones along the way.

What Can I Realistically Expect the Costs to Be?

The cost of passing a bond issue might be similar to passing a tax increase through a referendum. Somewhere between $500 and $1,000 might get the job done, but in a larger area you can benefit from the economies of scale. You might be able to do it with $15,000 to $25,000. It is difficult to predict how much a successful campaign will cost. Some professional fundraisers may be able to help you if they have experience in this area. Remember that you will have to raise this money from outside sources if you can't use library money to promote the referendum.

You cannot pass a bond election without someone spending some money. Some promotional activities will be free, but most of them will cost money. So expect to succeed without spending some money. If you can, use the library to provide information and let the Friends or some other groups or individuals pay for the pure promotional part of the campaign.

SUMMARY

There is no special formula on how to get a bond issue approved. Internal and external variables are at work all the time. They determine the success of getting a bond issue passed. The timing may be a problem because of an economic downturn; or interest rates may be high; or other agencies have projects on the ballot that are more worthy at the time. Just remember these techniques and how to use them:

- Make sure you have the support of the community and political leaders.
- Establish an overpowering need and make sure everyone gets the message.
- Create a compelling vision of the new library.
- Do everything you can to predict how the vote will go before you put the bond issue on the ballot.
- Postpone the vote on the bond issue if the feedback you get suggests insufficient support.
- Get help. Get more help. Get all of the help you can recruit.
- Pull out all of the stops and get supporters to do everything they can.
- Never doubt victory.

BIBLIOGRAPHY

Josey, E.J., and Kenneth D. Shearer. 1990. *Politics and the Support of Libraries*. New York: Neal-Schuman. Experienced library professionals have each written a chapter, making it a standard work on library funding. Topics cover the gamut from library politics at the national level to working with those who control library funding at the local level.

Shout!!! Library Advocacy: Teleconference for School Librarians, Library Trustees and Directors, Anne Abrams, Idaho State Library, 1998, videocassette. This video has practical advice on how to conduct a bond issue election campaign and lobby local state representatives.

Chapter 5

Pass a Referendum for Regular Funding

DESCRIPTION

The best place to get more money for your library is at the ballot box. If this option is open to your library, figure out what it takes to get the issue on the ballot and go for it. You will need the support of most of the people in your community. An increase that is voted on by the people is usually there forever. Except in a few states, once a tax for library operations is on the books, it stays on the books. You don't have to go out year after year to raise the same money to maintain your budget.

Passing a referendum to increase regular funding may sound easy, but it is not. It takes a lot of work and sometimes requires the right political connections. You start by getting the issue on the ballot and then persuading the taxpayers to vote for it.

In Ohio a share of the state income tax funds public libraries. In 1986 they repealed the intangibles tax for libraries in favor of a library and local government support fund, based on the proceeds of a percentage of the state personal income tax. Ohio might become a model for local library funding in other states.

PURPOSES

Increasing the library's operating budget is the main reason for using a referendum. It can give you the money you need for more books, more computers, more staff, better salaries, and better maintenance of the building. Winning a tax referendum gives a morale boost to the staff and the board, too. If you have been operating on a shoestring for several years, the extra breathing room afforded by a revenue increase is good

for everyone's mental health. Few other fundraising methods can produce as dramatic a result as passing a tax referendum.

BENEFITS

A tax referendum can benefit a library in the following ways:

- The financial benefit is long lasting.
- It is renewable year after year.
- It eliminates the need to do additional fundraising.
- The money can be used for whatever purpose the library board
  deems prudent.
- It enhances the library's visibility.
- Staff energies can be more focused on serving the public.
- It gives the people a chance to say how much they appreciate the
  library.

EXAMPLES

According to Karen Givens, librarian of the South New Berlin (New
York) Free Library, "Our success story involved petitioning the taxpayers in the school district to allow for additional taxes to go toward supporting the operation of the library. Since that measure was
whole-heartedly endorsed by the people, we have not needed to do additional fundraising since" (Swan, 1990:76).

The mayor of Ida, Illinois, was a helpful member of the Friends. With
his assistance, the Friends wrapped a crepe paper blue ribbon around
the entire library building to publicize the election. They also wrapped
blue ribbons around all of the trees on city property to remind people
to support the library. Newspapers and television stations from the neighboring large city of Rockford, Illinois, covered the event. The referendum passed by 72 percent.

HOW TO DO IT

The first step is to get the referendum on the ballot. Libraries that have
access to an initiative petition can push for a referendum by securing
signatures on a petition to have the issue put on the ballot. A certain
percent of the voters who cast ballots in the last election need to sign
the petition. If you can get enough signatures you can get the issue on
the ballot. If the local governing body has the authority to put referenda
on the ballot, they may be willing to do it for the library and let the vot-

---

Ideas for Promoting a Budget Increase

- Create a list of things the library will do with the new money.
- Create a financial sheet that includes current revenues and expenditures as well as proposed new revenues and expenditures.
- Make a list of all the services of the library.
- Gather property tax information that compares the amount of money the library gets from an average taxpayer to the entire tax bill he or she pays.
- Create an attractive brochure and pass it out at the library and wherever you can.
- Put the information on the library's Web page.
- Get as much free publicity as you can in the newspaper, radio, and television.
- Get someone to pay for advertising in the newspaper, on the radio, and on television (it may be illegal to use library money to promote the mill levy increase).
- Get someone to pay for yard signs and get volunteers to put them up all over town about a week before the election.
- Contact service clubs and offer to do a program for them and talk about the library issue on the ballot.

Figure II-5-1 Ideas for Promoting a Budget Increase

ers decide whether or not to give the library more money. It lets them off the hook for raising taxes.

Once the issue is on the ballot you have to pull out all of the stops and let people know why they should vote for the tax increase. People want to know how much the new tax will cost them personally. Figure out what the new tax would be on an average priced home in your city and include the information in the publicity you pass out.

Tell the people why the library needs more money. Even though the things the library has to buy today cost a lot more than they did twenty years ago, you don't need to remind people that their dollars are not going as far as they used to.

A few ideas for promoting the library's cause in a referendum are shown in Figure II-5-1.

RESOURCES

One of the best tools you have is the library statistics you have kept over the years. Many of the people who will vote on the referendum will not care how your library compares to other libraries. They will pay attention to the history of support for your library. Use the statistics you have to your advantage.

Use a computer to generate spreadsheets, charts, and graphs. Use these displays to show why you need more money for the library.

Voter registrations are public records. You may be able to gain access to this information and send personal letters to every voter in the city.

Create a video spot announcement for television. Keep it short and focus on the good things the library does for the people. Use a tag line like "Vote yes for the library."

SPECIAL CONSIDERATIONS

This is a legal initiative and must be done in accordance with state law. Hire a lawyer or get the city or county legal department to draft the referendum that will be on the ballot. Don't try to do it yourself. You could leave out an essential part and the whole action could be voided.

PITFALLS

Don't ask for the referendum to be put on the ballot, if you aren't relatively certain it will pass. You may need to enhance the library's visibility and performance before you ask for more money.

In some states it is illegal to use tax funds for political purposes. If you plan to spend any money to promote the passage of the referendum, make sure it comes from sources other than library tax funds.

Keep all of your publicity and promotions positive. Avoid identifying individuals who may have been responsible for the library's financial ill health.

Don't withhold your request for additional taxes because of a bad economy and you don't want to burden the taxpayers. If you don't speak up for the library, some other agency will come forward and get the money you thought you were saving the taxpayers. If you need the money ask for it.

Don't settle for an incremental increase that will only partially solve the problem and force you to make the effort again in a few years. This is the time to think boldly. Go for at least a 25 percent increase. You will have to work just as hard to get a lesser result. If people are going to vote for a mill levy increase for the library, they will be just as likely to vote for one mill as two.

FOR SCHOOLS AND ACADEMIC LIBRARIES

If you are in a school library, your library should be included in a district referendum. If you are not included, find out why. School librarians have to be very vigilant to make sure they get their share of the school district's resources. It usually means keeping the superintendent informed about the activities of the library and seeking the opportunity to request additional funding.

Academic libraries are in the same boat. They are at the mercy of those who allocate institutional resources. Unfortunately, school and academic libraries lack access to the ballot box when it comes to getting more money.

CHECKLIST

Use this checklist to plan for a referendum. It will help you remember some of the key points.

1. Is it legal for the people to vote to increase their taxes so the library can have more money?
2. What do you have to do to get the issue on the ballot?
3. Do you have the support of *every* person on your board?
4. Have you complied with the law that allows for the initiative on the ballot?
5. Have you contacted the proper legal authorities to draft the initiative for the ballot?
6. Once you have arranged to have the issue on the ballot, what appeals will you use to encourage the voters to approve the tax increase for the library?
7. What activities do you intend to use to promote the vote?
8. Is it legal to use library funds to promote the passage of the referendum?
9. If not, how will you pay for these activities?
10. What is your timeline for these activities?
11. How will you recruit volunteers?

GETTING RESULTS

If passing a referendum to get more money for your library is a strong possibility and you want to try it, use the following questions to help you get started.

What Do I Do Next?

Discuss this option with all of your board members. You may need to develop a preliminary proposal, similar to the one you would make to the general public. Make sure that each of them is 100 percent behind the effort. If you have the support of your board you can take the next step.

What Are the Policies and Procedures Needed?

Find out what the legal ramifications are. Talk with someone in the city legal department or someone at the state library. Find out what actions to take to get the issue on the ballot. Generally the governing body, by a majority vote, can place a tax issue before the voters. In some states if enough voters sign a petition the issue will be put on a ballot.

How Much Time Should This Method Take?

Timing is everything. It will take about a year and a half from the time you decide to advocate for a referendum until you see some of the money in the library's bank account. Planning with the board needs to take place about nine months before the issue is to be placed on the ballot. If the issue passes it will take another nine months for the new tax to be levied and collected.

When Can I Expect Results?

You won't be able to spend any of the money for about two years, but the results will be long lasting. Success at the ballot box could eliminate a lot of work with other fundraising efforts, but that doesn't mean you should give up on efforts that will help build a secure future for your library.

What Can I Realistically Expect the Costs to Be?

Costs to the library will depend on how much of the promotion expense you can get paid for by others. If you can get free airtime from radio and television stations this segment of your costs will be minimal. Newspapers may give you a free story or two, but don't count on a full-page advertisement for free. Costs will also depend on the number of voters you need to reach. Yard signs are effective, but they cost a dollar or more apiece. For the smallest of libraries, a war chest of $500 might get the job done, but in a larger area you can benefit from the economies of scale. Try to have between 10 to 25 cents per capita. Remember, you will have to raise this money from outside sources if you can't use library money to promote the referendum.

SUMMARY

Increasing the library's operating budget is the main reason for using a referendum. There is little difference between selling people on the idea of giving money to the library and asking them to increase tax support for the library. So, look first to the voters and sell them on the idea of providing more tax support for the library.

Here are the main points to passing a tax referendum:

- Passing a tax referendum is the most effective way to get more money for your library.
- The money can be used for whatever purpose the library board deems prudent.
- The financial benefit is long lasting.
- It eliminates the need to do additional fundraising.
- The campaign to pass a referendum enhances the library's visibility.
- It gives the people a chance to say how much they appreciate the library.

If you can articulate the library's need and can communicate it to the public, you are well on your way to passing a referendum.

BIBLIOGRAPHY

Bradley, Jim. 1995. *Passing a Library Tax Referendum by a Margin of Better Than 4-1*. Springfield, Ill.: Illinois State Library. Even though this book focuses specifically on Illinois, it has important implications for libraries in other states.

Budgets and Levies: Bring in an Expert, Phil Lenzini, Alliance Library System, 1999, videocassette. This video is very instructive for librarians in Illinois. It could have value for librarians in other states provided their state laws allow them to submit a levy increase for the library to the voters. This video deals with tax levy, budget hearing, budget and appropriation ordinance, truth in taxation, building and maintenance tax ordinance, special reserve fund ordinance, and working cash fund ordinance. The video may only be available through the Heritage Trails Library System, Shorewood, Illinois.

Childers, Thomas A., and Nancy A. Van House. 1993. *What's Good? Describing Your Public Library's Effectiveness*. Chicago: American Library Association. This book is based on solid research that can help you prepare for a referendum to increase funding for the library.

Rickert, Suzan, and Judy Zelenski, ed. 1988. *Campaigning for Libraries*. Wheat Ridge, Colo.: Central Colorado Library System. Learn the ins and outs of running a successful library referendum—from selling the need to the legal questions involved.

Steps to a Successful Referenda, H. Neil Kelley, 160 min., Illinois State Library, 2000, videocassette. The presenters in this video discuss how to successfully conduct a library referendum, how to defuse negative publicity, how to generate positive publicity, and how to target the audience. They also explain the laws governing library referenda in Illinois.

Turner, Anne M. 2000. *Vote Yes for Libraries: A Guide to Winning Ballot Measure Campaigns for Library Funding.* Jefferson, N.C.: McFarland. Persuading voters to support more taxes to support their library is difficult. Anne Turner recommends getting professional help because most people connected with libraries lack the experience to make it happen. Written for library directors, staff, board members, and Friends who want to know how to get people to vote for more money for the library—this book is a rare gem on the topic.

Chapter 6

Appeal for More Regular Funding

DESCRIPTION

When a tax referendum is not an option, the next best way to get more money for your library is to make an appeal to the governing body. In fact this is a regular occurrence in cities and counties all over the United States. Every year librarians develop and present budgets to their governing bodies, and they usually include some incremental funding enhancements.

You probably don't need help getting the status quo–type increases. As difficult as it may seem we are talking about making a plea for a significant increase in the library's share of the city or county's resources. We are talking about getting a renewable big chunk of money in the range of 20 to 25 percent or more—enough to make a big difference in the services the library provides.

PURPOSES

The reason for an appeal to the governing body is not just to get more money, but to offer more and better library services. Too often we get bogged down in the "more money" trap, and we fail to focus on the benefits to the public we serve. We want to be able to offer these services year after year without facing budget reductions.

BENEFITS

The single most important benefit of an appeal to the governing body is that any increase is a permanent increase. Unlike other fundraising activities in this book, you will not have to sell the idea again next year. The other benefit is being able to use the new money for ongoing operations as well as new services.

EXAMPLES

My first job as a library director was in Pickens County, South Carolina. I had to go before the county council every year and plead for more money for the library. It seemed that the library was on the bottom of everyone's priority list. In the 1970s it was a difficult task just to keep up with inflation. Sometimes it doesn't matter how valid or persuasive your appeal is—if the elected officials are not interested in the library, you won't get the extra money you seek. You may have to wait until the political climate changes to make your appeal.

During my third year in South Carolina, I used statistics to win the largest increase ever. The statistics showed that the library's share of county revenue had decreased over the past few years. The night of the budget hearing I taped charts and graphs all over the walls of the council's chamber. It may have looked funny, but it worked. Another year I presented a slide show to say, "It is time to be fair." The slide show won a John Cotton Dana Special Award, but the presentation fell on deaf ears.

When the roof of the Hays (Kansas) Public Library developed a terrible leak, the librarian went to the city administrator and told him that the library needed to increase the mill levy from four mills to six mills to help fix the roof. The governing body passed the increase unanimously and the library got the money. The roof was fixed and the next year the two-mill increase became part the regular budget.

HOW TO DO IT

To start with, the Friends, board members, etc. need to have contact with city/county officials throughout the entire year. You can't just go one time right before a budget hearing and expect to get what you want. You must cultivate your officials all year long. Let them know the good things that are happening in the library for their constituents. Say "thank you" whether you get a favorable response or not. You can't always be seen as asking for more money. That way when you do need their support and financial backing, you already have friends who are knowledgeable about library issues and concerns.

Having cultivated a relationship with members of the governing body, make a good case for the library. We have already discussed how performance precedes funding. If the library is already doing a good job and everybody knows it, selling the governing body should be easy. Every month Great Bend city officials receive a packet from the library that includes a copy of the minutes of the last month's board meeting, a copy of the director's report, and a copy of the agenda for the upcoming meeting. Last year it was no surprise when they received a request from the library for a new roof. They had been reading about it almost every month for the past year.

Try asking a few influential friends to contact the city officials. The good will of a few prominent citizens is often worth more than the support of many common folk.

Generating Statistics for Budget Presentation

The next step is to gather statistics. The state library usually publishes public library statistics every year. You can use this information to compare your library to other libraries in the state. In Chapter 2 we discussed gathering statistics and using various arguments to make the appeal. Refer to Chapter 2 to review the questions and types of appeal.

Making the Presentation

Do your homework. Cover all of the details. Think like the council members will think. Envision your presentation from their viewpoint. Then envision yourself standing up in front of the council and making a flawless speech. Mentally rehearse it over and over again in your mind. Your confidence will strengthen your position.

The next step is to use the budget and existing conditions to illustrate your library's need. Start by analyzing the budget and determine the library's priorities. Use only the data, which will present the library's need. Be specific, yet brief in describing the situation. Know exactly what you want. Make a specific request. Ask for a dollar amount. Be silent after you ask for the money. Wait for questions.

RESOURCES

Circulation statistics and a computer may be the best tools you can have to prepare an appeal to the governing body. A modern spreadsheet program can make quick work of tabulating data and turning it into easy-to-read charts and graphs. Pick out the best three or four graphs that convey your message and use them. Don't try to overwhelm members of the council with more data than they can absorb.

A video recorder is also a handy tool. Make a video of children in story hour or adults learning to use the computer at the library. If space is an issue take some shots of the crowded shelves. Keep the video under ten minutes. The best video piece I ever did was a 30-second public service announcement for television. In rapid succession it showed a montage of people using the library. The tag line was "There is more than you know at your library." It was not produced to influence voters or the city council, but it was an effective public relations piece.

The best arrow in your quiver may not be a piece of equipment, but an individual—maybe a board member, who has pull with members of the governing body. Use whatever resources you have to make your presentation as good as it can be.

SPECIAL CONSIDERATIONS

Sometimes no matter how good your presentation is or how convincing you may sound, if those who control the purse strings have no interest in the library, you may not get what you want. If you have done everything possible and you still come away empty-handed, don't get angry or upset. Letting your emotions show can only hurt the image of the library. Don't give up. Try again next year. You may have to wait until the political climate changes. If you keep the pressure on, you will succeed.

PITFALLS

Not everyone feels the way you do about libraries. Make allowance for alternative views. Listen to other people. They can help you sharpen the focus on the planks in your platform.

Make sure you have the support of every board member before you go to the governing body for an increase. One board member who does not agree that the library needs more money can scuttle the whole deal.

FOR SCHOOLS AND ACADEMIC LIBRARIES

The school board is the governing body for a school library. Unfortunately, school librarians do not have direct access to the school board. They usually have a building principal and a district superintendent between them and the school board. So, it is highly unlikely that a school librarian will ever have the opportunity to make an appeal to the school board for more money for the library.

Academic librarians need to work through the established hierarchy to get more regular funding. They don't usually have to worry about salaries because salaries for library staff members are controlled at the institutional level. Staffing levels are sometimes an issue.

The best thing academic librarians can do to enhance their regular funding is to win the favor of the deans and department heads. If the deans and department heads get what they want at the library, the deans and department heads will go to bat for the library at budget time—at least you hope so.

CHECKLIST

Here is a planning checklist to help you through the process.

1. Are there limits to the amount of increase the library can receive from the governing body?
2. Can the limits be exceeded under certain circumstances?
3. Do you have the support of the entire board to make the appeal to the governing body?
4. Have you preassessed the temperament of the members of the governing body?
5. Are you confident that you have the votes on council or commission to get the increase?
6. As you prepare for the appeal, what appeals will you use to get the governing body to approve the tax increase for the library?
7. What documents will you use?
8. Have you rehearsed your presentation?
9. Who will go with you to the budget hearing?
10. Can you envision yourself making the perfect appeal and getting the money you want?

GETTING RESULTS

If you think you have a good chance of getting more money for your library by making an appeal to the governing body you will want to use these questions and answers to help with your strategies.

What Do I Do Next?

Develop a preliminary proposal, similar to the one you would make to the governing body, and present it to your board. Ask them for their support, and ask them to critique the presentation to help you make it better. If you have the support of your board you can take the next step.

What Are the Policies and Procedures Needed?

There is nothing worse than a political miscue. Find out the right way to make your presentation. You need to develop a working relationship with the city administrator, who can help you weave your way through the political minefield if there is one. Generally, the governing body will set aside a particular night to hear budget requests from departments with the city. Sometimes if you can convince the city administrator that the library needs the money he or she will go to bat for you with the council and your appearance before the council will be a matter of supporting a "done deal." If a majority of the council votes to increase library funding, you get the money.

How Much Time Should This Method Take?

Timing is critical. The city administrator can tell when you need to make the presentation, but you need to be conferring with him or her several months to a year before to garner support and find out what you need to be doing to get ready. It will take about the same amount of time as it takes for a referendum until you see some of the money. Planning with the board needs to take place about nine months before the issue is to be placed on the ballot.

When Can I Expect Results?

City budgeting usually occurs in a yearly cycle. If the governing body approves your request and authorizes your budget at a higher level, you should see the new money at the beginning of the next fiscal year.

What Can I Realistically Expect the Costs to Be?

Costs to get the governing body to approve a significant increase for the library can be minimal. Preparing the budget proposal could take a lot of your time, but unless you spend money on a video presentation or some other promotional piece, you won't have to spend any money at all.

SUMMARY

Making a well-documented appeal to the governing body of your municipality may be the best chance you will have to gain a significant increase in funding for your library. Here are the main ideas for making an appeal to the governing body:

- Start by analyzing the budget and determining the library's priorities.
- Use only the data that will present the library's need.
- Be specific, yet brief in describing the situation.
- Know exactly what you want.
- Ask for a specific dollar amount.

- Assume they are going to give you the money you are asking for.
- When you finish your presentation, stop talking and sit down.
- Answer any questions as briefly as possible.
- Don't use the question and answer period to rehash points you have already made.

Every appeal to the governing body will not be successful. You have to be persistent. Your lack of success may have nothing to do with your presentation or the library's overwhelming need. It may have everything to do with the city's financial situation.

BIBLIOGRAPHY

Marchant, Maurice P. 1994. *Why Adults Use the Public Library: A Research Perspective*. Englewood, Colo.: Libraries Unlimited. Not only does this book tell us why adults use the public library, but it also serves as a model for conducting research in our own libraries.

Rounds, Richard S., and Margo C. Trumpeter. 1994. *Basic Budgeting Practices for Librarians*, 2d ed. Chicago: American Library Association. This is a solid basic book on budgeting for librarians. It covers various types of budgeting and includes income projections and expenditure estimates. The sections on writing a budget and making the presentation in person are especially worthwhile.

Van House, Nancy A., Mary Jo Lynch, Charles R. McClure, Douglas L. Zweizig, and Eleanor Jo Rodger. 1987. *Output Measures for Public Libraries*, 2d ed. Chicago: American Library Association. This book will help you decide which output measure to use in your presentation.

Chapter 7

Conduct Annual Campaign of Giving

DESCRIPTION

Annual giving is soliciting funds to support library services and programs. The Friends of the Library, the library foundation, or the development office usually conduct these annual campaigns, though it is not unheard of for the library staff to conduct a direct mail solicitation as part of an annual fund drive.

Annual fund drives can be conducted in a variety of ways. Public radio stations turn over their on-air programming to the development staff and they ask people to call in and pledge gifts. Most universities use a direct mail approach—sending out solicitations two or three times a year. Others call people on the telephone or go visit donors in person. All these approaches work. The main idea of an annual fund drive is to do it at least once a year.

PURPOSES

Annual giving is the yearly appeal a library makes to all patrons and friends for unrestricted gifts that can be used immediately to meet the library's most important needs—including library and computer resources, facilities maintenance, and renovation. Annual giving funds allow a library to solve problems as they arise, and seize unexpected opportunities.

BENEFITS

Funds from annual campaigns are usually unrestricted. Therein lies their unique benefit. If you get them you can spend them for any good library purpose. The materials budget is a popular target, but these funds do not have to be spent on books unless the donors have specified how they want their gift to be used.

Annual campaigns keep the library's need in front of the people—at least every year. People get used to receiving a request for a gift to the library and they give year after year without thinking too much about it.

EXAMPLES

The Grosse Point (Michigan) Public Library puts the names of everyone who donates to their annual giving campaign on their Web site. The donors are listed by category of giving. The library organized a development office to manage gifts and bequests it received. They use the money to increase programs for senior citizens, expand technology resources, and expand youth and adult services and programs (Grosse Point Public Library, 2000).

Eastern Montana College Foundation in Billings, Montana, organizes its annual fund drive committees according to the size of the gift to be solicited—$1,000, $500, $250, $100, and so on. The development director uses an effective approach to let volunteers select the size of the gift they want to solicit. The size of the gift donors seek matches the size of the gift they will give. If a donor is going to solicit $1,000 gifts he or she is expected to give $1,000.

HOW TO DO IT

The first year of an annual campaign for giving is the most difficult because you are starting without a list and little, if any, experience. As you persevere you will develop both. You will build on the success of previous years and build the quality of the list of donors as you progress from year to year.

Develop the Prospect List

You start by developing a prospective donor list and entering the names on your computer. Be careful not to get the cart before the horse. You need to decide how gifts will be solicited before you create your donor list. Will you use direct mail, matching gifts, telephone solicitations, or face-to-face requests? Your decision will affect the names on the list. Less personal methods of solicitation allow for less targeted selection, but you can have more people on the list. Telephone or face-to-face solicitations call for a carefully selected list.

Another way to get the names of prospects is to brainstorm. The same rules apply. No suggestion is passed over. Every name mentioned is written down.

Here are a few other possibilities:

- Library users.
- People who have given books to the library.
- People who have made memorial gifts to it in the past.
- People who have volunteered service to the library.
- Share lists with the community college.
- Guest registers from special events at the library.
- High school alumni lists.
- Country club list.
- Chamber of Commerce list.
- Voter registration lists.

Some of these lists will produce better results than others, but your best chances for success are to contact those who have already given something to the library.

Get Information About the Donors

Next look up the names and addresses and telephone numbers and enter the information on the database for each prospect. If you are creating a long-term list you will want to keep more information for each donor.

You will want to keep track of:

- Name
- Address
- Telephone
- E-mail
- Employer
- Age
- Family
- Church
- Work
- Volunteer
- Where they live—census tract
- Political precinct

Sample Prospective Donor Form
Confidential

Name _____

Spouse or contact _____

Home telephone _____

Home mailing address _____

City, state, zip _____

Business or employment _____

Business address _____

City, state, zip _____

Business telephone _____

Personal information: _____

      Family _____

      Church _____

      Hobbies _____

      Talents _____

Special comments: _____

_____

_____

Giving History

Year	Amount	Solicitor	Suggestion for next year
____	_____	_____	_____
____	_____	_____	_____
____	_____	_____	_____
____	_____	_____	_____
____	_____	_____	_____

Figure II-7-1 Sample Prospective Donor Form

Gathering and entering this information for every household in town could be a big job. Use volunteers or staff or a combination to set up the database. Remember that these are confidential records and should be shared only with those who have a need to know.

You may want to create a form for your computer that looks like the Sample Prospective Donor Form above.

Evaluate the Prospects

Once you have compiled the list of prospective donors, it is time to do your research and rate prospects. The purpose of rating prospects is to develop a consensus as to the giving potential for each prospect. Knowing their capacity to give and their interest in your library is the key to evaluating prospective donors. Before you start asking, you need to know their potential for giving and how willing they will be to make a gift. Otherwise, you could miss a potentially large gift or embarrass yourself by asking too little.

One way to evaluate the prospects is to invite the division heads and team leaders to breakfast and let them forecast the maximum gift each prospect might be willing to give, using these categories:

- More than $1,000
- $1,000
- $500
- $250
- $100

After the team leaders have rated the prospects, the development director and the chair of the committee make the final rating and assign each prospect to a category by amount. Then they invite the $1,000-team members in to suggest the names they would like to be assigned. Generally peers ask peers for money.

Assign the Prospects to the Committee Members

Once you have assigned the prospects to the solicitors, invite everyone in for your kickoff breakfast and give them the names of their prospects. Send them out to contact each person on their list. Do it at a breakfast because the purpose of this meeting is to get everyone involved, and they will have all day to go out and ask for money. Encourage all of the solicitors to make all of their calls that day. If you have the kickoff at night, the enthusiasm will be gone by the next morning.

Thank your solicitors for volunteering and praise them for their gifts (everyone should have made a gift by now). You announce the amount of money raised so far. People like to help with an effort that is well on its way to success.

Regular Reports

Each individual accounts to his or her team leader as the fund drive progresses. Team chairs stay close to their team members and report to their committee chairs, which in turn report to the chair of the steering committee. Every donation is a success and needs to be celebrated. Use competition between teams. Praise success.

End on Time

End on time and celebrate—even if you don't reach your goal. Dragging it out won't help your cause. Invite all the workers and the big gift donors to a big party to celebrate the success of your fundraiser. If you are short, who knows one of them may kick in another $10,000 or more to make up the difference.

Evaluate Your Success

After all the volunteers and donors have been thanked, take the time to evaluate your success with the committee chairs. Count the money. Count the new donors and make sure the information about them is correctly added to the database. Make a list of new donors who might be willing to volunteer to work for the campaign next year.

RESOURCES

The best resource you can have for an annual campaign is a powerful computer and database management software. You might consider investing one of the software packages specifically designed for fundraising. Fundraising software is designed to track prospects, donors, pledges, members, grants, gifts, and solicitations. They offer power, flexibility, and ease of use to make managing an annual campaign a lot easier.

You need a good source to find prospective donors. Perhaps the best way to find prospective donors is through a well-connected committee. Every committee member should be able to add 20 or more qualified leads to the donor list.

You also need a whole bunch of dedicated volunteers who will not only give of their time and talents, but also of their money. A volunteer without his or her contribution will not be an effective member of the team.

SPECIAL CONSIDERATIONS

Timing the annual campaign could be important. The best time of the year to ask people for money is during November and December. Even though every other organization in town is asking for money, too, you have just as good a chance as they do—maybe even better because you are from the library. Studies have shown that people are more generous around the holidays. The worst time to have an annual campaign is January and February.

It is a good idea to select a time for your annual campaign and stay with it year after year. People will begin to look for the library fundraiser and be ready to give.

Pick one method of asking and stick with it. If you always use direct mail don't switch to telephone solicitation. It will confuse your donors.

PITFALLS

Beware not to let funds from the annual campaign become part of the library's regular budget, but rather try to save them for a rainy day or take advantage of opportunities that will benefit the library.

Use local volunteers to solicit funds. I personally dislike smooth-talking professional fundraisers. They can make a lot of money for your library and all you have to do is pay them. But they can leave a very bad impression about your library—so bad that you may never be able to overcome it.

Sometimes we have to deal with objections. They might say, "The library already gets my tax money. Why should I give to the library, too?" Start by agreeing with the person who thinks his or her taxes are enough. He or she does pay taxes, and taxes are the best form of support for the library. Point out that taxes aren't enough to provide the level of service the community is asking for. Everyone pays taxes, but they should also contribute to it with a gift.

FOR SCHOOLS AND ACADEMIC LIBRARIES

School and academic librarians can make good use of annual campaigns of giving, provided you have a Friends of the Library group or some other volunteer group that is willing to help the library. Schools can enlist members of the P.T.A., but do not send out school children to solicit funds for the library. Alumni of schools, colleges, and universities are some of the most loyal donors you can find. All you need to do is tap into their pipeline of giving and hang on to it.

CHECKLIST

If you are thinking about initiating a campaign of annual giving, this checklist will help you decide if you really want to do it or not.

1. Do you have an existing volunteer group like a Friends group whose members are ready to take on a work-intensive project?
2. Do you have a paid staff member like a development director executive secretary to staff the work of the volunteer committee?

3. Are members of this group willing to make a gift themselves, before they ask others to give?
4. Are members of the group committed to take on the annual campaign year after year?
5. Does your community have a tradition of philanthropic giving?
6. How would your community respond to an annual campaign of giving to the library?
7. Are matching gifts a viable option in your community?
8. Do you have access to a computer and the necessary software to make the program work?

GETTING RESULTS

An annual campaign is a great way to let people know, on a regular basis, that the library needs their financial support. Doing it every year will tell people that you are serious about fundraising for the library.

What Do I Do Next?

Discuss conducting an annual campaign with the library board and the Friends of the Library. Work with the foundation board if the funds will be used to fund the endowment. Don't try this method on your own. Get some help. Especially find someone with money and sound leadership skills to chair the committee.

Learn from the success of others. Find out what development directors in large libraries have done and ask for their advice.

What Are the Policies and Procedures Needed?

Make sure the library board and the Friends of the Library support the annual giving campaign. Meet with them to discuss and develop the plan. If they are willing to help by making a donation themselves and securing donations from others, how can you fail?

How Much Time Should This Method Take?

The first year you do an annual campaign will take three to six months to organize and plan and a month to six weeks to do the soliciting. After that you will be able to build on previous experience. Then planning and soliciting altogether should take no more than two months.

When Can I Expect Results?

The money should start coming in as soon as the volunteers go out and start soliciting money. It could take up to a year if you solicit and accept pledges. If the money goes into the endowment, money from the investment could be slow coming in.

What Can I Realistically Expect the Costs to Be?

You can spend $1,000 or more on fundraising software, which is a must if you plan to continue the campaign on a yearly basis. A one-page brochure will cost about $1,000 to print plus development costs. Don't try to cut corners here because people who give at the level you need want to feel part of a class act. Count on spending some money for the kickoff breakfast and the closing party for the volunteers.

SUMMARY

Annual giving is the solicitation for funds to support library services and programs every year. The Friends of the Library, the library foundation, or the development office usually conduct annual campaigns for the ongoing support of the library. Here are the main points about annual campaigns:

- Annual giving funds allow a library to solve problems as they arise, and seize unexpected opportunities.
- Annual campaigns keep the library's need in front of the people—at least every year.
- The best people to include on the donor list are those people who have given books, memorial gifts, or money to the library before.
- Once you have compiled the list of prospective donors, it is time to do your research and rate prospects.
- Thank your solicitors for volunteering and praise them for their gifts.
- Evaluate the success of your annual campaign.
- Make a list of new donors who might be willing to volunteer to work for the campaign next year.
- Consider buying fundraising software that is designed to track prospects, donors, pledges, members, grants, gifts, and solicitations.

BIBLIOGRAPHY

Corson-Finnerty, Daniel Adam, and Laura Blanchard. 1998. *Fundraising and Friend-Raising on the Web*. Chicago: American Library Association. Computer laser optical disc. As the role of the World Wide Web expands, the opportunities for libraries to benefit financially will increase. This will show you how to organize and conduct an annual campaign using the Web and other resources.

Denham, Rudi. 1999. *Fundraising: A Virtual Guide for Small Medium-sized Public Libraries* [Online]. Available: www.bcpl.gov.bc.ca/qc/finsupp/FundraisingVirtualGuide.html [2002, February 17]. This Web site has some wonderful information about conducting an annual campaign of giving.

Greenfield, James M. 1994. *Fund-Raising: A Guide to Annual Giving for Professionals and Volunteers.* New York: John Wiley. This is a basic text on the fundamentals of fundraising. It covers the basics of direct mail solicitations, annual giving, membership drives, and gift renewals.

Chapter 8

Build Endowment

DESCRIPTION

An endowment is built from assets not needed by the library for immediate projects or operations. Money could come from cash gifts, securities, stocks, or real estate. These assets are invested and the earned income is used to support library activities. Creating and building an endowment is a job for the library foundation. If you don't have a library foundation, organize one or wait until you have one to build an endowment. See Chapter 8 for suggestions on organizing a foundation.

PURPOSES

The purpose of an endowment is to provide an avenue for initial and continued giving of money and other assets that are invested. A portion of the proceeds from the investments must go to the library every year, but most of the money can remain intact to earn interest. The library can use the money any way it wants to, unless the foundation board puts strings on the way the money can be spent.

BENEFITS

Endowment funds can provide a significant level of financial stability for the library. An endowment can enhance the library's ability to plan for future needs. An endowment gives the library more independence to follow its dreams without being encumbered by its dependence on public funds. An endowment can be used to leverage additional funds from other organizations.

EXAMPLES

The Belleville (Kansas) Public Library Foundation was established in 1992 as separate and distinct from the Friends of the Library. Its goal was to obtain and manage a permanent endowment. A seven-member foundation board manages the endowment. The library board appoints members to the foundation board.

Leah Krotz, Director of the Belleville (Kansas) Public Library, says, "In 1997, we conducted a major fund drive, kicked off by a $35,000 bequest. We used this as a local match to obtain a $30,000 LSTA grant and raised an additional $38,000 in local funds. The fund drive allowed us to completely renovate the library, automate our collection, provide computers for staff and public access, and start the Foundation's endowment fund. With additional donations and bequests, the endowment has grown to about $85,000.

"Most important of all, we provided superior library service. This made it easy to ask for money because people knew they were giving to something worthwhile and valuable to the community."

Leah offers these tips for beginning a fund drive:

1. "Have a plan and specific goals. Think about the questions potential donors might ask, and be prepared to answer them. How will your project benefit them?
2. Choose really good people to be on your board, task force, or fundraising committee. Select people with various talents like publicity, writing and desktop publishing skills and legal or financial knowledge. Also select some members with money who will give leadoff donations, and some people who are evangelists for the library and will talk about how wonderful it is.
3. Keep meetings brief and well organized. Establish committees or task forces to work on various projects so that meetings don't get bogged down in details.
4. If you have several groups, make sure each has clearly delineated responsibilities and goals" (Krotz, 2001).

In Medford, Wisconsin, the library foundation has a permanent endowment with a mission to benefit the community by raising, managing, and distributing funds to support library offerings and service. They use a giving tree to recognize donors in four levels of giving.

Some Sources for Endowment Funding

- Other foundations. Some foundations only give to other foundations.
- Deferred giving. Some individuals would love to see their bequest go to an endowment to provide a long lasting benefit to the library.
- Large corporations. If your library serves some of their employees, you may have a chance at a nice gift.
- Annual campaign of giving. Foundation board members should be asked to give and solicit donations every year.
- Local businesses. They seemed to be the ones who are hit by every fundraising effort to pass through the neighborhood, but for some it is their way to give back to the community.
- Wealthy individuals. Some people are wealthy because they have held onto their money. They may be willing to give you some of it, if they know that their money will be invested rather than spent outright.
- Membership fees. The foundation could assess membership fees.
- General public. Some people would rather see their gifts invested rather than spent for something.
- Earned income. Much of the interest earned can be reinvested in the endowment.

Figure II-8-1 Some Sources for Endowment Funding

HOW TO DO IT

Building an endowment can be a long and painstaking process fraught with frustration and disappointment. But everyone who has done it has said that it was worth the effort. The first step is to organize a foundation if you don't already have one. The two purposes of organizing a foundation are to 1) create a place where gifts will be tax deductible for the donors, and 2) provide a shelter from taxation on nonprofit investments. The best place to start is with the book *First Steps in Starting a Foundation* by John Edie. This book will take you step-by-step through the process.

Once you have the foundation in place, you can begin to build an endowment. It will take about two years to obtain the 501 (c) (3) designation by the IRS. Many large donors require this designation so they can have their gifts qualify as tax deductible. This is not something you can go out and do tomorrow. It takes careful planning and lots of help from other people, including lawyers and supportive advocates.

Sources of Funding

Where do you go to find the money to build an endowment for the library? You start with the foundation board. Everyone who is on the board should have already made a significant gift to the foundation for the endowment. If they haven't they shouldn't be on the board, because their ability to secure significant gifts from others will be severely limited, if not totally blocked. To be convincing solicitors they have to give themselves before they ask others to give. For more information of soliciting donations see the chapter on soliciting door-to-door, page 217.

Figure II-8-1 provides a few other sources to try.

Learn From These Steps

Building an endowment is very much like conducting a capital campaign. In fact you could conduct a capital campaign to build an endowment. It is logical then that you start with a feasibility study. (See Chapter 4 and Chapter 8 and Capital Campaigns.) A feasibility study will tell you if there is enough support in the community to build an endowment. The feasibility study will begin the process of building relationships with the influential people in the community. This is the first step towards increasing the library's constituency and building a strong network of potential donors.

Try to get a lead gift from a wealthy individual in the community or from a foundation. Nothing promotes giving better than having a strong base to build on. Raising significant funds early on will encourage donations and inquiries about the endowment. The public relations value of two or three large gifts cannot be underestimated. They will give the organization visibility and credibility. Challenge grants work well to help you leverage gifts from the community. (See Secure Matching Grants and Gifts, pages 273-279)

You will be more successful at building an endowment if you will include some of the following:

- Connect with as many constituents as you can and ask them for their input.
- Hire a professional fundraising consultant to help identify funding sources.
- Build relationships with locally influential people.
- Use positive relationships with foundation and corporate leaders to gain access to other foundations and corporations.
- Start with a big bang to gain maximum visibility for the endowment.
- Use startup donations to leverage other gifts.

Investing the Assets

Managing the assets of an endowment offers special challenges. How do you preserve the security of the principle and still gain the highest rate of return? This is one task I would turn over to a professional trust officer in a bank, unless a member of the foundation board is astute at managing a stock portfolio.

RESOURCES

The best resource you can find will be a good professional fundraising consultant who will conduct a feasibility study and tell you if you can succeed in building an endowment. The feasibility study will cost between $5,000 and $10,000, but it will be worth it.

The next best resource will be a book on how to establish a foundation. Check the bibliography in this section for one that will meet your needs.

Another essential resource is a good attorney to help fill out the application for the 501 (c) (3) designation for the IRS.

You will also need good leadership and committed volunteers to succeed in building an endowment.

SPECIAL CONSIDERATIONS

If you don't think you can handle establishing a foundation on your own and building an endowment is over your head, find out if your community has a local foundation through which donations that require a 501 (c) (3) designation can pass to your library. If such a foundation exists contact the director and find out how to have money for your library passed through them. This is a good alternative to doing everything yourself. It opens the door for a wider variety of grants and gifts.

PITFALLS

The worst thing that can happen to your foundation is to get it organized with a board that will not give and will not solicit donations. All of your plans will be dead on arrival. You would be better off to have done nothing than to have a nonfunctioning foundation board.

Be careful to distinguish gifts to the library and gifts to the foundation for the endowment. If the foundation board is not actively seeking gifts, they may want to claim gifts to the library designated for books for the endowment.

Make sure you have a broad base of support from everyone in the community, including people with discretionary funds to give away.

FOR SCHOOLS AND ACADEMIC LIBRARIES

If you are in a school library let the district handle an endowment.

If you are in an academic setting it will be better to get a special designation for the library within the endowment supported by the institution. You might want to have your own solicitors who will seek donations for the endowment specifically for the library.

CHECKLIST

Use this checklist to assess your library's readiness for an endowment or to evaluate the operation of the one you already have.

1. Is your library connected with an organization that can administer the endowment?
2. Do you have leaders within the organization who will make substantial gifts to the endowment?
3. Will these leaders be willing or able to solicit sizeable gifts from the community?
4. Is there support from ordinary citizens for a library endowment?
5. Does this organization have a 501 (c) (3) designation for charitable giving from the IRS?
6. Does this organization have the startup resources to start an endowment?
7. Do you have a unifying goal or purpose for the endowment?
8. Do you believe an endowment for the library would work in your community?
9. Do you have the money to hire a professional to conduct a feasibility study to determine if an endowment for the library would be a good idea at this time?
10. Are you willing to work to spearhead the establishment of an endowment for the library?

GETTING RESULTS

The results of building an endowment will be positive and long lasting. The more supporters you can involve the more successful the effort will be.

What Do I Do Next?

Start with a few individuals who are committed to building an endowment. Empower this group of people to recruit other volunteers. Help them set up the foundation first and then put together the endowment. Don't try to force something to happen. It could backfire. If you are the librarian, provide support services and stay out of the way.

What Are the Policies and Procedures Needed?

The Internal Revenue Service has some narrowly defined requirements for organizing and managing an endowment. IRS Form 1023 must be used to apply for this status. A copy of the form is available online at http://nccs.urban.org/irsforms/1023.pdf. You will also have to file a Form 990 with the IRS. The state will also have laws and procedures for incorporating a foundation.

Don't overlook the customary protocols for recognizing donors. You could turn the first gift to the endowment from a new donor to the last gift from the same donor.

How Much Time Should This Method Take?

Organizing a foundation and setting up an endowment could take more than five years.

When Can I Expect Results?

Even though the foundation is required to give away five percent of its income every year, don't count on any real money from the endowment for at least ten years.

What Can I Realistically Expect the Costs to Be?

If you hire a lawyer (recommended) to fill out the 501 (c) (3) application, you could spend $1,000 or more. Try to find an attorney in the community who is interested enough in the library to provide his or her services pro bono. The application fee to the IRS for the charitable tax-exempt status will be $500 or more. The cost for creating a good looking brochure could be $500 to $1,000 depending on how elaborate you make it and the number of copies you print.

SUMMARY

Creating and building an endowment is a job for the library foundation. An endowment is built from permanent assets, which could include money gifts, securities, stocks, or real estate. Here are the main points to remember when setting up an endowment:

- Endowment funds can provide a significant level of financial stability for the library.

- Members of the foundation have to be the first people to give. Their giving empowers them to go out and solicit additional gifts.
- Building an endowment is like conducting a capital campaign. A feasibility study will tell you if there is enough support in the community to build an endowment.
- Be careful to distinguish gifts to the library and gifts to the foundation for the endowment.

BIBLIOGRAPHY

Edie, John. 1997. *First Steps in Starting a Foundation*, 4th ed. Washington, DC: Council on Foundations. This is the bible on starting a foundation. It is a basic tool that explains the options available to those who want to set up a foundation, then gives them step-by-step instructions to do it. It will also tell you the legal requirements you need to know.

Moerschbaecher, Lynda S., Barbara G. Hammerman, and James C. Soft. 2001. *Building an Endowment: Right From the Start*. Chicago: Precept Press. This books starts at the beginning of building an endowment and takes the reader step-by-step through the process.

Chapter 9

Solicit Funds Door-to-Door

DESCRIPTION

Soliciting for donations door-to-door, sometimes called grassroots fundraising, is asking people for money face-to-face. When you use this method you are assuming that everyone you contact is a constituent of the library. Some of the people you solicit may never have been in the library, but that is all right. They can still believe that the library is a public good that deserves their support.

Soliciting door-to-door doesn't take too many workers in a small town, and it works well because volunteers are asking their neighbors for a gift to the library. It will work well in larger communities, but you will need more volunteers and assign them to homes near where they live. You will not be able to contact every resident in a large city.

PURPOSES

This can be an extension of a capital campaign, but it could also be used to raise money for other purposes, too. Besides a new library you could conduct a door-to-door campaign to raise money for more books, a new computer system, carpet for the children's department, or just about anything the library needs.

BENEFITS

Soliciting door-to-door brings in extra money, and it is free and clear. You don't have to give the donors something for their gift, except a receipt and a thank you note. The public benefits because the library can improve services with every gift. Giving to the library also gives people a good feeling about themselves and the library. They may even resolve to use the library more often after making a contribution.

EXAMPLES

In Youngstown, New York, the library raises over $9,000 each year by going door-to-door in the community. Volunteers make personal solicitations and letters are sent to previous patrons and sponsors. The community feels a part of the library committed to its success.

HOW TO DO IT

Door-to-door soliciting requires planning, organization, and volunteer training. If it is part of a capital campaign, organizing volunteers to go door-to-door could be part of the capital campaign committee. The volunteers will not be expected to solicit large gifts, but they will be expected to make a contribution similar in size to the donations they are soliciting for. The minimum suggested gift for a door-to-door solicitation should be at least $100 or a monthly pledge of $10. Your volunteers will, of course, accept a gift of any amount, but starting solicitation should be for $100, or a three-year pledge of $300.

If you plan to do this on an annual basis, see the section on annual giving or annual events.

Getting the Names

If this is not an annual event and you are not planning to do it again any time soon, you may be able to assign volunteers to cover certain blocks and not worry about making a list of names. You could use a city directory to help the volunteers by giving them the names of people who live at a particular address.

Otherwise you may want to use a brainstorming session. (See the section on a capital campaign on page 72.)

Organizing the Committee

You need about one volunteer for every five people to be contacted. Organize the volunteers into logical teams of about five people per team and have a team captain for each team. A logical organization could be by neighborhood, by size of gift to be solicited, or self-selected into groups they feel comfortable with.

Training Volunteers

Hold a meeting with all of the volunteers. Fill them with product knowledge (What does the library do? How is it funded? What does it need?). Give them a copy of the case statement. Come up with a list of eight to ten reasons why people should donate to the library. Brainstorming works well for this part of the meeting. Ask them why they think people will want to give to the library. Make sure everyone gets a copy of the list.

Next, come up with two or three scenarios for making the first approach. Have the volunteers learn them verbatim and practice giving them to each other. Then have them give the pitch to someone outside the group like a friendly prospect. Make sure they follow the script. Rehearse the answers to objections, too. This gives the solicitors a security blanket. Everyone will be able to go out and recite the script, but the highest achievers will probably use a combination of all the scripts. Their approach will become natural.

Practicing for Confidence

Create a positive experience for your solicitors by having them practice until they overcome their natural fear and hesitancy. Plan a contrived experience that will always allow them to win. The volunteers will become so drilled in the experience that their responses will become automatic. With practice a fundraising contact can become like a piano recital—so well practiced that the audience can't tell you are nervous. It will be a lot easier. You don't want the presentation to sound canned. Strive for a naturalness that exudes confidence. Confidence is a key to asking for money. Training and drilling your volunteers can make them more effective.

Regular Feedback

Individual workers account to their team leader and turn in money and receipt copies on a daily basis. Team chairs stay close to their team members and report to their committee chairs. They in turn report to the chair of the whole committee. The secretary or treasurer makes deposits daily and keeps a running balance for reports to the group. Every donation is a success and needs to be celebrated. Competition between teams is a good motivator if it is handled right. Consider prizes like a steak dinner for the teams that solicit the most money. It will foster competition and will reward excellence. Praise success consistently and constantly.

Refer back to Chapter 5 for more ideas to help volunteers solicit donations.

RESOURCES

The best tool your volunteers can have is a copy of the case study, so they can share with their prospective donors how the library will spend the money they give. Very few people will give money to an organization without knowing how it will be spent.

Training and practice sessions will also be helpful to the solicitors. These sessions will improve their confidence and effectiveness.

SPECIAL CONSIDERATIONS

Door-to-door soliciting assumes that everyone you contact is a constituent of the library. That may not be true, but it is close enough to make the effort. Not everybody will give. Those who do give will make it worthwhile.

This is a good technique if the potential donors are expecting it. An advertisement in the newspaper or sending a direct mail piece before the volunteers knock on the door could give the campaign a big boost.

If your door-to-door solicitation could become part of an annual campaign, record the names and addresses of the people who give and add them to your donor database.

As with all fundraising techniques you need to evaluate whether or not door-to-door soliciting will produce the results you want. If you don't have enough volunteers to cover most of the town you may not raise the money you need.

PITFALLS

Some communities have regulations about soliciting for donations door-to-door. Find out what the rules are in your town and follow them. Get permission for your group if it is necessary.

- Don't send children out to solicit for the library. They get pressed into doing it too often for the schools as it is.
- Don't send a door-to-door solicitor to the home of someone that has already made a significant gift.
- For safety's sake send solicitors out in pairs—especially after dark, if they go out at all in the evening.

FOR SCHOOLS AND ACADEMIC LIBRARIES

School libraries will probably be successful soliciting door-to-door, but there are probably better ways to get more money for the school library.

Asking for an outright donation might be more effective than trying to sell a candle or some candy that nobody wants. Don't try to solicit outside the district. Let the district raise the money for a new school library from a bond issue.

I believe academic libraries could find more effective and efficient ways to raise money because not as many people consider themselves constituents of an academic library.

CHECKLIST

This checklist will help you organize for a door-to-door solicitation.

1. Can you describe why you have chosen door-to-door solicitation over other ways to get more money for your library?
2. Can you describe your project in ten words or less?
3. How many volunteers will you need to make this effort successful?
4. How will you recruit volunteers?
5. How much will you ask for at each home?
6. Is your case statement understandable to someone who reads at a fifth grade level?
7. How will you get the names for volunteers to contact?
8. What will you do to train the volunteers?
9. How do you plan to organize the committee?
10. How will you reward excellence?

GETTING RESULTS

Being successful at raising money with door-to-door solicitation will require the support of many volunteers. They have to be committed to the project and be ready to step outside their comfort zones.

What Do I Do Next?

The first step is to find a committee chair that has the leadership skills to lead the campaign. The next step is to find volunteers who will give and then solicit donations. Then develop the case statement, so the volunteers will have something to show the need.

If you decide to accept pledges, figure out a way to collect the pledges. Otherwise much of the effort will be in vain.

The librarian can become involved as one of the volunteers or he or she can support the efforts of the committee.

What Are the Policies and Procedures Needed?

Be aware of any city ordinances against door-to-door solicitation. If there are restrictions, get permission before beginning the effort.

Establish policies and procedures for volunteers to follow. It could be a good idea to send solicitors out in pairs and restrict solicitations after dark. You will need to have rules for turning in donations and making reports to the team leaders and the committee chair.

The best book I know of on the business of door-to-door solicitation is *The Grass Roots Fundraising Book* by Joan Flanagan. It has some great suggestions from people who have been in the trenches.

How Much Time Should This Method Take?

As in a capital campaign, don't let a door-to-door campaign drag on—even if you don't reach your goal. Start to finish you should take about six months to organize and do a door-to-door campaign. The actual period of solicitation should take no more than three months—preferably only a month to six weeks.

When Can I Expect Results?

The money should start coming in as soon as the volunteers go out. Donations that come in the form of pledges will take a little longer, but not more than a year, unless this is part of a capital campaign.

What Can I Realistically Expect the Costs to Be?

Your major expense will be the case statement you prepare for the donors and the volunteers. If you send it out to be printed commercially, you can spend $50 to $100 per thousand sheets, or more depending on how elaborate it is. Other costs could be minimal. You may need to use the time of some library staff members to receive the money and make deposits in the bank. Budget three to five dollars per volunteer for a celebration party to recognize and thank the campaign workers.

SUMMARY

Some of the most effective fundraising is friend-to-friend and face-to-face. Door-to-door soliciting is this kind of fundraising. Besides helping to get a new library, a door-to-door campaign could raise money for more books, a new computer system, carpet for the children's library, or just about anything the library needs. Soliciting door-to-door brings in extra money without strings. You assume that everyone you contact is a constituent of the library.

Door-to-door soliciting requires planning, organization, and volunteer training. Try the following:

- Organize the volunteers into logical teams of about five people per team.
- Have a team captain for each team.
- Hold a meeting with all of the volunteers.
- Give them a copy of the case statement.
- Train your volunteers to help them be more effective.
- Teach your volunteers that they can only win or break even.
- Help them practice their approach.
- Give your volunteers the power to succeed.

BIBLIOGRAPHY

Edles, Peter L. 1993. *Fundraising: Hands-on Tactics for Nonprofit Groups*. New York: McGraw-Hill. This book shares tested fundraising techniques that really work. The author gives us the benefit of his many years of experience in this goal-oriented book on fundraising.

Flanagan, Joan. 1982. *The Grass Roots Fundraising Book*. Chicago, Ill.: Contemporary Books. This book gives some great ideas on how to raise money in your community. It has some great community-based "how to do it ideas."

Mutz, John, and Katherine Murray. 2000. *Fundraising for Dummies*. Troy, Mich.: Hungry Minds Inc. This book is not for dummies, but it is easy to use and you will find the information you want about fundraising. The section of grassroots campaigns will be helpful to those who are planning a door-to-door campaign. This is a good reference tool for board members and volunteers.

Sturtevant, William T. 1997. *The Artful Journey: Cultivating and Soliciting the Major Gift*. Chicago: Bonus Books. The author relies on the experience of other professionals who have solicited large gifts. He tells us what he is doing and why. This book is a must read for anyone who faces the prospect of soliciting a large gift.

Chapter 10

Lobby for More State Aid

DESCRIPTION

State grants in aid to libraries come from appropriations made by the legislature. The governor signs them into law. So to get an increase in state aid you need the support of the legislature and the governor. The state library usually administers the grants on some sort of a population formula. In 2001 the following states received no state aid at all: Idaho, Iowa, Louisiana, South Dakota, Vermont, Washington, and Wyoming. Public libraries in Hawaii are totally funded by the state. The average per capita state aid for all states excluding Hawaii is $1.58.

If state aid is a way of life in your state, you can become involved in the legislative process and help to increase state aid for the libraries in your state.

PURPOSES

The philosophy behind state aid is that all residents of the state benefit from the resources of each public library, and the state has an obligation to contribute to the support of all libraries that provide this public good. For libraries, the main purpose of state aid is to augment library budgets. The money can usually be spent for most library purposes. In Kansas, grants-in-aid money may be used for construction, repair, debt reduction, or basic utilities. Other states may have similar restrictions.

BENEFITS

- More money is the obvious benefit, but other more subtle benefits make increasing state aid worthwhile.

- Once state aid has reached a certain level it usually stays on the books at that level. Even though state aid is in perpetual danger of being cut by the legislature, it is usually a stable source of funding. Every year librarians fight to keep what they have and try to get a little more.
- State aid is a lever against the loss of local funding. State legislatures have insisted that local funding not be reduced. Otherwise local governing bodies might be tempted to let increases in state aid replace local funding and leave the local library the same amount of money.
- Struggles in the legislature over state aid keep the focus for funding on libraries. In the end it provides visibility for local legislators at home. Even in towns with a population of 500 or less, a dollar per capita makes the local legislator look good.

EXAMPLES

State Aid in Kansas

Kansas librarians are trying to sell the state legislature on the idea that the state should be supplying at least ten percent of the revenue for public libraries. They contend that because local libraries provide library services to those beyond their own taxing districts, and all Kansas libraries have enhanced the education, economic development, and quality of life for all Kansans, the state should pick up a larger share of the cost. They point out:

- Kansans without a local library have access to service at nearby communities.
- Through interlibrary loan and reference services, every Kansas resident has access to the resources of major libraries in Kansas and the nation.
- Libraries offer cost effective access to electronic databases through statewide database licenses.

They concede that local units of government should be expected to fund most library operating costs, but are asking the state move from providing less than five percent of the costs of library services to ten percent of the cost of providing local library service.

State Aid in South Carolina

In South Carolina the program of state aid to county libraries has been funded continuously since 1943. Participating libraries must be legally

---

Sample Arguments to Support an Increase in State Aid

- "Public libraries serve many people who live outside their own service area."
- "The entire state is a community of library users."
- "Interlibrary loan is just as costly to the lender as it is to the borrower."
- "Per capita state aid in our state aid is less than the cost of a roll of Life Savers."
- "Our state ranks tenth in the nation in per capita income, but our per capita state aid for libraries ranks 40th in the nation."

Figure II-10-1 Sample Arguments to Support an Increase in State Aid

established, provide countywide service, maintain levels of county funding, and meet certain standards of service. Local maintenance of effort requirements has encouraged county governments to increase local support for libraries. In 1978 state aid was increased to $1.00 per capita, which librarians in many other states envy.

State Aid in Maryland

In 1998 Maryland counties benefited from a substantial increase in state aid for libraries, raising the per capita amount of state aid from $8.25 to $9.25.

State Aid in Kentucky

In 1995 the Kentucky Library Association was recognized by ALA/LAMA for their public library advocacy campaign that dramatically increased state aid for libraries. They trained volunteers to be forceful and effective advocates with legislators. The volunteers communicated library needs to legislators in a variety of focused approaches. The result was an increase in state aid for Kentucky libraries (ALA/LAMA, 1995).

HOW TO DO IT

Legislative action to increase state aid cannot be done in secret, even though many deals and concessions will be made outside the view of the public. You cannot do it all by yourself, so learn how to become an effective team player. In most states the state librarian is the team captain. The chair of the state library association's legislative committee assists him or her. Members of the legislative committee are the precinct captains across the state. These people must be well acquainted with the legislative process and the key players.

The push for more state aid starts with a plan and a rationale. There has to be a justifiable reason to request more state aid. You can't just

Suggestions for Lobbying the State Legislature

- Organize the library community involving the state library as an information gathering and dissemination unit.
- Generate ground-swell support by involving public librarians, board members, and patrons.
- Sponsor legislative receptions in the library. Invite local legislators and their constituents.
- Encourage the state library association to sponsor legislative workshops.
- Make sure that the legislative committee is comprised of librarians affiliated with both political parties.
- Know the issues yourself and make sure others do too.
- Hold "Library Legislative Day" at the capitol during the legislative session.
- Learn how to communicate with your legislators using letters, telephone calls, and personal visits.
- Stay abreast of pending legislation as it works its way through the legislative process.
- Make timely contacts with your legislators.

Figure II-10-2 Suggestions for Lobbying the State Legislature

walk into the legislature and say give us more state aid because we need it. I have seen a few effective arguments in support of increased state aid (see Figure II-10-1).

These arguments coupled with a visible need like technology or materials have been effective in securing state aid increases. Unfortunately, as persuasive as these arguments seem, they are just the beginning of winning action in the legislature.

Introducing the Legislation

Start with the governor's budget as the first place to go to introduce your request for increased state aid. Present your case succinctly and forcefully. If the governor supports your request by including the increase in the budget he or she submits to the legislature, you have made a big step forward. Now it is up to the opponents of state aid to get it out of the final budget.

The next step is to get a powerful legislative committee to sponsor the bill if the governor doesn't support your request. The dealmaker is to gain the support of the leaders in the majority party. If the Republicans are in control of both houses in the state legislature, it is much better to have the chair of a key committee who is lukewarm about libraries introduce your state aid bill than to have a Democrat who cares deeply about libraries do it. That is just the way politics works.

Rules for Communicating with Legislators

- *Be brief.* Keep your letter to a half page if possible and never more than one page. You may include a fact sheet if you want, but don't count on them reading it. Put all the important stuff in your letter.
- *Be specific.* Identify the piece of legislation you are concerned about, by bill number if possible.
- *State your position.* They need to know how you feel.
- *Explain the benefits.* Tell how their constituents will benefit if they vote the way you want them to.
- *Urge their support.* Ask them specifically to vote on the measure in support of your position.
- *Ask for a response.* You are asking them to commit to a position and let you know how they intend to vote.
- *Close.* Offer to provide additional information if they need it. Sign your name and mail it.

Figure II-10-3 Rules for Communicating with Legislators

Lobbying the Legislature

Once you get your bill introduced it is time to pull out the stops and involve librarians and trustees in a statewide lobbying effort. A few lobbying suggestions can be found in Figure II-10-2.

Rules for Writing Legislators

You can be more effective when you know and understand the custom for communicating with legislators. Keep in mind the rules of Figure II-10-3.

A letter from the librarian is important, but a letter from board members and patrons will have an even greater impact. It may take special encouragement. Try giving them this information and drafting a sample letter. Urge them to put the ideas into their own words. Identical letters to one legislator from several people lessens the value of all letters.

Handwritten letters from individuals have the most influence of all. They are the letters legislators read first. Individuals have nothing to gain except better service from their library. Librarians are seen as the local experts on library matters, but if they are not careful they can be perceived as self-serving advocates of the library.

Don't overlook the benefits of immediacy afforded by e-mail. E-mail is almost as quick as a telephone call, and probably preferred by most legislators. E-mail messages can be very short and some of the formalities of a typed letter can be overlooked. But don't overlook the respect due to a person in an elected position.

Just as fundraising is selling, so is legislative lobbying. You are trying to persuade a group of legislators that more money for state aid to public libraries will benefit them, their constituents, and the state. Don't give

---

Sample Letter to a Legislator

Representative Bill Williams
123 State Capitol Building
Topeka, Kansas 66612

Dear Representative Williams:

House Bill 2345 provides $800,000 to help libraries link to the statewide information network. Your support of this bill will help every library in Kansas tap into the excellent information databases. No matter where they live, people in Kansas will be able to get what they want when they go to their libraries because their library will be part of the automated information system.

Please vote in favor of House Bill 2345.

Sincerely,
Librarian

Figure II-10-4 Sample Letter to a Legislator

up on the first try. It usually takes two or three years, maybe more, to get a new piece of legislation through the process. Legislators have to understand that you are serious about your proposal. Your persistence tells them that you are serious.

RESOURCES

Take advantage of the power of technology. Communicate with constituents by e-mail to get them to contact their legislators. E-mail coupled with a statewide electronic mailing list could be the best tools in your arsenal. Timely contacts with legislators are critical to the success of any legislation.

Sharpen your skills in writing persuasively, communicating effectively in person, and learning to speak with a paucity of words. Build a relationship with the legislators who represent you the people in your town in the legislature. Learn to listen to them, rather than expecting them to listen to you all of the time.

SPECIAL CONSIDERATIONS

If your state association has a library legislative day make every effort to attend and make plans ahead of time to visit your legislators.

- Make an appointment to visit the legislator in his/her office.
- Be prepared to discuss specific bills relating to library funding.
- If they ask questions that you don't know the answer to, say, *"I'll find out about that and get back to you."* Then do it.

- Contact the legislators when they are home during legislative recesses.
- Attend legislative coffees or brunches, and other social events. This will show your support for the legislative process.

Be sensitive to the mood of the legislature. Sometimes lobbying with a full-court press harms the cause more than it helps it. A few times in the Kansas Legislature the leaders have asked the state librarian to "call off the dogs." Libraries were going to get as much as the legislature could give them.

PITFALLS

Make sure that all librarians in the state are unanimous in the legislation they want. It only takes a few vocal librarians who disagree with the majority to kill your whole effort. Legislators will say, "Come back when you get your act together, and you can all agree on what you want."

Be pleasant when you contact your legislators. Most of them really do try to serve the majority of their constituents.

Don't remind your legislator that you voted for him or her in the last election and your vote in the next election will depend on his or her vote on library legislation. Elected officials are not impressed with such tactics. They were voted into office by a majority of the voters and they are confident of their position.

Extreme Caution: Laws for lobbying must be observed to the letter. Since they vary from state to state, make sure you know what the laws in your state are. You may not be able to do some of the suggestions in this section because laws in your state prohibit library personnel from lobbying and forbid the use of library money to promote legislative action. Some state laws only allow librarians to inform people of a bond proposal, election, etc. They cannot lobby or tell people how to vote. In this case you will need to use outside groups such as the Friends or nonprofit committees formed exclusively for lobbying. In some states nonprofits can only spend a certain percentage of their budget on lobbying or they can lose their nonprofit status.

FOR SCHOOLS AND ACADEMIC LIBRARIES

Everything in this section can apply to school and academic libraries. I have seen academic librarians be very successful when they aligned themselves more with the legislative effort of their institution than the public library effort. School librarians have done the same thing. It all depends on the political climate, but for the most part school and academic libraries fare better when they remain part of their institution's legislative effort. Then they have every right to claim their share of the reward.

CHECKLIST

Here is the checklist for legislative action to increase state aid for libraries:

1. Have you participated in the planning of the legislative effort?
2. Is everyone unanimous about the issues to be pressed for?
3. Are you sure your information is correct?
4. Who else in your community agrees with you? Can you get them to go with you to lobby the legislature?
5. What has been done to make sure all media venues are informed of your effort?
6. Have you attended public meetings to show your support for the legislative process?
7. Have you kept your emotions in check?
8. Have the lobbying duties been shared across the state? Are key members at risk for burnout?
9. Have you recognized that there are good, well-intentioned people on both sides of the issue?
10. Are you prepared for the long haul?

GETTING RESULTS

Unless you are the chair of the library legislative committee, you will undoubtedly find yourself in the role of a follower rather than a leader. Don't let that keep you from participating in the effort.

What Do I Do Next?

Contact the state library or the chair of the library legislative committee. Find out what legislative efforts are being pursued. Offer to help. Attend the meetings of the legislative committee. Offer to contact constituents in your area to make them aware of the issues and provide information.

What Are the Policies and Procedures Needed?

Political activity for librarians is treading in sensitive territory. Be careful to abide by the law. If the law says you cannot be involved in advocating for state aid, don't advocate, provide information to those who can advocate. If you go to visit your legislator in the capitol, provide information. The rules in every state are different and you need to find out what they are in your state and abide by them.

How Much Time Should This Method Take?

Getting an increase in state aid can take up to five years or more. Even then you cannot be sure that you will be successful. Some states don't even have state aid, and there is very little hope of getting it any time soon.

When Can I Expect Results?

Most state budgets are prepared every year. Money appropriated this year will generally be sent out in the next fiscal year. Don't count on replacing all the computers in your library with an increase in state aid. Increases tend to be small and relatively insignificant. In some states librarians consider themselves lucky to keep the state aid they won several years ago.

What Can I Realistically Expect the Costs to Be?

Using e-mail and other electronic methods of communication can keep the costs down. If you plan to travel to the state capital to meet with legislators you can expect to incur some travel expense.

SUMMARY

As you plan to lobby for more state aid keep these ideas in mind:

- State grants in aid to libraries come from appropriations made by the legislature and signed by the governor.
- The main purpose of increasing state aid for libraries is to augment library budgets.
- The state librarian is the legislative team captain. The chair of the state library association's legislative committee assists him or her. The members of the legislative committee are the soldiers across the state.
- Use the arguments that will work best in your state.
- Lobbying the legislature is crucial to the success of the effort. Band together with other librarians to press for action.
- Use the checklist for legislative action.

BIBLIOGRAPHY

Library Advocacy: Influencing Decision Makers. 1999. Chicago: American Library Association. This brochure focuses on the need for increasingly more sophisticated legislative advocacy on behalf of libraries and the millions of people who depend on them. The techniques and messages described can be used at the local, state, and national levels.

Chapter 11

Write Foundation/ Corporate Grant

DESCRIPTION

Foundations are established to assist organizations that espouse the same values they do. Their giving benefits a cause or group of people. Corporations are established to increase the assets of the shareholders. They can be very generous, but they like to see their giving benefit the corporation or their employees. When you write a foundation or corporate grant proposal you are asking them to give you some of their money to do something in your community that they think is worthwhile.

Foundations have their own funding priorities. Spend time researching and identifying potential foundations that look as if they have the best fit to the type of program or target audience you are seeking funding for.

Only about 12 percent of all charitable giving comes from foundations and corporations. Libraries receive a very small percentage of that 12 percent. The pie is still very large. So don't despair. Go for it if after careful research you think you can qualify.

Corporate Grants

If you are applying for a corporate grant, emphasize the benefits of your project to the employees of the corporation. Does a major corporation have a production plant in your area? Have they made grants to libraries before? Write to corporate headquarters and ask for a grant application. If nobody in your town works for the XYZ Corporation and they don't have a plant within fifty miles of your town, don't waste your time submitting a grant proposal.

Foundations

If you locate a foundation you think might fund a project you want to implement, contact the grant officer and ask for an application and a copy of the guidelines during the preliminary research stage. Then throughout the application process call and ask questions. Get acquainted with the grant administrator. It is his or her job to see that the grant applications that come in are the best they can be. The administrator has a vested interest in your success. You can't just submit every grant from research through directories. You have to get to know the foundation staff and allow them to assist you in putting together a winning proposal. Sometimes success is based on whom you know rather than what you know.

Some foundations support only agencies dealing with the youth or the elderly or a specific ethnic group. Some of these may also give money to libraries. Your job is to find a foundation that has funded the type of project you want to do in your library. Refer back to Chapter 3 on Grants for more information on foundations.

Civic Foundations

Most international major civic groups—Lions, Rotary, Kiwanis, Optimists, etc. have a foundation that is funded by donations of the member clubs. They make grants to local clubs for needed nonprofit projects. The Lions in Delphos, Kansas, received a matching grant from the Lions Club International Foundation to help remodel an old bank building to turn it into a library and a meeting room. If you can team up with one of these groups they may be able to secure a grant to help with a library project.

PURPOSES

The main reason you write a foundation or corporate grant is to fund a particular project. Projects are as big as new buildings or as small as a new copier. You have an idea to provide better service at your library. You cannot afford to initiate the service with your current budget. If you think your idea/project will make a big difference in the community, and all you need is a little help to get started, write a grant proposal to a foundation or a corporation.

BENEFITS

Foundation and corporate grants are usually large enough to make the difference between completing a project and not completing it. Projects they fund are often beyond the reach of the community working alone, but the grants usually carry a healthy match or commitment from the people. This commitment gives local citizens a sense of ownership and pride in the project.

EXAMPLES

Kanopolis, Kansas, has a new library thanks to a local salt mining corporation. The library was built in three phases. The mining company paid to have the shell of a metal building erected (Phase I). The library and the community finished the inside and furnished it. The second phase added a meeting room, a serving area, and expanded restrooms. The third phase added the children's department.

Delphos, Kansas, got a new library thanks to the Lions Club International Foundation. Tom McGavran, a member of the local Lions Club was responsible for writing a successful grant proposal. His effort netted the local club the largest grant ever awarded in Kansas by the Lions International Foundation. His practical advice may help other grant seekers.

On a much larger scale the Bill and Melinda Gates Foundation formed a partnership with public libraries to provide computers that are connected to the Internet. The giving is focused on low-income communities—poverty level at 10 percent or above. This low threshold of participation has made it possible for everyone in the United States to have access to the Internet and digital information at their libraries. In addition to computers and software, the foundation has provided technology training and ongoing technical assistance. Every library that qualified (poverty level at 10 percent and above) and applied for a grant received at least one computer. Larger libraries received more than one computer based on population.

HOW TO DO IT

The size of your project could make a difference in the way you present your proposal. A small project could be very informal, but a large, highly competitive grant could require a formal proposal.

Small Project

The application for a small local grant may be as simple as writing a letter. You simply:

- Tell who you are.

- Define your need.
- State what you want to do.
- Tell how you are going to accomplish it.
- Show your budget and ask for a specific amount.
- Explain how you plan to keep the project going.
- Outline how you will evaluate the project.

If you have received a grant from this foundation before, write the letter and ask for the money. Make sure the grant administrator knows the application is coming.

Large Proposal

You will need a more carefully developed proposal if you are asking for a sizeable grant from a new source. If they don't have a form to complete you will have to organize your own proposal.

Here is a basic outline using as a sample the need for a new building:

- *Identify your organization.* We are a public library in a town of 50,000.
- *Give a little history.* The library was built in 1939 under the Works Progress Administration.
- *Identify your problem.* Our 50-year-old library is over-crowded and in need of repair.
- *Document your specific need.* The library was originally built to serve 5,000 people. It was remodeled and expanded to 15,000 square feet in 1953. The standard for a library in a town our size is 50,000 square feet. There is no room for expansion at our present location, etc.
- *State your objectives.* We want to build a new 50,000 square-foot building near the population center of our town.
- *Describe your activities.* The site has been selected and has received enthusiastic support from the community. We have a contract with a local architect to design the building. A local fundraising committee has been formed and a bond election is scheduled for next spring, etc.
- *Describe the required resources.* The estimated cost of the building is $5,000,000. (Include a copy of the budget with anticipated revenue by source.)
- *Outline the plan of evaluation.* Our project will be successful when people can enjoy the new library. We expect that circulation and other usage measurements will increase dramatically after the new library is built.

Winning Tips for Grant Writers

- *Contact your regional Foundation Center Cooperating Collection.* Many are housed in libraries and have trained librarians who can direct you to many sources on grant writing and fundraising.
- *Obtain copies of 990-PF report.* This is the form each foundation must file with the IRS each year. Copies are available from the state attorney general's office. Limited copies may be available through your regional Foundation Center.
- *Call the secretary of the funding agency.* Ask for forms guidelines for submitting a grant proposal. Ask for suggestions or ideas. Try to find out what makes a difference to the grant readers.
- *Call former recipients of grants.* If they are not applying again, they may be willing to give you a few pointers.
- *Follow the submission guidelines.* Pay special attention to length, content, and documentation.
- *Write succinctly.* It's difficult to see around extra words to find out what you want to do. A tightly crafted presentation that outlines who you are and what you want to do is easier to evaluate.
- *Be specific:* Provide a strong and credible description of the need for a single project that reflects a community need.
- *Define your goals, your methodology, and your evaluation criteria precisely.* Ensure that your project has clear, realistic, and measurable results.
- *Demonstrate how the project is tied to your library's future.* Give the reviewers a vision of your library in the future and link your proposal to that vision.
- *Consider other ways the funder could help you.* Beyond the money, is there technical assistance or in-kind support that could benefit your project just as much?
- *Communicate electronically when it is appropriate.* But don't fax your request and then follow up with a hard copy in the mail. This suggests a lack of preparation on your part.

Figure II-11-1 Winning Tips for Grant Writers

Matching Your Proposal to the Grant Requirements

Applying for a grant is like looking for a job. The funding agency is the employer and you are the applicant. In a hiring situation, the employer is looking for the applicant that best matches the job requirements. Your task is to learn as much as you can about the company and the job and create the image that your qualifications match their job requirements. The most effective resumes are rewritten to match the specific requirements of each job.

You need the kind of help you can find in books like *The Foundation Directory* and the *Corporate Foundation Profiles*—both are published by the Foundation Center. Many states have published a directory of foundations for their state. Check with the Foundation Center's Cooperating Collection in your state to see if your state has a statewide foundation directory. These directories list agencies that award grants within the state. Make sure you have the latest edition. A three-year-old foundation directory is practically worthless.

Winning Tips for Grant Writers

Figure II-11-1 provides some suggestions that may help give you an edge at winning grant funding.

RESOURCES

The Internet is a powerful resource for grant writers. It would take several volumes to hold all the sites I found offering suggestions for writing successful grants. One of the more bounteous sites is *The At-a-Glance Guide to Grants*, www.adjunctadvocate.com/nafggrant.html. It has multiple links to grant writing aids and tutorials. The links are a resource to all researchers and grant writers.

- *Advice for Grant Writers*, www.depaul.edu/~ospr/apply/advice.htm, is posted by the Office of Sponsored Programs and Research at the De Paul University. It has well-selected links to very helpful sites.
- Hints for Preparing Funding Proposals, www.science.iupui.edu/Wilson/GrantSk.IUPUI.html, has timely suggestions for grant writers.
- Proposal Writing Short Course, www.fdncenter.org/onlib/prop.html. This is The Foundation Center's proposal writing site.

The bibliography of this book lists several good books on writing grant proposals.

SPECIAL CONSIDERATIONS

Grant writing is a complex process, one that requires time and energy. Give yourself plenty of time to do it. Start thinking about your project well before the proposal deadline. Gather references even while you do other tasks. Find out as much as you can about the foundation or corporation you are applying to. If possible, get copies of past successful grant applications. Study the main themes and objectives, and the points that made them successful.

Many foundations and corporations require a copy of the letter from the IRS designating your library as a 501 (c) (3) agency. If you don't have 501 (c) (3) designation, obtaining it takes time and is a lot of work. It often requires the expertise of an attorney. You may be able to go through your city or find a community foundation that acts as a pass-through agency for other community organizations that need 501 (c) (3) designation.

PITFALLS

Make sure the foundation or corporation you are applying to supports the kind of program or activity you want to fund. Otherwise your grant will be lumped into the category of "does not fit well within our programs" and will likely not be competitive.

You can avoid the pitfalls of approaching a corporation for funding. Here are some of the big reasons grants are not funded:

* Lack of preparation.
* Improperly addressed mail.
* Lack of understanding of the prospect's interests.
* Failure to know the donation policies and procedures of the prospect.
* Asking for too much money.
* Asking the wrong person.
* Failure to give the donor several funding options.
* Failure to say thank you effectively.

FOR SCHOOLS AND ACADEMIC LIBRARIES

Foundation and corporate giving can be effective ways for school and academic libraries to get money for a particular project, like the enhancement of a collection that is important to a local corporation or a learning lab that focuses attention on a particular subject. Building projects are still the purview of the school district or the university. Even if you need a bigger library it is still best to work within the organization.

CHECKLIST FOR WRITING A WINNING FOUNDATION OR CORPORATE GRANT

After you have written your grant proposal, but before you send it, review it once more by asking yourself these questions:

1. Are the purposes of the grant aligned with the funding objectives of the foundation or corporation?
2. Have you captured the grant reviewer's attention?
3. Have you stated your case without vagueness on the first page of your proposal?
4. Have you stated exactly the needs addressed by your proposal?

5. Have you stated specific objectives for your project?
6. Is every word in your proposal easy to understand and free of jargon?
7. Does your proposal have a fresh approach to solving the problem you outlined?
8. Do you clearly describe what you are going to do and how?
9. Have you described what the end product will look like when you finish?
10. Does your proposal have all of the necessary signatures?

GETTING RESULTS

You can develop the special relationships and skills you need to help you become successful at writing corporate or foundation grants.

What Do I Do Next?

Find a grant source that best matches the project you want to do and make sure the agency funds grants to libraries in your area of the country. Discuss the possibilities with library staff and board members. They can help you develop a fundable project. Follow the "How to do it" section of this chapter.

What Are the Policies and Procedures Needed?

Every funding agency has its own policies and procedures. Once you receive the application and guidelines, read and follow the grant guidelines to the letter. Call the grant administrator to clarify anything you do not understand. Begin the writing process early to give what you have written a chance to age before you edit it for the final time. Confer with others to refine your application.

How Much Time Should This Method Take?

From finding a potential grant to submitting the final application should take from three to nine months. If you try to do it in less than three months, your grant will show it and may lack the polish necessary to be successful. Getting the money could take another three to six months depending on the timeline of the funding agency. In some cases you can expect the check as soon as the grant award is made.

When Can I Expect Results?

Once you get the money you will have a certain amount of time to spend it and implement the project. Along the way certain recognition activities like photos for the newspaper will be required. Before you know it the funders will be asking for an evaluation. So be sure to have evaluation activities in place the minute you offer the service to the public.

What Can I Realistically Expect the Costs to Be?

Some foundations and corporations require a local match, either actual cash or in-kind. This match could be as high as 50 percent, but it could be zero. Every grant I have ever seen required some expenditure on the part of the recipient. If it isn't in the form of a required match, it will come in the form of expenses you didn't see when you started the project. Just count on shelling out at least 10 percent of the grant from your own funds to cover unexpected contingencies.

SUMMARY

Foundations and corporations have their own funding priorities. If you apply for a corporate grant, emphasize the benefits of your project to the employees of the corporation. Keep these points in mind as you prepare your grant proposal:

- If you apply for a foundation grant align the purposes of your project with the objectives of the foundation.
- Use foundation or corporate grant funding for special projects, not ongoing operations of your library.
- The application for a small project could be very informal.
- A large, competitive grant could require a highly developed formal proposal.
- Make sure you understand the application requirements before you start to write.
- Take advantage of as much help as you can get from all the sources you can find.

BIBLIOGRAPHY

Blum, Laurie. 1996. *The Complete Guide to Getting a Grant: How to Turn Your Ideas Into Dollars*, rev. ed. New York: John Wiley & Sons. From starting with an idea to following up after the project is complete *The Complete Guide to Getting a Grant* is worth the money. The basics are here but so are some little-known strategies.

Ezell, Tom, Carole Nugent, and Creed C. Black. 2000. *The Grantwriter's Start-up Kit: A Beginner's Guide to Grant Proposals*. San Francisco, Calif.: Jossey-Bass Publishers. This video and workbook will help you get started on the process of writing a successful grant proposal to a foundation.

Grant Your Wish: Learn From the Professionals How to Write a Successful Grant Proposal, Sergio Gonzalez, 30 min., Successful Images, Inc., 1998, videocassette. Well organized and to the point, this video outlines the basics of writing a foundation grant. It presents twelve key elements of a proposal, why some proposals get funded and others do not, and where to get a list of funding sources.

Hale, Phale D. 2000. *Writing Grant Proposals That Win*, 2d ed. Gaithersburg, Md.: Aspen Publishers, Inc. This is a must read for anyone who plans to write a grant for anything. The chapter on private-sector differences delineates the critical differences between government funding agencies and private agencies.

Karges-Bone, Linda. 2000. *The Grant Writer's Guide: How to Become an Expert Grant Writer for Schools and Nonprofit Groups*. Torrance, Calif.: Good Apple. This book is written for teachers and school librarians, but every grant writer will benefit from using it. It stresses attitude and attributes an action to help grant writers get the money they need.

Miner, Lynn E., Jeremy T. Miner, and Jerry Griffith. 1998. *Proposal Planning and Writing*. Phoenix, Ariz.: Oryx Press. This book is for beginning grant writers who want to perfect a grant application and find funding agencies. The information is helpful, precise, and accurate. The methods have been field-tested for effectiveness.

Przeworski, Adam, and Frank Salomon. 1988. *On the Art of Writing Proposals: Some Candid Suggestions for Applicants to Social Science Research Council Competitions* [Online]. Available: www.javeriana.edu.co/cursos/aflorez/ssrc.htm [2002, February 18]. This Web site has some very helpful ideas. Check it out before you even think about writing a grant.

Ullman, Hannah, and Barbara L. Dougherty. 2000. *Six Flawless Steps to a Winning Grant Proposal*. Upper Fairmont, Md.: Barbara L. Dougherty, Inc. This short book is packed with the essentials of grant writing.

Chapter 12

Hold an Auction of Donated Goods

DESCRIPTION

Auctions are a great way to raise money for your library. Doing it right depends on the volunteers you recruit and your community's response. Every auction has to have enough of the right items to attract a crowd and get the people to bid. Bidders will come because they want to get a bargain. Others will come just to have a good time. Most will come to help the library.

Volunteers ask for gifts from businesses and individuals to sell at auction instead of asking for a cash gift. Some merchants respond well to giving an item for an auction. Their gift is valued at its retail price. The heart of a good auction is a master list of prospects and a wish list. It lists the names of prospective businesses with a contact person and address. It has another column for desired items (suggestions only) and another column for volunteers to sign up as a solicitor to the business.

PURPOSES

Auctions have several purposes, including recycling the inventory of some businesses in town.

- Auctions generate additional private funding for the library.
- They give the library another opportunity to tell its story and promote services.
- They promote annual giving from the business community.
- They provide an entertaining social event for adults. They give the

bidders something for their money besides a good feeling and a thank you.

- They give merchants a chance to be recognized publicly for their gift to the library.

BENEFITS

Auctions work best when they are part of the library's annual giving program. They can be an integral part of an overall successful fundraising plan. Here are a few benefits that can be realized, which are not generally attributed to other fundraising activities.

- The goods or products that are sold cost nothing.
- The money can be used for whatever purpose the library deems important.
- Merchants get a tax write-off for merchandise they donate.
- The people who buy items at the auction get a good deal while helping the library at the same time.
- Everyone who comes to the auction has a good time.
- If you hold an auction every year, people will look forward to attending it.

EXAMPLES

One library wrote to several famous Hollywood personalities and requested items for an auction. They received several unique items that sold for a lot more money than they might have had they not been previously owned by a celebrity. You will have to be very persuasive to get a celebrity you don't know to give you something of value.

For over 30 years the Barton County Community College Foundation has held annual auctions. These events have been successful because they were able to:

- Auction only quality goods.
- Draw a large crowd of bidders.
- Sell tickets at the door and in advance.
- Price the admission tickets within the price range of all people in the community.
- Secure free (donated) radio, television and newspaper advertising to help promote the event.
- Hold the auction at a convenient time and location.
- Ask local vendors to sell food/snacks on the premises.
- Limit silent auction to items valued at $100 and less.

- Limit live auction items to a value of $100 or more.
- Mail invitations one month in advance.
- Mail the auction catalog one week in advance.
- Get the auctioneer to donate his services.
- Have the use of the building donated.

HOW TO DO IT

Organization is the key to a successful auction. The auction coordinator is in charge. Since everyone involved with the auction is a volunteer you may want to let the Friends of the Library handle the auction.

The auction coordinator does the following:

- Serves as community representative/liaison in the promotion of the event.
- Provides overall support in planning efforts.
- Generates ideas for and carrying out the securing of unique auction items.
- Takes responsibility for selling tickets and putting up posters.
- Handles arrangements and set-up the day prior to the event.

Once the coordinator is in place, he or she may call as many committee chairs as necessary to get the job done. One or more committees will have to secure the items to be auctioned. Committee members who solicit for gifts need to sell the "joy of giving." If they are approached right, people who give will feel part of the cause. You know best how to define the cause for your library. If you are to solicit items to be auctioned, be specific and ask for what you want. If you want a ten-speed bicycle, ask for a ten-speed bicycle. Otherwise you might end up with a screwdriver. You can start high and work down, but it is difficult to move up once you have made your first request. If they won't give a ten-speed bike maybe they will give a coaster wagon. If they don't want to give merchandise ask for a cash gift.

You could divide your auction into three categories.

1. Door prizes—valued under $20, given away at auction by the number on the ticket stub.
2. Silent auction items—valued under $100.
3. Live auction items—valued over $100.

Next you create a master list of prospects, wish list, and volunteer solicitors. I hope you get some good ideas from this sample master list.

Develop a Prospective Donor and Wish List

Here is an example of a short master gift list:

Master Gift List for an Auction		
Prospects and wish list		
Prospect	Item Wished for ...	Volunteer
A to Z Mini Storage Abraham Zlotski 1928 Wall Street	Storage for one year	_____
*AAA Sporting Goods Bob Adams 1987 Main	Pair of jogging shoes	_____
*Hometown Video Robert Rabbit 243 North Broadway	50 free video rentals	_____
*American Security Bank Howard Ericson 98 South Main	Millionaire for a day	_____
Andrew's Television Andy Berlin 123 North Main	Portable TV	_____
Art Emporium Debbie Crockett 243 East First	Framing of one picture	_____
Auto Electronics Bill Boxley 5654 Rock Island Road *Previous donor.	In-Dash CD player	_____

Figure II-12-1 Master Gift List for an Auction

Make up your own prospect and gift list based on this one. The Chamber of Commerce membership list is a good source. Make a list of all the retail merchants in town and create a list of possible gifts for your solicitors. Send a letter to all prospects on the Master Gift List a week before personal calls are made.

After the commitments for auction items are complete, make arrangements to either have them delivered to the place of the auction, or have them picked up by volunteers. Make sure everything will be at the auction the night it is held.

Create the Catalog

Once you have all of the auction items lined up, it is time to create the catalog. Use this document to attract people to come to the auction and create enthusiasm to buy. You create interest in each item by the way you describe it. Find someone who is adept with words. Ask him or her to write a clever 25-word description of each item. Be sure to give each item a number and include the donor's name or business and the estimated retail value.

Make a statement about the purpose of the auction. Remind your bidders that your auction is a benefit auction for the library. Mention the benefits and tell them if they purchase an item for more than the estimated retail price they can count the difference as a tax-deductible contribution. Your catalog gives you a chance to recognize your workers and donors. Make sure everyone who volunteered or made a contribution is named in the catalog.

Printing the Catalog

The library may have to pay for the printing of the catalog. You can use a computer to create the pages for the catalog, but it is a good idea to use a commercial printer to produce mass quantities. The catalog will look nicer and will help the auction bring higher prices.

Charge for Admission

You need to decide whether or not to charge for admission. It is obviously a way to enhance the income for the library. Many Friends groups hold an annual auction of quality merchandise where membership in the Friends of the Library is the admission price. Membership in various Friends groups runs $5.00 to $25.00. If other people want to come to the auction they can join the Friends group at the door. You can also make some money selling tickets to people who do not plan to attend the auction. They consider it a donation.

Setting the Date

You want as many people as possible to come to your auction. The best way to insure that is to pick a day and time when people are normally off work and have time to spend with others. Friday night is your best bet. Try not to schedule it on top of something that is already scheduled, like a high school football game. If your auction is an annual event, hold it the same day of the month every year; e.g. the last Friday night in March. Remember, the purpose of setting the date for your auction is to insure a good crowd. It may take time, but if you persist, it won't be long before you will have a successful annual event that people will eagerly anticipate each year.

RESOURCES

The best resources you can have to help you with auctions will be the learning experiences you develop as you document your experiences and use them for the next auction. Keep a file of the forms you develop, the lists you prepare, and the names of people you can count on for help. Even as you are putting the finishing touches on this year's auction look forward to the one for next year.

Other tools include a computer with desktop publishing capabilities, a good public address system, and a good printer.

The auctioneer is a key player. It is better to find someone who does it for a living, than to honor the president of the board by asking him or her to do it. A professional auctioneer can get the most money from every item for sale. A gift of some value is an appropriate way to say thank you to the auctioneer. Some flowers, a dozen golf balls, or a bottle of wine would all be nice gifts depending on the personal preferences of the person.

SPECIAL CONSIDERATIONS

Remember the tax write-off for an auction goes to the merchant who gave the gift, not the person who bought it. The merchant can claim only the cost of the gift, not its selling price. Promote the tax benefit when you solicit the gift. Most companies can count it as a business expense or a charitable contribution. The person who buys the item receives merchandise in return for his purchase. He may look at it as a contribution to your cause, but he is really buying something. The buyer can claim a tax deduction if he pays more for the item than it would sell for in the store.

You can't expect to get everything free. Sometimes you will have to pay for: printing, use of the hall, janitor service, advertising, etc.

People think they are going to get a bargain at an auction. Play up that angle. Create an atmosphere of competition. Keep these points in mind:

- Cater to your audience—give them what they want.
- Establish your criteria for giving up front.
- Take care of your donors—a toaster this year may become a TV next year.
- Organize your auction well—give each volunteer a job to do and let him or her do it.

PITFALLS

Here are a few don'ts:

- Don't make it too exclusive. Auctions are for people who want something for their money.
- Don't schedule your auction on top of another community event. People will have to choose between your auction and the other event.
- Don't have your auction on Sunday if you rely on tourists. They will have gone home by midday Sunday.
- Don't spend too much money. Every dollar you spend to put on the auction will take away from the profits.
- Don't buy items to auction. It is possible you won't get your money back.
- Don't accept poor quality, used items, or junk. Nobody wants to pay $5.00 for admission and then bid on something that is not worth the money.

FOR SCHOOLS AND ACADEMIC LIBRARIES

Auctions can work well for school and academic libraries. It is an overall good way to get more money for your library. It could become the annual moneymaking event for any organization.

CHECKLIST

Use this checklist to avoid a last minute snafu:

1. Have you contacted the auctioneer to confirm necessary arrangements?
2. Have you made arrangements to have auction clerks?
3. Have last minute arrangements for the building been covered?
4. Are all items up for bid at the site of the auction?
5. Have all advance tickets been accounted for and the money turned in?
6. Have food and beverage arrangements been finalized?
7. Is the temperature in the building right for the occasion?
8. Is seating set up and adequate?
9. Do you have plenty of programs for walk-in bidders?
10. Are registration materials in order including bidders cards?

GETTING RESULTS

There is a fair-like quality to an auction. The excitement and enthusiasm can lead to larger than expected gifts—especially when two or more bidders compete for an attractive item. If everyone gives their best efforts to the auction the results will be very rewarding.

What Do I Do Next?

Make sure everyone knows why you are having an auction. Find a committee chair—preferably someone who has been working on the committee for at least a couple of years. Check out all possible locations for the auction and reserve a date as soon as possible. Look to the Friends for leadership and volunteers. Don't try to do it with library staff members. Follow the "How to do it" section of this chapter.

What Are the Policies and Procedures Needed?

Learn the IRS rules for taking tax deductions on donated goods. The purchaser of an auction item receives no tax deduction unless the fair market value of the item is less than the purchase price. Check out the sales tax laws in your state. You may be required to collect and pay sales tax. If you plan to serve liquor at the auction find out what liquor laws apply and abide by them.

How Much Time Should This Method Take?

Planning for next year's auction begins with the evaluation of this year's auction. Ask, "What went well? How could we improve on the good things that happened? What pitfalls do we need to avoid next year?" Actual planning should begin about six months before the date of the auction. Establish a timeline to help the committee understand what is coming up. After that you will be able to build on previous experience.

When Can I Expect Results?

The money should all be in as soon as the auction is over. Spend the money the way you told the people you were going to use it. If the money goes into the endowment, it could take some time to see the investment produce income for the library.

What Can I Realistically Expect the Costs to Be?

The biggest expense will be creating and publishing the auction catalog. Depending on the use of color and how elaborate it is, you could spend between $2.00 and $5.00 for each catalog. Count on $2.00 per person if you serve free refreshments—more if you serve liquor. Charging $5.00 or more admission will help offset the cost. The costs for renting the venue for the auction can be $500 to $1,000 or more, unless you can hold it in the library or some other place free. You will still have the cost of custodial services for setup and cleanup. If the auctioneer charges for his or her services, count on spending $500 to $1,000. Plan on spending $50 to $100 for a gift or flowers, even if the auctioneer's services are free.

SUMMARY

Benefit auctions give people a chance to support a worthy cause, socialize, have a good time, and get something for their money. It is a great way to involve the entire community in a variety of ways. Merchants donate goods from their stores. Purchasers receive something for their money. Here are the main points for conducting a benefit auction:

- Auctions work best when they are part of the library's annual giving program. If you hold an auction every year people will look forward to attending it.
- Organization is the key to a successful auction, and the auction coordinator is the key to the organization. Auctions are great activities for the Friends of the Library.
- The auction catalog gives you the opportunity to make a case for library fundraising. A nice looking catalog will help the auction bring higher prices.
- Make sure all of the last minute details are checked and double-checked and you will have a successful auction.

BIBLIOGRAPHY

Understanding and Advising Nonprofit Organizations. 2001. St. Paul, Minn.: Continuing Legal Education. This book is for lawyers who advise nonprofit groups about their fundraising activities. It includes a section on auctions and raffles, which will be of some value to those who plan auctions.

Winter, Maureen, and John Winter. 1999. *Going . . . Going . . . Gone: Successful Auctions for Non-profit Institutions,* 2d ed. Palm Beach Gardens, Fla.: Target Funding Group. This book will help you pay attention to the details—a key to the success of any auction. This comprehensive guide gives you some practical and creative ideas on how to organize and stage an auction.

Chapter 13

Organize Regular Annual Events

DESCRIPTION

Annual events are moneymaking activities you do year after year to raise money for your library. Most annual events give the donors something in exchange for their money like a homemade craft or a food item. Other activities like a home tour or a fashion show will entertain them. After a while you may dread the pending annual event, but the people will look forward to it. They like annual events that benefit the library because they offer an opportunity to meet their neighbors in a social setting and have a good time.

The most important ingredient of an annual event is its regularity. Downtown merchants often have sidewalk sales the last Saturday in July. Retailers put out the merchandise they haven't sold for a year or two. Customers come early to take advantage of discounts up to 80 percent. People enjoy repeating a positive or pleasurable experience like getting some real bargains. Library annual events can build similar public anticipation.

It is beyond the scope of this book to cover every annual event ever held by any library. As soon as I think I have listed them all someone will come up with one I didn't list, but you will get the idea.

- Fashion show—The more elegant the more money you can make. Volunteers do the modeling; retailers provide the clothes; and the library provides the venue. Add a luncheon, a reception, or a free drawing for an article of clothing from the show.
- Flea market—Use the library parking lot. Sell the spaces to vendors and charge the public an admission fee. Give away door prizes or sell snacks and beverages.
- Garden tour—Ask four to six people who are famous for their gar-

dens in your community to host a tour. Advertise and sell tickets. Have the tour on a Saturday and arrange for refreshments along the way.

- Raffle—Some quilting groups like the Mennonite ladies have a reputation for making fine quilts. Raffling one of their quilts or an exotic trip can bring in big bucks.
- Poetry rendezvous—solicit poems for the anthology you publish. Invite a featured poet to read his or her poems. Offer others the opportunity to read and sell their published poems. Charge an entry fee and sell the anthology.
- Street dance—If you can get a local band to play for free and sell tickets ahead of time you could make a lot of money.
- Street fair—Sell space to vendors and have plenty of opportunity for the library to make money from other concessions.
- Wine tasting—The winery sets up the wine as an advertisement. You charge the guests or accept donations for the opportunity to come and drink the free wine. It can be a big social event.
- Bike tour—Hire a guide and provide camping and meals for the group. Charge participants for the opportunity to explore new places.
- Book banquet—Hold a banquet for the Friends or some other support group. Admission is a $50 donation or a new book for the library.

PURPOSES

The main purpose of annual events for the library is to supplement the library's income every year. It is nice to have additional money to buy things the library cannot afford with its regular budget. It may be easier to have one big annual event than several smaller events throughout the year.

BENEFITS

If you have an annual fundraising event, it won't be long until all you have to do will be to update and plan for contingencies. Annual fundraising events are great because:

- People like them and count on them.
- Annual events create great visibility for the library.
- You will become proficient at making them successful.

When we persist in doing something it becomes easier for us to do.

The task itself may not change, but our power to do it will increase. We become good at annual events because we do them over and over again. The better we become, the easier they are for us to do, and we make more money doing them.

EXAMPLES

In Woodstock, New York, the major fundraiser for the library is the annual Library Fair, which is held on the last Saturday of July (rain or shine) every year. They sell books, clothes, furniture—you name it, they sell it. They have a large raffle with a trip as the first prize. There is always plenty of food and entertainment, and a special "kiddieland" for entertaining children. This fair has been going on for about sixty years, and it is easy to see why tradition is on the library's side. Volunteers do all of the work. It costs about $6,000 to put on, but they bring in $25,000 or more every year.

The Friends of the North Castle Library in Armonk, New York, raise about $20,000 a year with a juried art show. This outdoor event draws 200 exhibitors and thousands of visitors. They ask for a donation at the gate. The artists and crafts people bring their wares for exhibit and sale. The event is enhanced with food booths, and raffles. Over the years the library has used the money for both building projects and equipment purchases.

HOW TO DO IT

Annual events require strong organization and lots of volunteers to make them work. Start with good leadership. The chair of the committee must be tireless and be able to work with all segments of the community. It is wise to bring in new people at the top level to be trained to take over the leadership roles.

Organizations sponsor the same annual event every year because the workers become proficient at it and they learn from their mistakes. After each event is over you really need to evaluate the success of the event and make notes for the people who are going to do it next year. Drop what didn't work and introduce a new element only if it has great promise.

Decide what you are going to do and stick with the plan. Organize with the same committees. Assign the same tasks to each committee. Recruit as many volunteers as you need and meet with them as often as necessary. Make sure everyone knows what is going to happen when the day of the event arrives. Make lists and share them with the team leaders or committee chairs.

Be consistent with your date year after year. If you start with your street fair on the last Saturday in July, have the last Saturday in July be used for that event every year from then on.

Besides having plenty of volunteers to do the work, the key to success of most annual events is having as much as possible of the stuff you are selling donated. If it is an ice cream social have the ice cream and cookies donated. If you are having a street dance have the musicians donate their services. If you have to pay for very much of the stuff you won't make very much money.

The next key is to sell lots of tickets. Sell them to everyone, especially to people who don't plan to come. Include a chance on a door prize or raffle if they buy a book of tickets. Do a good job of publicizing the event.

RESOURCES

The cumulative memory and evaluation of those who have worked the event year after year will be your most valuable resource. You will develop a routine based upon the successes and failures (learning experiences) of others. Develop a calendar that starts right after the completion of the most recent event. Set markers along the way that indicate the date by which certain tasks must be accomplished—similar to other events that require a lot of planning. Don't meet too often with the committee because people get burned out with too many meetings, but keep everyone informed with letters, phone calls, or e-mail messages. They need to know what is happening and when their next assignment is due.

Think of time as a wonderful gift. Think of all the small things that get done behind the scenes that culminate in a big successful affair. Let time be your friend by staying on top of each task, rather than watch it become your enemy because you left everything until the last minute.

SPECIAL CONSIDERATIONS

Any fundraising activity could become an annual event. In fact, all annual events started out as single moneymaking activities. They seemed so successful that those running them said, "Let's try that again." Soon the fundraising committees became the "fashion show committee" or "the pancake feed committee" or the "book sale committee." These committees become very proficient in organizing and carrying out the annual event. After the completion of each year's carnival or luncheon they evaluate their success. They ask, "What went well?" Then they ask, "What could we do better?" Their answers helped plan and refine next year's event.

Annual events require an influx of new volunteers every year because someone will always drop from active participation. They may become ill or too busy and leave the organization. Don't count on the same people year after year for a long time. You always need some new blood.

PITFALLS

Don't sponsor a wine-tasting event where a predominant religion frowns on the use of alcoholic beverages. They may not picket the event, but they probably won't come either.

Don't have your annual event on a day when you know that a neighboring town is having their biggest community celebration of the year. You won't be able to attract the crowds you need to make your event a success.

The concept of annual moneymaking events suggests two weaknesses in the way the library is funded:

1. The library is not receiving enough money from its normal sources of funding.
2. Most of the people who come to the event are nonconstituents because they will only give money to the library if they get something in return.

Both of these points may not be true in every situation, but the income from annual events can easily become a replacement for adequate funding from regular sources.

Annual events are a lot of work and people will burn out. If you are involved in an annual event right now or are thinking of starting one, take a look at what you are doing and figure out if it is worth it.

FOR SCHOOLS AND ACADEMIC LIBRARIES

School libraries often have annual events called book fairs. (See the section on new book fairs, page 299.) They work well in schools and are a natural source of enhancement revenue. Other annual events might work well if they do not conflict with other moneymaking projects connected with the school.

Academic libraries can and do hold successful annual events, though they are usually related to the mission of the library. As with school libraries, those in charge need to make sure their annual event does not conflict with other events planned by the institution.

CHECKLIST

Use this checklist to help plan your next annual event.

1. What went well with the last annual event?
2. How much money did you net from the last annual event?
3. Were the benefits including the money worth the effort?
4. What do you plan to do differently next year?
5. Who will be in charge of next year's annual event?
6. Was he or she involved in this year's event?
7. How will you secure donations of the main goods and services for the event?
8. How will you handle ticket sales? What incentives will you offer to get people to buy more tickets than they need or plan to use?
9. How will you know if your annual event was successful?

GETTING RESULTS

Giving an annual event your best effort will usually pay off well after the second or third year. Since every annual event is different and requires different leadership skills, the suggestions that follow are general in nature.

What Do I Do Next?

Success with annual events requires a special understanding of the community. An ice cream social in a town of 100 people can produce a thousand dollars or more and leave the people looking forward to the next one. The same type of an event fifteen miles down the road or in a larger community might fail and nobody knows why. The best thing you can do is to find something that works and repeat it every year.

After a while, organization and planning will become second nature and soon extensive advertising will not be necessary. Let the people who have done it before do it again. Encourage them to bring in new people so they can pass on the leadership to others as the dynamics of the community changes. Do what works in your community.

What Are the Policies and Procedures Needed?

People who buy things from library moneymaking projects get no tax deduction. They might even have to pay sales tax. Some states allow occasional selling for fundraisers to be exempt from sales tax. Don't assume that to be the case in your state. Find out the sales tax laws and comply with them. If you plan to serve liquor at any event, you may not be able to do it where minors are present. Find out what liquor laws apply and abide by them. Gambling is usually regulated by the state. Do not assume that because you are raising money for a nonprofit agency that you are exempt from any laws that normally apply to commercial establishments.

How Much Time Should This Method Take?

Most annual events that last for an evening or, at most, a week will require up to a month of planning. After the event count the money. Put it in the bank. Pay any outstanding expenses and spend the rest.

When Can I Expect Results?

Some annual events are huge affairs and take a full year to plan and put on. It will take a year or more to benefit from these productions.

What Can I Realistically Expect the Costs to Be?

Costs will vary from event to event. Some of the more common items to carry an expense you may not be able to avoid are:

- Promotional materials and advertising
- Programs
- Tickets
- Amenities
- Rent for the event location
- Food, if served by the hotel
- Performers from outside the area
- Travel expenses for individuals coming from a distance
- Honoraria or thank you gifts for special guests
- Security
- Custodial expenses
- Contingencies

Develop a budget in your initial planning and stick to it. Otherwise a fundraising event could turn into a fund-loser.

SUMMARY

Annual events are moneymaking activities you do year after year to raise money for your library. Most annual events give the donors something in exchange for their money like a homemade craft item or some food.

Here are the most important things to remember about annual events:

- The main ingredient of an annual event is its regularity.

- The main purpose of annual events for the library is to supplement the library's income every year.
- Annual events require strong organization and lots of volunteers to make them work.
- Annual events require an influx of new volunteers every year because someone will always drop out.
- Planning from the successes and failures of the most recent event is essential to success.
- Selling things to make money for your library is sometimes more work than it is worth.

The side benefits of increased visibility and adding nonconstituent names to your donor base may make the difference. When it comes to fundraising, you have to start somewhere. Try selling something the people will buy. If you have a well-developed, generous constituency, solicit a donation rather than sell something.

BIBLIOGRAPHY

Amos, Janell Shride. 1995. *Fundraising Ideas: Over 225 Money Making Events for Community Groups, With a Resource Directory.* Jefferson, N.C.: McFarland. If you are looking for some moneymaking ideas, this book has lots of them. They run the gamut from men-only beauty contests, to tearooms, to cakewalks, to kissing booths. Every event is described in detail along with the workers and tools needed.

Basics for Board Members: An Overview of Fundraising. 1994. New York: Jeanne Sigler and Associates. This video was prepared to help board members overcome their fear of asking for a gift. It also includes segments on capital campaigns, annual fundraising events, the benefits of giving, and foundation and corporate giving.

Chapter 14

Set Up Retail Sales with Shop in the Library

DESCRIPTION

Having a retail shop in the library is not a new idea, but only a few libraries have them. Museums have had them for years—selling items related to their collections. Library shops sell books, T-shirts, book bags, trinkets, gifts, and postcards. Well selected, gently read books that have a new appearance could make good money for the store if they come in free and leave at half the retail price. If the library has a distinctive logo or has famous objects like the lions in front of the New York Public Library, the shop will have items for sale that use these features. These items are unique and make attractive gifts.

Library stores may not offer every bestseller, but they should have books by local authors and books relating to local history and genealogy.

Volunteers from the Friends group or the library foundation usually staff the shop. The hours for the shop may not match library hours, but they are usually open when traffic is heaviest.

With the advent of the Internet, retail shops in libraries have become virtual stores, making it possible for people to shop online. Customers do not have to go to New York City to get a book bag with pictures of the lions on it. The virtual store could make more money than the one in the library.

Because space is precious, shops in libraries tend to be small and can only stock a few items. Some libraries like the Meriden (Connecticut) Public Library have decided to take the shop out of the library altogether, and set up a separate store.

PURPOSES

Shops in the library give people the opportunity to express their love for reading, literacy, or freedom of access, through their purchases. The profits from the sale of library logo merchandise could go directly to the endowment fund or to the Friends of the Library for their support of library projects.

Shops in the library also enhance the library's visibility—especially if tourists know the shop has unique items related to the history of the area or the library.

BENEFITS

Besides giving the Friends an ongoing project, a shop in the library could enhance tourism and take advantage of local tourism efforts.

The shop in the library can provide a real benefit for the shopper who is looking for the truly unique gift. People who shop for unique gifts expect to pay a premium for one-of-a-kind items.

EXAMPLES

Marcia Trotta, Director, Meriden (CT) Public Library shared the story of the shop her Friends group operates for the benefit of the library.

"The Friends of the Meriden Public Library operate a retail store that is located in the business district of our city. It is not part of the library building. Its purpose is to provide a means to sell high quality, used paper and hardcover books, videos, DVDs, software, etc. in order to raise funds for the library.

"The store provides an ongoing source of income for enhancements to the library through the Friends. The proceeds are never used as operating funds. Rather, the funds are used to provide seed money for a new project, or pay for major enhancements. The store also serves as part of the library's outreach efforts in the community—enhancing public relations, and promoting literacy.

"Materials are sold at very low prices, and many are even given away, especially to children.

"We also invite local authors to include their items in the store. The local land-trust organization wrote a book on hiking. The store gave them an outlet for sales and visibility" (Trotta, 2001).

The Library of Virginia operates a shop that has "something for everyone" with proceeds going to support the mission of the Library of Virginia. Items for sale include books, postcards, note cards, souvenirs, and high-quality products (The Library Shop at the Library of Virginia, 2002).

The San Antonio Public Library runs a used bookstore called The Book Cellar. Volunteers from the Friends of the San Antonio Public Library staff the shop. They sell hardback books for $1.00 and paperback books for 25 to 50 cents. Premium books sell for the price marked on the book, usually for about $5.00. All of the proceeds go to the library for its activities and materials. The shop is open seven days a week from 11 A.M. to 3 P.M.

They also sell magazines, comic books, records, videos, audio books, T-shirts, and book bags.

The Book Cellar is the main source of income for the Friends. They turn about $30,000 a year over to the library from the profits (San Antonio Public Library, 2001).

HOW TO DO IT

Every successful business needs a business plan. A shop in the library is no exception.

Developing a Business Plan

A good business plan outlines an accurate view of the future, and established down-to-earth expectations and long-term objectives for the new enterprise. It sets parameters and rules for operating the business. The business plan becomes the venture's most persuasive document for outside support. Don't "pass go" without one.

A well-developed business plan is just as important for an established venture as it is for a new one. It serves five important functions:

- It helps the manager focus on developing the business and cultivating prospective customers.
- It gives the manager a basic structure for pursuing long-range business strategies.
- It is a tool for explaining the business to other interested parties like bankers, investors, or board members.
- It contains a benchmark for measuring and improving performance.
- It provides a vision of the establishment's alignment for everyone involved with the project.

A business plan will be the roadmap for your shop. It will tell your staff, your suppliers, and your board where you want the business to go. The plan will help you make management decisions. Here are the basic elements of a business plan.

Elements of a Good Business Plan

- *Decide what business you are in.* If the library shop is in the used book business, say so and build the business around that concept. It is better to start with one product line and expand your offerings than to try to sell anything and everything and end up with products you can't sell.
- *Develop a marketing plan.* Decide what you want to do and how much you can afford to spend on advertising. You can't just open the doors and expect people to beat your doors down.
- *Determine the sales potential for your shop.* If the shop is in the library, what kind of traffic will you have? How many tourists will you be able to attract? Sales potential is not easy to assess, but it is essential to the success of your shop.
- *Determine your pricing policies.* The only way your shop can sell things at low prices is to have low-priced merchandise. You have to decide who your clientele will be. If people are looking for a top-quality, unique gift, they probably won't go into a used bookstore.
- *Decide what you are going to do about advertising.* This is a tricky balance. Sales will depend on advertising, but a shop in a library will attract a lot of traffic without advertising.
- *Figure out how you will get the merchandise you plan to sell.* If you plan to have quality gifts that carry the library's logo, you will have to find a supplier that will do this custom work for the shop. You can get all of the used books you need from library patrons.
- *Develop a procedure for stock control.* Lots of times people will enter a shop, look around, and leave because they didn't find what they wanted. You need to have several products in several price ranges. If you offer three different book bags, you need to have enough of any one of them to take you to the next shipment of the ones that are out of stock.
- *Set the standard for stock turnover.* You will need to get rid of merchandise that has been handled a lot by customers, but not purchased. Don't leave over-handled items on the shelf alongside of brand new things. It will cheapen the look of everything on the shelf.
- *Convert all of your plans into dollars.* Everything in your business plan has to have a dollar value on it. Add everything thing up and see how it fits into your business plan. You need to know what it will take to make your shop profitable before you make too many commitments.
- *Establish a bookkeeping system.* You have to keep good records to know if your shop is making any money or not.
- *Create a vision for your shop in the library.* Have a clear idea what it will take to accomplish the vision, and share your vision with the other people involved in the venture.

Figure II-14-1 Elements of a Good Business Plan

Staffing is one of the most costly expenses associated with any retail outlet. Using volunteers could be the difference between success and failure in a shop at the library.

Marcia Trotta provided some sound tips for setting up a library store:

1. "Secure a retail location, in a good traffic area, that is either donated or has an affordable rent. You will not want to spend your earnings for rent on a building.
2. "Secure donations/gifts. Buying things to sell will cut into your profits.
3. "Make sure that you have space to sort out donations and store them until they are needed.
4. "Install the necessary fixtures in the store. You need to have displays, book shelves, a check out area.
5. "Write a formal business plan, including a marketing plan and a budget. In order for an operation of this type to be successful, it must be run in the same manner as a small business.
6. "Have an operations committee develop the policies for the operation of the store. They develop the daily operations plan. They decide the hours as based on the needs of the community.
7. "Have someone designated as day-to-day operations manager for the store. It is his or her job to recruit staff (volunteers in this case), schedule their work, organize the stock, display the materials in the store, arrange for cleaning, etc.
8. "The business plan should have a method of bookkeeping and deposits of cash into appropriate accounts.
9. "Make sure to evaluate the process regularly. This will alert you to things that may need to be changed in order to have the operation run smoothly" (Trotta, 2001).

RESOURCES

Every store needs fixtures, telephone service, materials for sale, and money for advertising.

Finding the right vendor to produce quality one-of-a-kind-items with the library's logo is essential to success.

If you sell gently read books in the library shop, you will need a steady stream of top-quality used books. Select only the top ten percent of books you receive as gifts.

Volunteers are a key resource. Train them well and teach them to be dependable.

Use the Internet to create another opportunity for people to buy.

SPECIAL CONSIDERATIONS

If you decide to have a shop in the library make sure that it is as attractive as you can make it. I have been in lots of used bookstores and most of them are dingy and cluttered with books piled everywhere. It is better to have three or four shelves with almost new books than to have a shop full of books no one wants to look at.

Make sure the library shop has good visibility to traffic in and out of the library.

Register the library's logo as a trademark and protect it. Then make sure that the library shop has exclusive rights to use it.

PITFALLS

Staffing the shop could become your biggest nightmare. Don't staff with library personnel—even to fill in. Use volunteers and close the shop if they don't show.

Don't buy cheap trinkets to sell in the store; buy quality items that people will pay good money to have or to give as gifts.

Limit the number of items you sell. You don't want to have your operating funds tied up in things you can't sell.

FOR SCHOOLS AND ACADEMIC LIBRARIES

I can't see a store in a school library working very well. School libraries would do better to have a book fair once a year.

A shop in a university library is a good idea. Just make sure you don't compete with the college bookstore. You wouldn't want them to see your store as infringing on their turf. Stock only quality items.

CHECKLIST

Use this checklist to help you decide if you want a shop in your library or to help you take a look at the one you have.

1. Do you have a room in the library that could be used for a retail shop?
2. Would the room be visible to patrons of the library as they came and went?
3. Is there enough tourism in your town to make the shop a viable entity?
4. Is there an organization like a Friends group or foundation with members that are willing to manage and staff the shop?

5. Does the library have a distinctive logo or a piece of art that could be used as the basis for custom-designed items to sell?
6. Does the library have a Web site that could provide customers with online access to the shop?
7. Does the community have many local authors who would like to promote their books in the shop?
8. Does the group that will run the shop have a business plan?
9. Do enough people in the community want to see a shop in the library to make it a success?
10. Can you envision a successful retail store in the library or any place in your community?

GETTING RESULTS

A store in the library has exciting potential if you have the space. You have to be in it for the long haul for the best results.

What Do I Do Next?

Since this is a project for the Friends, let them make the first move. Work with them to make it a success. If you are planning to build a new library or remodel your existing one, consider making a small room with good access and visibility available for a store in the library.

What Are the Policies and Procedures Needed?

The library and the Friends must have a policy that clearly defines the role of each organization. Make sure the public understands that the library store is run by the Friends of the Library.

Again, sales tax laws will apply. Make sure the store complies with the law.

How Much Time Should This Method Take?

It could take a year or more for the store to show a profit. Furnishing the store and buying items to sell will require a sizeable investment. Don't expect to make any real money for a year.

When Can I Expect Results?

If you are fortunate and turn a profit sooner than a year it would probably be wise to plough the money back into the store for at least two years. From then on about every other dollar you earn could be transferred to the Friends treasury.

What Can I Realistically Expect the Costs to Be?

Many retail businesses fail in the first year because they are undercapitalized. If the Friends don't have at least $5,000 they can afford to lose, a store in the library may not be a good risk.

SUMMARY

Having a retail shop in the library is a great idea for some libraries. Having enough space and having enough dependable volunteers are critical to its success. If you decide to try it keep these ideas in mind:

- Sell only quality products. If all you plan to sell are used books, think twice. It may not work or be as profitable as you hope it will be.
- Expand your wares to include books, T-shirts, book bags, umbrellas, toys, trinkets, gifts, and postcards.
- Offer bestsellers because some people can't wait till their turn comes on the waiting list to borrow a book they want.
- Carry books by local authors and books relating to local history and genealogy.
- Have things in your store that will be attractive to tourists.
- Make your store a virtual store by offering your wares on the Internet through the library's Web site.
- Determine in advance how the profits will be used.

A retail shop in the library could be a real moneymaker if you can keep your costs down and charge enough to make money on every item you sell.

BIBLIOGRAPHY

Hupalo, Peter I. 1999. *Thinking Like An Entrepreneur: How to Make Intelligent Business Decisions That Will Lead to Success in Building and Growing Your Own Company.* St. Paul, Minn.: HCM Publishing. This is a good book for your library and for anyone who wants to start a new business. If you are serious about establishing a shop in your library, you will want to read every word.

Segel, Rick. 2001. *Retail Business Kit for Dummies.* New York: Hungry Minds, Inc. This is a step-by-step book on how to set up a retail business—a good book for any librarian who wants to help the Friends group set up a store in the library.

Trotta, Marcia. 2002 (forthcoming). *Starting and Operating a Library Store: A How-to-Do-It Manual*. New York: Neal-Schuman. This book emphasizes the importance of a business plan before starting a shop in the library.

Chapter 15

Secure Matching Grants or Gifts

DESCRIPTION

Matching grants or gifts can double or triple contributions from donors. Are you overlooking this form of corporate giving? This is how it works: an employee from a participating corporation makes a gift to an eligible institution like your library and the employer matches or doubles the contribution up to a predetermined amount. Most matching gifts are capped at between $500 and $1,000, even though they vary among institutions, programs, and services.

Your library may already have donors who qualify for a matching donation from their employers, but they just don't know about it. You may be able to recruit many more donors if they know their gift to your library would trigger a similar gift from their employer. Generally the matching ratio is one-to-one, although some corporations do match two-to-one for universities, colleges, and arts and culture organizations. Do a little snooping around to find out how to take advantage of this often untapped resource of extra money.

PURPOSES

Libraries are among the agencies that are frequently eligible for this type of giving. Matching gifts can be part of a capital campaign, which you may be able to leverage into larger donations. This is a good way to encourage giving from the community.

Matching gifts can also be a component of an annual giving campaign. Matching gifts could be used for whatever purpose the library deems necessary at the time. The gifts might not be as large as for a capital campaign, but the overall benefit to the library could be exceptional.

BENEFITS

Matching grants or gifts could be the easiest money you will ever raise. It is an easy way to bring attention to your library and promote awareness of corporation and foundation matching gift programs. It can also set the stage for other types of financial assistance in the future.

Once it is established it can be maintained with very little effort. A letter or telephone call to the donor will let him or her know that it is time to make the annual gift to the library. Once the pledge is made the matching gift can be solicited at the same time.

The recipients aren't the only ones to gain. Companies also receive benefits. Their corporate relations and communications, and overall image improve. Employees appreciate corporate support of their commitment to the community. The public sees management and workers coming together for the common good. Matching gift programs also furnish low-cost publicity and are flexible enough to meet a variety of objectives and corporate budgets. These are just some of the reasons your library should seek funding from corporate-matched giving.

EXAMPLES

One of the best examples comes from public radio. Before their "on-the-air" fund drive, employees and volunteers solicit challenge grants from local underwriters. Radio staff members get on the air and challenge listeners to call in and pledge a certain amount, which will be matched by the challenge grant offered by the company or personal underwriter. It is a way of encouraging increased giving.

The Sara Lee Foundation Matching Grants Program encourages Sara Lee employees to support eligible nonprofit organizations. The minimum employee contribution that will be matched is $25. Gifts from $25 to $1,000 are matched dollar for dollar (Sara Lee Foundation, 2001).

The Lutheran Brotherhood's "Branch Challenge Fund is a program through which branches raise funds for community organizations or individuals in need. Branches apply to have their fundraising projects matched on a dollar-for-dollar basis, up to a designated amount, by the Lutheran Brotherhood" (Lutheran Brotherhood, 2002). I know of libraries that have benefited from this fund.

"The Gannett Foundation, a corporate foundation sponsored by Gannett Company, Inc. serves local organizations in those communities in which the Gannett Company, Inc. has a local daily newspaper or television station. The program makes contributions through grants and a matching gifts program to qualified nonprofit organizations to improve the education, health and advancement of the people who live in Gannett communities" (Gannett Foundation, 2002). Another source of matching grants is the Wal-Mart Foundation. Their mission is to serve their associates and customers with compassion and integrity. Their emphasis is on their associates, children, families, the local community, and other local programs that improve the quality of life in communities where there is a Wal-Mart store. During certain times of the year they allow nonprofit organizations to hold fundraising events in front of their stores. Then they match money raised up to a certain amount. Find out more about the Wal-Mart Foundation at www.walmartfoundation.org/about.html or call your local Wal-Mart store.

HOW TO DO IT

Since it's not difficult to advocate for your library and encourage individuals to donate qualifying gifts, matching gift programs are one of the most cost-effective projects you can promote. Following annual gifts with little additional effort, you don't have to solicit corporations directly, and your organization doesn't have to compete with other agencies for corporate attention.

More than 1,000 American companies have adopted corporate matching gift plans to help support nonprofit organizations. You can find out if a company in your town supports matching gifts by calling the personnel or community relations department. Ask if they have a matching gift program for their employees. If they do, ask for a copy of their guidelines. Find out if your library is on the list of qualified recipients. If you are not on the list find out what you need to do to get on it.

Corporate managers may have overlooked the benefits of matched giving. Point out that matched giving is good for morale. Giving money to charity is a personal sacrifice for the employee. When staff members know that their employer supports the causes they support they will feel good about working for the company. Matched giving also spreads the benefit. It is a good way to make relatively small donations to a large number of charities. Best of all, matched giving has a positive impact on the corporate image.

Once your library is on the list, you have to solicit donations from the employees. It is probably better to get on the list of several of the major employers, maybe even some of the smaller ones too, then make a general solicitation, naming all of the companies that match the gifts of their employees.

RESOURCES

Get or create a list of local companies that offer matching gifts or grants when their employees donate to a charitable cause. A city directory might tell you where individuals work, if they give that information when they return the directory information form. Some directories have this information on a CD-ROM database. If one is available try using it to create a potential donor list. From this donor list you could create a generic direct mail appeal. You could say something like this in the letter:

"The following companies in our area provide matching gifts to organizations like the library." (Then list the companies.)

"If you work for one of these companies a gift of $50 from you to the library would mean a total gift of $100."

Go on to mention the library's need or project for which funds are being sought.

(See also the chapter on Direct Mail Campaigns, page 315.)

SPECIAL CONSIDERATIONS

The main issue here is getting your library on the list of charities for which the company will match a gift from an employee. Some companies will not donate to organizations that have a regular source of income like tax funds from the city or county.

If you are conducting a capital campaign or some other form of solicitation like direct mail or door-to-door, try to get a company to offer a matching challenge grant that will be realized as the community donates to the same cause.

Use the matching gifts you receive to encourage more matched giving. If a company has only recently included the library on its list of acceptable charities, recognize the first donor and the company with a picture and a write-up in the newspaper. Recognize substantial gifts that come in later the same way.

Matched giving might give you a good opportunity to introduce or remind donors that they can use their credit cards if they want to. See the chapter on using the library's Web site to solicit gifts.

PITFALLS

Make sure you understand the terms of the challenge or matching grant and convey that information accurately to the public. Misunderstandings can occur easily when emotions are high and money is involved.

When they do, the library has to deal with the negative public relations that follows.

Receipt and acknowledge every gift with a thank you note. Failure to take care of donors will backfire quickly and dry up the pool of giving in the community.

FOR SCHOOLS AND ACADEMIC LIBRARIES

Colleges and universities have always been the big recipients of matched giving. Their fundraisers have aggressively sought corporate funding to match the gifts of alumni. They probably do this best of all. Now other agencies are beginning to find the value of this source of funding.

School libraries may be able to tap into this source of funding, but it will be more difficult because their alumni tend to remember their college libraries first. It might be because academic libraries have development officers and schools do not.

CHECKLIST FOR GETTING MATCHING GRANTS

This checklist will help you establish and take advantage of a program of matched giving for your library.

1. Do you know which employers in your community offer to match the gifts of their employees?
2. Do you know which companies might consider offering a challenge grant to the community to help your project succeed?
3. Are you aware of the benefits matched giving offers to large corporations?
4. Do you know someone who has been successful at raising money by using matched gifts?
5. Do you have a method in place to solicit matched gifts?
6. Do you have a mechanism to recognize and thank donors?
7. Do you have a program to accept pledges for three to five years?
8. Do you allow credit or debit cards as a form of payment?
9. Are members of the library staff trained to receive matching gifts?
10. Have you set a goal for income from matched giving?

GETTING RESULTS

Matching gifts are the sleeping giants of fundraising. Because libraries have a natural constituency many more people will give if they know their employer will match their gift.

What Do I Do Next?

Contact the corporate officer in charge of charitable giving. Ask him or her if the corporation would be willing to issue a challenge grant of a certain amount to be matched by gifts from their employees or the community.

What Are the Policies and Procedures Needed?

Each corporation or employer that has a matching gift program will have procedures and policies they follow when matching a grant. Your job is to find out what they are and inform their employees about them.

How Much Time Should This Method Take?

Matching gifts can take as long as six months or longer to secure. If the library is not on the company's list of agencies that could receive matching gifts, it could take a year or more for the library to achieve that status. If the company only funds agencies that receive all of their income from fundraising, the library will never get on the list.

When Can I Expect Results?

Results from matching gifts could begin to come in as soon as donors realize that the library needs a donation and that their employer will match their gift up to a certain amount.

What Can I Realistically Expect the Costs to Be?

This is not a high-dollar effort. Building relationships of trust and confidence with corporate executives can take time and sometimes money for social occasions. An occasional lunch or an after-hours drink may be appropriate, but we are not looking at more than $100.

SUMMARY

Matching grants or gifts could be the easiest money you will ever raise. Matched gifts can be used effectively to stimulate first-time gifts, offer an inducement for large donations, or reactivate former donors. Here are the important points to remember about matching grants or matched giving:

- Many American companies have adopted corporate matching gift plans.
- Matching grants or gifts can double or triple contributions from donors.
- Matching gifts can also be a component of an annual giving or capi-

tal campaign. Matching gifts could be used for whatever purpose the library deems necessary at the time.

- A matched giving program will bring attention to your library and promote awareness of matched giving programs.
- Matching gift programs are one of the most cost-effective fundraisers you can promote.
- You can use the matched giving program of a corporation to leverage even larger gifts.

You could be missing out on a powerful source of income if you are not taking advantage of the matched giving available in your community.

BIBLIOGRAPHY

Joint Task Force on Matching Gifts. 1990. *Guidelines for the Administration of Matching Gift Programs*. Washington, D.C.: Council for Advancement and Support of Education. This guide provides an overview of procedures for soliciting, receiving, recording, and acknowledgment of matching gifts.

Chapter 16

Use Recognition to Enhance Giving

DESCRIPTION

Most of the time we think of donor recognition as a reward for their donations, but it can also become a way to increase giving after the initial gift has been made. Our job as fundraisers, according to Arthur Frantzreb, an author and professional fundraising consultant, is to "Create the desire to give; then to give generously; then to give recurringly; then to give ultimately by bequest." Recognition of donors will keep them giving on a recurring basis. It is a little like suggestion selling. When we go to a convenience store for a beverage, the cashier always asks us if we would like a candy bar or a bag of chips. We don't need to be that overt, but we need to be looking for the next gift.

PURPOSES

While the main purpose of recognizing donors is to say thank you for their most recent gifts, the secondary purpose is to prepare them for the next gift. Every time we recognize a donor we should be looking forward to the next gift and how best to reward the donor for his or her generosity. Well-developed methods of recognition allow us to do that in a tasteful way.

BENEFITS

Recognition is a way of giving the donor something as a reward for his or her gift. It helps the donor to feel good about the first gift and it paves the way for additional giving. Donor recognition if done right provides a steady flow of money into the library.

EXAMPLES

Recognition can also mean something less tangible, but more precious to the donor.

Benefiting From a Personal Visit

The head of a Topeka, Kansas, youth advocacy sent out a direct mail piece to several people in the neighborhood that his agency served. The young man was hoping to raise $2,500 in gifts ranging from $25 to $50. When a check for $500 came in he decided to deliver the receipt and thank you in person. The donor's housekeeper admitted him into the donor's home. When the donor came into the room, the young man introduced himself as the head of the youth organization and said that he had come by to thank the man for his generous gift.

They sat and visited for a while—the old man talked about his family and the head of the youth agency talked about the programs of his agency. As the younger man got ready to leave, the donor asked the housekeeper to get his checkbook. Over the protests of the younger man that he wasn't there to solicit another gift, the donor wrote another check for $400 to the youth agency.

This is not the end of the story. A few days later, the young man went back to deliver the second thank you note. He was invited in and had a nice visit with the old man making sure he knew that he was not there to solicit another gift. Again the man called for his checkbook and wrote another $400 check to the youth organization. A simple direct mail solicitation had turned into a $1,300 gift, just because someone took the time to say "thank you" in a personal way.

Following Up with a Visit

A few years ago I offered a loaf of my famous (in Great Bend) cinnamon bread to anyone who gave $50 to the library. At the end of the campaign I made the bread and delivered it to the donors. It was another chance to say thank you and recognize the donors. Some of the people opened their doors just wide enough to receive the bread. Others insisted that I come in and visit with them. Most of these people were older and lived alone. They just wanted to talk. These visits made it easier to solicit donations the next time around.

Letting Passive Solicitations Speak for Us

The Medford (Wisconsin) Public library uses the giving tree with brass leaf-shaped nameplates to recognize donors of $500 or more and passively secure donations to their endowment.

Some fundraising groups have used recognition bricks with customized messages to raise money for a building project. Bricks are engraved with customized memorial messages created by the donors. The bricks are used to pave a walkway or patio near the library. Gift level starts at $100 and goes up depending on the size of the brick or the number of bricks.

A few years ago I attended the dedication of a new library in Minneapolis, Kansas. Lots of important people were there and the president of the board recognized all of them. They had two large plaques with engraved brass nameplates and a giving tree with little brass leaves on it to recognize various levels of donors. The large plaques were full. They had no room for more nameplates. I suggested to the president of the board that they needed to buy two more plaques otherwise people would think they didn't need any more money. The next time I went there they had new plaques on the wall with names already on them. Whatever we do to recognize donors, we never want to send the message that we don't need any more money.

HOW TO DO IT

Start with a well-developed, clearly defined policy on giving. We discussed this more thoroughly in Chapter 1. Make sure that various levels of giving are tied to specific methods or recognition. Inform the donor and follow the policy. This is a critical first step.

In her Master's thesis, *Thanking Miss Daisy: A Study of Donor Attitudes Relating to Recognition,* Kathleen M. Clark uncovered some interesting attitudes about fundraising that might be helpful to library fundraisers. Here are some of the attitudes I was able to extrapolate from the charts she presented:

- Almost all donors said that some form of recognition was important to them. They seemed to be more concerned to know that the gift had been received than being thanked.
- About half of all donors considered recognition unimportant because their reward came from personal satisfaction. The other half disagreed.
- More than half of the donors surveyed agreed that recognition of their gift would influence future giving. But a significant number said that they would give to the organization without receiving recognition.
- Over 70 percent of respondents said that written acknowledgment should be sent within a month or sooner. To the rest it didn't seem to matter.

- Seventy percent of donors who gave over $100 said that receiving a prompt acknowledgment was important.
- When asked what form of recognition they preferred donors responded in this order:

1.	Handwritten note	24 percent
2.	Other	23 percent
3.	Typed letter	22 percent
4.	Seeing name on printed donor list	12 percent
5.	Printed card	10 percent
6.	Phone call	7 percent
7.	Plaque or certificate	2 percent
8.	Premiums	2 percent

Overall Kathleen Clark found that recognition was a motivator for additional giving. Based on her findings and my experience and if I had the time, I would create a handwritten thank you note and deliver it to the donor in person if I wanted to encourage repeat giving. Only people in the smallest of libraries could really do this. But then again, what would you be willing to do to thank someone who had just given your library $100,000 or more.

After we understand this principle we need to make the public aware of the library's donor recognition program. Use moments of public recognition for donors to explain the library's gift policy. Use flyers in the library, newspaper photo ops, and personal visits to promote giving to the library. Let everyone know that the library is open for business and accepting donations. Public acknowledgment is a key to using recognitions to promote additional giving.

Using Methods of Recognition to Encourage More Giving

In Chapter 1 we discussed donor recognition. As you reconsider these ways to recognize donors think about how you could leverage the recognition to get another gift (see Figure II-16-1).

RESOURCES

Use the Internet to find different ways to recognize donors and find vendors of unique recognition methods. Learn from other librarians.

If you use recognition plaques make sure you have a good source for getting the nameplates engraved.

Maintain a good relationship with the people at the local newspaper. Recognize them for helping you recognize donors to the library.

Using Donor Recognition to Leverage Additional Giving

- *Hold a large banquet in his or her honor.* If you are short of your fundraising goal and everyone knows it the donor could come up with enough money to put you over the top.
- *Put the donor's name on the new wing of the library.* If the original gift fell short of funding the new wing let the donor know and he or she might make up the difference rather than see the new wing completed without furnishings.
- *Have a fancy reception at the library in the donor's honor.* Announce your next fundraising effort and let everyone there know what you plan to do.
- *Invite the donor and a few friends to a fancy restaurant for supper.* Offer a more lasting type of recognition and ask for an additional gift.
- *Put the donor's name on a piece of furniture or equipment in the library.* Once the piece of furniture has been delivered and the recognition plate is in place, invite the donor to the library to see the new addition. Suggest a companion piece to the one you just added.
- *Invite the donor and his or her spouse to lunch with you and the president of the board.* During the luncheon try to discover what the couple is really interested in. You may be able to turn that interest into a project for the library and another gift from the couple.
- *Put the donor's name on a recognition plaque.* Suggest the next higher level of giving to put his or her name on another plaque.
- *Pose for a picture with the donor giving a check to the library.* Give the picture to the local newspaper with a story about the donation. Use the opportunity to publicize the library's gift policy and recognition for levels of giving.
- *Give the donor a framed certificate of recognition for his or her home.* Offer the donor a framed art print as a premium for a higher-level gift.
- *Give the donor a premium like a coffee mug, a blanket, or a book bag.* Appeal to the donor's sense of generosity by suggesting an additional comparable gift without the premium.
- *Send a personal letter of thanks from the library director.* Offer a premium for the next level of giving.
- *Put the donor's name on a memorial bookplate inside the cover of a book.* Thank the donor and encourage him or her to think of the library the next time he or she wants to make a memorial gift.
- *Send a handwritten thank you note.* Ask the donor to remember the library the next time he or she wants to remember a loved one or just feels generous.
- *Put the donor's name on the library's Web page.* This would work well if you changed the list every year.
- *Say thank you in person.* Some people require no more recognition than a simple thank you. Say thank you again and tell him or her how glad you are that they thought of the library.
- *Give the donor a good feeling about his or her gift.* Try to find out what else would make the donor feel good and do it if you can.

Figure II-16-1 Using Donor Recognition to Leverage Additional Giving

SPECIAL CONSIDERATIONS

Communicating the library's giving policy requires proficiency and diplomacy. Whether you are soliciting a gift or receiving an unsolicited one, make sure the donor understands the library's policy. It is helpful to agree upon the recognition with the donor before the gift is made. It doesn't matter if the gift is a box of used books or a boxful of money, the donor needs to understand the policy and know how he or she will be recognized for the gift.

PITFALLS

Donor recognition is an arena where people can get their feelings hurt. Misunderstandings and unmet expectations can quickly incur the wrath of an already emotional donor. The last thing you want to do is to alienate a rich donor, or even a poor one for that matter.

The fallout from not having a well-articulated gift and recognition policy in place can cause irreparable public relations damage. Misunderstandings can severely hurt already bruised feelings of a bereaved family member. Make sure you communicate your recognition policy to the public and the staff.

FOR SCHOOLS AND ACADEMIC LIBRARIES

Since the patron traffic in schools brings in few if any donations, the use of donor recognition to encourage additional giving may be limited. It is possible for the parents of a deceased child to want the child to be remembered by a memorial in the school library. School librarians and principals need to be ready for this possibility, but the chances of something like this happening are remote.

Academic libraries can and do benefit greatly from a donor recognition program. They could have a memorial lounge with a donor wall that has all kinds of plaques and photos. The gift policy is the key to evenhanded recognition.

CHECKLIST

Use this checklist to assess donor recognition in your library.

1. Does your library have a well-articulated gift policy in place?
2. Can all staff members explain the gift policy to potential donors?
3. Are the levels of giving clearly defined with appropriate distinctions for each level?

4. Is the general public aware of the library's gift policy and levels of recognition?
5. Are donor recognitions elegant but tasteful?
6. Are donor recognitions placed where people can see them?
7. Do donor recognition efforts lend themselves to both active and passive gift solicitation?
8. When a gift comes into the library has a particular staff member been assigned to write the thank you note and handle the recognition?
9. Does the library have a working relationship with members of the media?
10. Does the library's donor recognition policy encourage donors to give "generously; then to give recurringly; then to give ultimately by bequest"?

GETTING RESULTS

Recognizing donors appropriately is probably the best way to encourage additional giving. The results are long lasting and worth the effort.

What Do I Do Next?

Start with the recognition section of the library's gift policy. Consider each form of recognition and look for ways to use the recognition for the most recent gift to secure the next one. If you recognize donors by putting their name in the Friends newsletter, ask a recent donor to write a short piece for the newsletter on the importance of regular giving to the library.

What Are the Policies and Procedures Needed?

The library's policy on giving may need to be revised—especially if more modern forms of recognition, such as the donors name on a Web page, are not listed. Make sure that staff members follow through on assignments to recognize donors with thank you notes and acknowledgments.

How Much Time Should This Method Take?

Public recognition of donors will plant a seed in the minds of other donors. Gifts can begin to come in immediately or it can take several years to see recognition of one donor produce a similar gift from another donor.

When Can I Expect Results?

You can expect results in three to six months, but because this is a passive technique it may take years to produce a significant gift. You can help it along by drawing attention to various forms of recognition offered by the library.

What Can I Realistically Expect the Costs to Be?

Depending on the number of brass plates and the size, a recognition wall plaque can cost $100 to $500. The giving tree starts at about $500. Other forms of recognition cost little or nothing. Listing a donor's name in a newsletter or on the library's Web page costs nothing. A personal visit to deliver a thank you note is just part of your job.

SUMMARY

Using donor recognitions to encourage additional giving requires skill and tact. Recognition of donors will keep them giving on a recurring basis.

The main points of this section are:

- The main purpose of recognizing donors is to say thank you.
- Recognition is a way of giving the donor something as a reward for his or her gift.
- A well-planned recognition program can prepare donors for the next gift.
- Donor recognition if done right provides a steady flow of money into the library.
- Donor recognitions take many forms. One size does not fit all.
- A well-articulated gift policy is the heart and soul of recurring giving.
- People can get their feelings hurt if donor recognitions are not handled right.
- All library staff members need to know and understand the library's gift policy.

BIBLIOGRAPHY

Clark, Kathleen M. 1997. *Thanking Miss Daisy: A Study of Donor Attitudes Relating to Donor Attitudes*. Thesis/dissertation/manuscript. This is a Master's Degree thesis that will be helpful to fundraisers that want to know more about donor attitudes. It gives us some revealing information about recognition and donor attitudes. I was able to borrow it through interlibrary loan.

Successful Capital Campaigning, Gary W. Phillips, Phillips Communications, 1994, videocassette. This video gives us the essential elements of a successful capital campaign, including appropriate donor recognition, formulating realistic goals, developing the campaign statement, identifying potential donors, and training the campaign staff.

Chapter 17

Use the Library's Web Page to Solicit Gifts

DESCRIPTION

This is a simple idea that lets you ask people for money without facing them and asking them directly. You can do it. Many libraries now have their own Web page on the Internet. All you need to do is to create a link from the library's main page to pages that tell your prospective donors what you need the money for and how they can make a donation.

PURPOSES

This technique is a good way to reach constituents and encourage them to give money to your library—maybe for the first time. Since this is a passive technique, you can't count on it to bring in big bucks for a project with a close deadline. Use it to build your donor base and put the money in the bank or spend it on something you need right now, like books.

BENEFITS

The benefits of using the library's Web page to promote giving to the library are:

- It will help you send a message to more of your constituents that the library needs their help.
- It will help you communicate your mission and message to millions of people.
- It provides you with an inexpensive, yet very accessible way to communicate and advertise.

- It will attract people who may not be constituents now, but may be willing to give you money once they see your message.
- It can be another part of your overall fundraising strategy.

EXAMPLES

Two good examples are:

- The University of Waterloo, www.lib.uwaterloo.ca/Gifts.html
- Peters Township Public Library, www.ptlibrary.org/Fundraising.html.

The message is straightforward. "The library encourages gifts and donations, which are considered an important source of additional revenue. They are also a meaningful way for patrons to support the library and its role in the community. Their message is clear, and straightforward. They want people to "make a bequest, establish a trust fund, send a check or give us cash" (Peters Township Public Library, 2002).

In the Great Bend (Kansas) Public Library we have had a Web page, www.ckls.org/~gbpl/, since 1996. Until 2001 it did not include a solicitation for donations. The main page has a link entitled *"Make a gift to the Library."* This link takes the potential donor to a page that explains our need and shows them our wish list as well as "Other ways to give to the library." Each of the items on the wish list has a link to its own page. On these pages we explain the need for the item in a little more detail and then give the donor the opportunity to use a credit card or send a check.

Until a few years ago this fundraising idea had not been heard of, let alone tried. Some libraries have tried it, allowing patrons to use their credit cards as a method of payment for donations.

HOW TO DO IT

If you are going to use a Web site to solicit gifts for your library you need to know how to create documents in HTML (Hypertext Markup Language). Basically HTML is a standardized protocol on Internet browsers like Internet Explorer or Netscape.

The markup language tells the browser how to display what you have written. It uses angle brackets, "< >," sometimes called carrots, to hide instructions to the browser. It is reminiscent of early word processing programs. You use a beginning tag and an ending tag. For example if you wanted to display text in bold type you would put a beginning tag like this "<B>," telling the browser to begin showing the text that follows in bold typeface. The text follows and a "</B>" turns off the bold type.

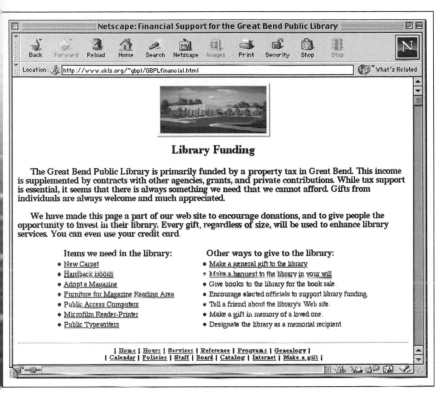

Figure II-17-I Example of Web Page Solicitation

This is a very simple example. Hundreds of books have been written on HTML and many institutions offer classes on HTML. If you are going to create a Web page for your library you will need to learn how to use HTML. You can also pay someone to create your Web page, but maintaining the page can get expensive if you have to pay someone to update your page every time you want to make changes.

Online security is essential if you are going to accept credit cards as a form of payment. Your donors need to feel that their personal information is kept confidential. Don't try to develop the secure software yourself. Pay for an encrypted software package called shopping cart. Some banks specialize in online commerce. Their representatives can direct you to sources for encrypted software.

Fundraising is just one of the benefits of learning HTML. You can also use the skill to write other pages to promote the library and its services.

RESOURCES

An HTML text editor can be very helpful. These editors will help you create HTML pages without keying in all of the code. While it is essential to learn the tags and what they do, it is very handy to have an editor to take away much of the drudgery of code writing. The two editors I use are PageSpinner for the Macintosh and DominHTML for the Windows environment. PageSpinner is an award-winning Web authoring package for Mac OS. It supports HTML 3.2, HTML 4.0, XHTML 1.0, and others (www.optima-system.com/pagespinner/). DominHTML by Domino Computer Services is for Windows 95 and above. If fancy wizards and templates in HTML editors put you off, try DominHTML. It is a text-based HTML editor with many unique features. There are no wizards to get in your way, just a bunch of neat tools to help you generate HTML pages quickly and easily (www.fyi.net/~abass/domino/editors.htm).

When creating a Web page you will sometimes have mistakes and you will need to troubleshoot them. These editors will let you see the HTML code so you can find the errors easier.

The next hurdle to having a Web page for your library is finding a provider to host your page. Several Internet companies will host pages for individuals and businesses for a fee. Some will allow their Internet customers a limited amount of space on their server as part of their monthly service charge. You simply have to check around to see what is available.

Once you have all of this in place, it is time to begin with the library's Web page. *Fundraising for Libraries* is not a book on writing pages for the World Wide Web. I just want to give you a few ideas for your page, including ideas for fundraising as part of your page.

SPECIAL CONSIDERATIONS

Here are a few questions to consider:
1. Who is going to see your Web page?
2. What message do you want to convey?
3. What do you want them to do after they have seen your Web page?
4. How will you tell them what you want them to do?
5. How will you ask them to give money to the library?
6. What will you use as graphics to help the donor visualize the results of his or her gift.
7. How will you provide security for online giving?

A solicitation on the Web page could also include an easier way to give. Andrea Lapsley at the Houston Public Library says, "We take memorial and tribute gifts by credit cards. For our special events we also give people the option of paying for tickets or tables by credit cards. Many people charge $5-10,000 tables. We take Mastercard, VISA, Diner's Club and American Express to pay for fines, fees, etc.

"We have credit card machines at the Central Library and our six regional branches. Any credit card information we take in the Development Office, we write up the slip and then go down to circulation to use the machine. We send the donor a copy of the credit card slip and turn the other copies into our business office to handle the remainder of the processing. Having the option of using credit cards has enabled donors to make a gift over the phone rather than writing a check and sending it in to the library" (Lapsley, 2001).

Al Escoffier of the Burlingame (California) Public Library says, "Our Library Foundation has set up a system to enable donors to donate using Visa. It also helps at fundraisers, since so many people these days use credit cards to buy or donate. Probably 2/3 of the guests at our fundraiser charged their purchases. We used the Visa on our direct mail campaign recently as well. I highly recommend it. It makes it easier for the donor and the recipient" (Escoffier, 2000).

PITFALLS

I do not recommend trying to create a Web page for your library on your own. Find someone to coach you or take a class on writing Web pages. You will be glad you did.

- Don't try to cram everything on one page. Your message should fit on one screen without having to scroll down.
- Do keep in mind that pages look different with different browsers and on different computers. Use graphics sparingly. They can clutter up the page and they make your page load more slowly.
- Make sure you mention your fundraising message on the first page. If you don't, potential donors may never see it.
- Update your Web page often. Nothing will turn people away faster than stale information on your Web page. If you are in the middle of a capital campaign, use the familiar "thermometer" to let donors track their success and yours.
- Let people know about it. Put its address on your stationery, on your business cards, and any other publications you put out. Write an article about it for the local newspaper.

SCHOOLS AND ACADEMIC LIBRARIES

If you are in a school or academic setting this may be one of the things you can do. It is very likely that your institution will have a Web page and all you need is some space for the library. You may be big enough to have a Web page with your own domain. The sky is the limit and you could really make some hay with this one.

CHECKLIST

Here is a checklist for using the library's Web site to solicit gifts:

1. Does our library have a Web site?
2. Is there space on the first page to put a link that suggests making a donation to the library?
3. Does someone in the library update and manage the Web site?
4. Does the library have a mechanism for handling unsolicited gifts and recognizing donors?
5. Does the library have a "wish list" to share with people who may want to make an unsolicited gift to the library?
6. Does the library take credit cards to facilitate online giving?
7. Do library patrons know about the library's Web page or the opportunity to give online?

GETTING RESULTS

Using the library's Web page to solicit gifts can produce positive results for the library. Publicity experts say it takes seven "tellings" to make individuals aware of a new product. This is one way of telling the public that the library needs a gift from them.

What Do I Do Next?

Start with the library's Web site. If you don't have one, build one or have someone do it. Create several pages that explain the library's need and ask for a gift. You can ask for a general gift, a specific gift, or ask the donor to leave a bequest to the library.

What Are the Policies and Procedures Needed?

The firm that hosts your Web site may have some restrictions or policies that could affect how you word your page, but generally anything you want to do will be well within any policies the hosting server will have.

How Much Time Should This Method Take?

It will take at least a month to set up the Web site and possibly another month to get the virtual shopping cart working. It may take a lot longer than that to get someone to notice the solicitation.

When Can I Expect Results?

The Great Bend Public library has had its Web site and gift solicitation in position for a year. People have paid for lost books using their credit cards. They have also used their credit cards to pay for genealogy searches. No one has ever sent a gift to the library using our Web page.

What Can I Realistically Expect the Costs to Be?

Here are the basic costs. Count on about $1,000 or more to have someone create a basic Web page unless you have someone on your staff that can do it. An "e-commerce account" that lets people give money to the library using credit cards will cost about $1,300. The software license for an encrypted secure shopping cart will cost $400. You will need someone to bring all of this together and make it work. I am not a professional Webmaster, but I was able to do it for the Great Bend Public Library.

SUMMARY

Using the library's Web page to solicit donations is a passive technique that could yield big rewards. It can help you promote giving to the library, and it will help you send a message to more of your constituents.

The most important points to remember about Web page solicitation are:

- Learn how to use HTML. Take a class or find a tutor. You can hire someone to create your Web page, but maintaining the page can get expensive if you have to pay someone to update it every time you want to make changes.
- An HTML text editor can be very helpful. These editors will help you create HTML pages without keying in all of the code.
- Don't try to cram everything on one page. This can clutter up the page and make your page load more slowly.
- Update your Web page often. Nothing will turn people away faster than stale information on your Web page.
- Once you get your library's Web page up, let people know about it. Remember you never get a second chance to make a first impression. Your Web page may be the only impression you make.

BIBLIOGRAPHY

Allen, Nick, Mal Warwick, and Michael Stein, eds. 1996. *Fundraising on the Internet: Recruiting and Renewing Donors Online.* Berkeley, Calif.: Strathmoor Press. This book is for development officers, membership committee chairs, directors, and executives of associations. *Fundraising on the Internet* delivers the goods if you want to use the Internet to raise money for your library. It covers all the basics, and then it takes you to the next level.

Corson-Finnerty, Daniel Adam, and Laura Blanchard. 1998. *Fundraising and Friend-Raising on the Web.* Chicago: American Library Association. As the role of the World Wide Web expands, the opportunities for libraries to benefit financially will increase. This book shows you how to weave a Web strategy whether you are just getting your Web page started or you already have a well-developed Web presence.

Web Sites:

The University of Waterloo Library, www.lib.uwaterloo.ca/Gifts.html.

Peters Township Public Library, www.ptlibrary.org/Fundraising.html.

Great Bend (Kansas) Public Library, www.ckls.org/~gbpl/.

DominHTML by Domino Computer Services, www.fyi.net/~abass/domino/editors.htm.

PageSpinner, www.optima-system.com/pagespinner/.

Chapter 18

Have a New Book Fair

DESCRIPTION

Book fairs are very popular in school libraries and the children's department of public libraries. Not only do they encourage reading, but they also provide revenue for the school or the library. The book fair comes in transportable, freestanding bookcases filled with books. The vendor sets up the display, you sell the books or take orders, and the library gets a commission or free books for the children's department. It sounds like a good deal, but there are a few things you may want to know before you jump into the pond.

Book fairs usually feature as many as 3,000 books and over 500 titles in fiction, nonfiction award winners, best-selling series, classics, and popular new releases. They also include educational items—from learning games to computer software.

Some book fairs make it a family event. Parents with children come to the library to select and purchase the books they want and buy books to donate to the library. The organizers of the book fair provide ideas to help you bring in the parents. When parents participate students are motivated and the fair is a big success.

In a different version of a book fair, Friends groups hold them like a special event and invite authors who have their books available. Customers pay for the privilege of having an author personally autograph a copy of his or her book. The event lasts only a single day, and just the books by invited authors are available at the fair.

BENEFITS

In a time when technology seems to rule the world, libraries and books are hard pressed to claim even a modicum of attention. New book fairs are a wonderful way to speak out in favor of reading and book ownership. Book fairs are designed to raise the level of reading among children by drawing attention to new colorful books and making them available to own. Book ownership motivates reading. Libraries need all of the readers they can get.

PURPOSES

Book fairs help schools earn money for special projects by offering students, parents, and teachers the opportunity to purchase and enjoy books.

Companies that put on book fairs offer cash commissions to sponsoring libraries, but they may also provide free books to the library instead. Unless you really need the cash for some other project, free books are a good way to grow your collection. On the other hand you may not want to load your shelves with mass-market paperbacks.

EXAMPLES

The Big Piney (Wyoming) Elementary School Library has a book fair for four days every year in March. Science, arts and crafts, historical fiction, poetry, and popular fiction head the list of topics. Parents are invited to the school with their children to pick out books for themselves and the school library.

The Eric Friedheim Library of the National Press Club has a book fair in a class all by itself. This prominent event features authors with their most recent books. It brings in over 1,100 prospective buyers who get to meet the authors and buy autographed copies of their books. The event has become so popular that the library has had to limit the number of titles in the fair to 80 (National Press Club, 2001).

HOW TO DO IT

Select someone to be in charge of the book fair—usually a parent or a volunteer. Contact the sales representative of a company who does book fairs in your area. Scholastic Book Fairs are one of the largest companies (www.scholastic.com/bookfairs/index.htm).

A month or two prior to the book fair the company will send a planning kit to help the person in charge get ready for the fair. Just before the scheduled date of the fair the company will send promotional materials, which include posters and student and teacher book lists.

Publicity is critical to the success of every book fair. Everyone connected with the school or library in any way has to hear about the book fair. You have to do something to motivate them to come. Children performing something—a skit, a puppet show, or just singing will bring the parents. Other motivators include the special recognition for participation or the opportunity to win a prize.

Think of your book fair as a mini-bookstore with limited offerings and open over a limited time. Visit a local bookstore to get some merchandising ideas. Their display ideas will help bring your fair to life and create an interest to buy. Attractive displays make the difference.

Here are some display ideas to consider:

- Group books with similar topics together.
- Put books of the same reading level on the same table.
- Situate books for young children on lower shelves so they can have better access to them.
- Keep the special sale items near the checkout area.
- Keep the display racks and tables full of books. As books are sold replace them with more copies of the same book.
- Give the featured books a place of honor or prominence, and keep the display filled with books.
- Use the posters supplied by the vendor to make the surroundings colorful and attractive. Keep copies that are for sale near the checkout table.
- Put the cashier table near the entrance of the fair.

The sales representative from the company will have some good ideas for first-time book fair people. This is one fundraising activity that almost takes care of itself. It is definitely a turnkey deal. Your book fair will be a success if you follow instructions and keep the display full of books.

RESOURCES

The best resource you can have is a good person to volunteer to chair the book fair. You are probably too busy to handle it yourself. Give the job to someone else and take care of your own job.

Book fairs require a lot of room. Don't try to have one in a broom closet or an already crowded library. Make sure you have plenty of tables available.

The company will supply the books to sell at your fair. They also provide a planning kit, flyers, banners, signs, and other promotional materials.

Most book fair companies have a Web site to help customers get through the process step-by-step. They have suggestions for planning, promoting, and managing a book fair.

Try contacting other librarians who have held book fairs. They will be honored to share their successful ideas with you.

SPECIAL CONSIDERATIONS

Remember that book fairs in schools and libraries are a way for the book fair company to market its merchandise. You are in fact a sales agent for them. Because they do it as a way of doing business, they will become proficient at the task. You are taking advantage of their expertise. They benefit from your access to students and parents who might not buy their products if you didn't have a book fair.

PITFALLS

Book fairs seem to be a safe no-risk way to get more money for your library. If you are working with the representative of a company you know and trust, not much can go wrong. Here are a few things to watch out for:

- Avoid unfair competitions among students. A classroom with 30 children has an advantage over a class of 20 if you are measuring total sales instead of average sales per pupil.
- Avoid a "100 percent club." Some classes may have more children with limited means than another class. Peer pressure can be difficult for children who cannot afford to buy books.
- Avoid dragging your book fair out too long. Bring it in. Set it up. Sell the books in a few days. Take it down.
- Avoid trying to do all the work yourself. Spread the work around.

Most book fairs feature soft covered books. Some are mass-market paperbacks, printed on cheap paper and have only one or two color illustrations. Other books are trade paperbacks and are made of a higher grade of paper with four-color illustrations. Select only the higher quality books for the library collection.

FOR SCHOOLS AND ACADEMIC LIBRARIES

This is an activity made in heaven for school libraries. Everything in this section fits like a glove for school librarians. If you have never tried a book fair, consider one in the future. You will be surprised at the success you will enjoy. It sure beats selling cookie dough or candles.

Those connected with an academic library may prefer an author-type book fair. If many of the professors on campus have published books people will want to read, several of them may be willing to participate in a book fair.

CHECKLIST

Here is the checklist for holding a new book fair:

1. Have you shopped around for the best company for holding a new book fair?
2. Will you receive cash or books for the library as compensation for your library's participation?
3. Where will you hold the book fair?
4. Do you have the necessary permissions to have a book fair in your library or school?
5. Who will chair the book fair committee?
6. Do you have enough volunteers?
7. Is the date you have set compatible with other events in the community?
8. What is your plan for promoting the book fair?
9. How will you encourage parents and other adults to participate?
10. What will success look like when you achieve it?

GETTING RESULTS

Results will improve with experience. So try to have a new book fair every year and you will see better results as you learn from practice.

What Do I Do Next?

Schedule your book fair early—at least six months before you want to do it. You may have to wait a year for the book fair company to have an opening. Once you have scheduled the book fair stay in touch with the representative and learn what you can do before the event.

What Are the Policies and Procedures Needed?

Work within the guidelines for fundraising events established by the school board or library board. If you have to collect and pay sales tax, you may want to include it in the price of each book.

How Much Time Should This Method Take?

Most of the work connected with a new book fair will occur a month before the event and a week after.

When Can I Expect Results?

You can expect results six months after you schedule a book fair, unless you schedule it later than six months.

What Can I Realistically Expect the Costs to Be?

Costs will be minimal to nonexistent. All of the costs should be covered by the book fair company. This makes a new book fair one of the more attractive ways to get more money for your library. Don't count on making more than a few thousand dollars.

SUMMARY

Book fairs come to the library in transportable, freestanding bookcases filled with books. Parents with children come to the library to select and purchase the books they want and buy books to donate to the library. Here are the main points about having a book fair:

- Book ownership motivates reading.
- Book fairs raise the level of reading among children.
- Book fairs help schools earn money for special projects.
- Book fairs in schools and libraries are a way for the book fair company to market its merchandise.

BIBLIOGRAPHY

Book Fair Magic: Scholastic Book Fairs, 2000-2001, Scholastic Book Fairs, 2000, videocassette. This is a video about authors of books for children and the books they have created. It will provide a preview of a Scholastic Book Fair.

Scholastic Book Fair Basics. Web site: www.scholastic.com/bookfairs/choosing/basics.htm

Texas Book Festival. 1999. Austin, Tex.: Texas State Library and Archives

Commission. This resource has information and documentation about the Texas Book Festival, a fundraiser for Texas public libraries.

Usborne Book Fairs. 2001. [Online]. Available: www.usbornebooks.com/rfts.htm [2001, October 10]. An Usborne Books Book Fair can generate free resources for any library.

Chapter 19

Write an LSTA Grant

DESCRIPTION

The Library Services and Technology Act (LSTA) of 1996 is a section of the Museum and Library Services Act. The purpose of LSTA is to give individuals of all ages access to learning and information resources in all types of libraries. The IMLS provides funds to State Library Agencies using a population-based formula. Most state libraries have some form of competitive sub-grant to libraries.

The Goals and Priorities of LSTA are:

- Establishing or enhancing electronic linkages among libraries.
- Linking libraries electronically with educational, social, or information services.
- Assisting libraries in accessing information through electronic networks.
- Encouraging libraries to establish consortia and share resources.
- Paying costs for libraries to acquire or share computer systems and telecommunications technologies.
- Targeting library and information services to special populations including: people of diverse geographic, cultural, and socioeconomic backgrounds; individuals with disabilities; people with limited literacy or information skills; and underserved urban and rural communities, including children from families with incomes below the poverty line.

PURPOSES

LSTA outlines two broad priorities for this funding. They are:

1. Using technology for information sharing between libraries and between libraries and other community services.
2. Funding programs that make library resources more accessible to urban, rural, or low-income residents, and others who have difficulty using library services.

Each state has a five-year plan outlining its state programs. These programs support the LSTA goals, which are to:

- Establish or enhance electronic linkages among or between libraries;
- Link libraries electronically with educational, social, or information services;
- Help libraries access information through electronic networks;
- Encourage libraries in different areas and different types of libraries to establish consortia and share resources;
- Pay costs for libraries to acquire or share computer systems and telecommunications technologies; and
- Target library and information services to persons who have difficulty using a library and to underserved urban and rural communities (LSTA goals, 2001).

If you want to write an LSTA competitive grant, contact your own state library agency. Each state established its own five-year plan in which the competitive grants are defined. Some states have chosen not to offer competitive grants, but most states have them. The URL for directory of State Agencies is www.imls.gov/grants/library/gsla_cos.htm.

BENEFITS

The main benefit of LSTA competitive grants is the opportunity they give libraries to fund projects that might never be funded with local funds. Here are some other benefits of the LSTA competitive grants:

- They offer opportunities for beginning grant writers to succeed.
- They provide extra funding for narrowly defined special projects.
- They encourage an atmosphere of mentoring among colleagues.
- They give local libraries the chance to get some federal funding and brag about it.

EXAMPLES

A Special Populations Grant written by Joanna Runion, Library Director, in Smith Center, Kansas, was one of the best LSTA grant proposals I have ever seen. The grant proposal documented the needs of older citizens for large print books with published statistics. "In 1998 Smith County had the highest percentage of people over 85 in the United States. In 1998, 18 percent of the nation's population was 65 or older. In 2000, 35.5 percent of Smith County's population was 60 and older" (Runion, 2000).

The librarian localized the need with this statement: "We receive an average of 12 patron complaints per month that we do not have enough large print books."

In Dodge City, Kansas, the librarian focused on the need of pregnant teens and single teens with children. The statement of need includes the following: Ford County has seen a significant rise in several areas relevant to the target population. Increases in the following statistics have been noted:

- Births to single teens (13 percent increase).
- Births to mothers with less than a high school diploma (21 percent increase).
- Childhood death rate (14 percent increase).
- Infant mortality (85 percent increase).
- Reported child abuse and neglect (53 percent increase).

These statistics present a vivid word picture of the community need for the grant reviewers. The people in the library believed they could make a difference by providing valuable information to the 25 to 30 students in the alternative high school. Their solution took them out of their comfort zone in the library to other locations in the community.

Institutions do not have needs; people and communities have needs. Libraries and institutions are in the business of alleviating those needs.

HOW TO DO IT

Start by contacting the state library to find out if your state has LSTA competitive grants and what the categories are. In Kansas we have two grant categories:

1. Technology training and development
2. Special populations

Other states probably have similar grant categories. Review these suggestions and use the ones you think will help you:

- Take advantage of any grant writing workshops offered by the state library. Individuals who know the grant reviewers and know what they are looking for when they read grants will probably teach these classes.
- Find out how to apply for a grant. We have to submit letters of intent well before the grant applications are mailed. This step limits the paperwork of the state library staff.
- Get a copy of the application form, grant guidelines, and make sure you know the deadline date for applications.
- Get acquainted with the LSTA program administrator at the state library. Get to know him or her on a first name basis. Call to ask questions. Call to get advice. Call to get an opinion. The person in this position has a vested interest in your success.
- Review the grant guidelines to develop ideas for a project you want to do. Better yet, get involved in the process of establishing the grant criteria, if you can.
- Become familiar with the review process. Learn how your grant will be reviewed and by whom. Do the grant reviewers use an evaluation form? Get a copy for yourself if they do.
- Develop a project based on the needs of your community. Build a project around it like they did in Smith Center and Dodge City.
- Complete the grant application based on the information presented in Chapter 3. Make sure you keep your narrative within the space limitations of the grant guidelines. Follow the guidelines exactly.
- Secure the necessary signatures and mail your grant well in advance of the time deadline. There is nothing worse than to spend a lot of time and effort to write a grant and then have it disqualified because it arrived too late to be considered.
- Find out when and where the grants will be discussed and awarded, and attend the meeting. You may even get the chance to answer questions about your grant.
- If your grant is funded, go to work and make your project the best one funded. If your grant is not funded, learn what you could have done to make it better.

RESOURCES

Successful grants of other libraries could be the best resource you can find. While creativity and innovation are often rewarded, replicating a successful project of another library could be very worthwhile and fundable for your community.

Members of the state library staff often present workshops to help grant writers prepare LSTA grant applications.

Books and other training materials can also be valuable tools in preparing a grant application.

SPECIAL CONSIDERATIONS

Your ability to write is on the line when you apply for an LSTA competitive grant. Your written words are all you have to convey the urgency of the community need and what your library plans to do to fix it. Grant readers cannot read your mind. They can only read the words you have put on the page and make their decision on what you have said.

If you have never written a grant before, an LSTA competitive grant is a good place to start and learn by doing. If your grant is funded you will have the opportunity to spend the money and do what you plan to do to meet a community need. If your grant is not funded, you will have an opportunity to learn from the experience and to try again next year.

PITFALLS

Start early enough on your grant to plan well. Don't wait until the week before the application deadline to start writing the grant. You may be forced to leave out valuable information just because you don't have it. Start by writing a rough draft and then revise it several times. Take out the weasel words. Take out whole sentences if you can do it without losing meaning.

Failure to explain in detail how you will continue the project after the grant has expired could be very costly. Be sure to use numbers and dates and your firm commitment to carry on the project without grant funding.

Do not assume the grant reviewers know anything about your community or the need you plan to alleviate. You have to tell them.

FOR SCHOOLS AND ACADEMIC LIBRARIES

School and academic libraries are eligible for LSTA grants. The suggestions in this section are just as viable for librarians in these institutions as they are for other librarians.

CHECKLIST

Answer these questions about your grant before you type the final draft. Reconsider what you have written if you cannot answer a resounding yes to every question.

1. Is the need for service readily apparent and clearly expressed, quantitatively and qualitatively?
2. Does the application have a clear statement of the audience to be served?
3. Does the grant fit the priorities that have been established by the state five-year plan?
4. Is it obvious that the objectives and methodology of the proposal will alleviate the community problem or need?
5. Will the grant produce enhancements to library service programs that are measurably the result of technology?
6. Is it clear that the planned expenditures will make it possible to accomplish the goals and objectives of the project?
7. Does the evaluation methodology include how the project will be evaluated, what tools will be used, and who will do the evaluation?
8. Does the proposal show innovation and creativity?
9. Does the application show quality of effort including evidence of planning, clarity of expression, and conciseness?
10. Do the numbers add up?

GETTING RESULTS

When you have a chance to write an LSTA grant, use the following questions to help you get started:

What Do I Do Next?

Discuss the options with library staff members. They can help you brainstorm to develop a fundable project. Follow the "How to do it" section of this chapter. To avoid sending materials to librarians who do not expect to use them, some states require a letter of intent to apply for a grant. Send in the letter of intent and request the application form and guidelines.

What Are the Policies and Procedures Needed?

Once you receive the application and guidelines, read every word and read them again. Call the state library to clarify anything you do not understand. Begin the writing process early to give what you have written a chance to age before you edit it for the final time. Find out the processes the state library will use to evaluate the grant applications, and get a copy of the grant evaluation tools that will be used.

How Much Time Should This Method Take?

Writing the grant and getting it funded should take about three months. Getting the money should take another three months—maybe longer if the federal appropriation gets held up.

When Can I Expect Results?

Once you get the money you will have a year to spend the money and get the project implemented. Be sure to build evaluation activities into the implementation phase of the project.

What Can I Realistically Expect the Costs to Be?

The costs of writing an LSTA grant are minimal. Besides the time it takes for the grant writer to gather statistics and write the grant, the only costs are making copies and mailing the application.

SUMMARY

The Institute for Museums and Library Service provides funds to state library agencies to enhance library services through technology. State libraries may use some of the funds for a competitive sub-grant to libraries in their state. These funds can be used to:

- Establish or enhance electronic linkages among libraries
- Link libraries electronically with educational, social, or information services.
- Assist libraries in accessing information through electronic networks.
- Use technology for information sharing between libraries and between libraries and other community services.

If you want to write an LSTA competitive grant keep these points in mind:

- Contact the state library to find out if your state has LSTA competitive grants.
- An LSTA competitive grant is a good place to learn how to write a grant proposal.
- Start early enough on your grant to plan well.
- Attend the meeting where the grants are awarded.
- Don't give up if your first try is turned down.

BIBLIOGRAPHY

Miller, Patrick W. 2000. *Grant Writing Strategies for Developing Winning Proposals*. [United States]: P. Miller. This book has explicit information for grant writers. It focuses on fundamental phases of proposal development. It is designed to walk even the novice grant writer through the process of submitting a grant proposal.

Miner, Lynn E., Jeremy T. Miner, and Jerry Griffith. 1998. *Proposal Planning and Writing*, 2d ed. Phoenix, Ariz.: Oryx Press. This self-help book is for those who have never written a grant before. The authors share their tested techniques with their readers. This is a must-read for grant-writing beginners.

Chapter 20

Hold a Direct Mail Solicitation

DESCRIPTION

Direct mail is writing a letter to people to ask them for money. Your letter usually includes a brief statement of why you need the money and how you will use the donor's gift. You send a donor card, a return envelope, and a one-page case statement. You also send an attractive drawing of the planned new building if you are doing a capital campaign.

You have to be able to clearly state what you want to do and why people should give you money to do it. Direct mail takes just as much planning and effort as any other fundraising technique. All direct mail lacks is a friendly face to ask for the gift and hold the prospect's attention while you make the pitch. In fact you have about five seconds to grab and hold the prospective donor's attention, and you will never get another chance to make a first impression.

Direct mail soliciting is a method, not an event. You build enduring, mutually rewarding relationships with lots of donors. You don't necessarily ever meet them face-to-face. As you do direct mail year after year, donors get used to seeing your mailing and will respond if you send them a letter every year.

Some organizations have turned their direct mail campaign over to professionals and let them handle the whole project. Barring that, you will need a few volunteers or the time of a few staff members.

Direct mail sounds easy, but it is not. You could end up spending more of the library's time and money than you get back. It is not as effective as the door-to-door, face-to-face solicitation of a capital campaign.

Benefits of Direct Mail Fundraising

- Direct mail is easier than most other fundraising methods.
- Direct mail is a way to identify and enlist new donors.
- Direct mail fosters and sustains relationships with important donors.
- Direct mail reaches donors you can't afford the time or money to contact in other ways.
- Direct mail can be done year-round and on a schedule.
- Direct mail sustains contact with donors even when the fundraising committee is relaxing.
- Direct mail can be focused and personalized to send different messages at different times to different people.

Figure II-20-1 Benefits of Direct Mail Fundraising

PURPOSES

Direct mail is a donor prospecting tool. It will help you get the first gift, and the name of a new donor that can be added to your donor base. You move people from the list of nongivers to those who have given. The next step is to get them to give more. If someone sends you more than $50.00 in the mail, chances are they will give you much more when you visit them in person.

Direct mail is a great way to contact a lot of people without involving an army of volunteers. It is work that can be done almost exclusively by paid staff.

There are four reasons for preferring a direct mail solicitation to contacting people face to face:

1. If you have a small donor base and you want to enlarge it.
2. If your donor list is large and you lack the organization and volunteers to make the face-to-face contacts.
3. If you have a far-reaching alumni list and you strongly believe they will contribute.
4. If you have already built up your direct mail donor list and direct mail is part of your annual campaign.

BENEFITS

Direct mail has many benefits over other forms of fundraising (see Figure II-20-1).

EXAMPLES

A few years ago the library where I work was facing a money crunch. We decided to do a fundraising letter, even though our last effort achieved mixed results. We revised the letter until it would fit on one page. The letter explained the library's need. We created a donor card and a return envelope to send with the letter. Then we developed a list of 262 qualified donors. We discussed premiums, but everything we could afford seemed tacky. Believing that everyone including the librarian should give to their own fundraising effort, I volunteered the fruits of my avocation—fresh homemade bread. Everyone in town knew about my bread concession at the local farmers market. So I offered to deliver a fresh loaf to everyone who gave $50.00 or more to the library. We mailed the letters and money rolled in. Happy donors enjoyed a loaf of fresh bread and the library was $3,100 richer. Out of 262 letters mailed, 80 responses came back with money.

Sandy Sweitzer, Director of Development at the Durham County (North Carolina) Public Library enjoyed some great success with a direct mail solicitation. She said, "We sent out our first annual fund appeal to about 1,500 people, half of whom had given to the library in the past. The previous donors included Friends of the Library or participants in our centennial celebration a few years earlier. With just one simple letter we made $20,000 and have been cultivating donors ever since.

"A man walked in last week to say he had thrown out the first two fund appeals, but now wanted to discuss giving something to honor his wife who had just died. I tried to be polite and not trip over myself because I had never done this before. As we narrowed in on the discussion he said what he'd really like to do is give $5,000–$10,000 for a naming opportunity in the children's area. This demonstrated quite clearly the importance of using a basic annual fund appeal to get people thinking about the library as a place to give" (Sweitzer, 2001).

McCracken, Kansas, lost its high school back in the 1970s. So, when the library board needed money for a new library they appealed to the high school alumni by offering the new library as a home for school trophies and class pictures. They sent out a fundraising letter and raised several thousand dollars, most of it from one donor.

Direct Mail Planning Guide

What is the overall purpose of your fundraising effort?

How does direct mail fit in with other fundraising activities?

Is your contact list large enough to warrant a direct mail campaign?
Yes ___ No ___

Who is going to do the work?

Staff? Do they have the time?

Volunteers? Do you have enough of them?

What method will you use to encourage prospective donors to open your letter?

What is the main point of your letter? Why do you want the money?

What ideas do you have to grab the reader's attention? What will your lead be?

What is the emergency to your request?

How much money are you going to ask for?

What benefits will you offer your donors? Name on a plaque? A premium?

Will the letter have a postscript? What will it say?

What will the package contain?

How many people do you have on your list?

Is there anyone on the list who lives in town and might give more than $500?

What form of postage will you use? First class? Bulk rate stamps?

How will you handle the thank you notes?

Who will be in charge of recognitions?

Figure II-20-2 Direct Mail Planning Guide

HOW TO DO IT

Start by studying the direct mail solicitations you get in the mail. You can learn from the professionals by studying their direct mail solicitations.

Your job as a direct mail solicitor is to get the receiver of your piece to spend more than a few seconds with your request. A lot of direct mail pieces end up unopened in the trash five seconds after the prospective donor receives them. It will tax your skills as a letter writer and publicity design artist. *Maximum Gifts by Return Mail* by Roland Kuniholm is worth buying and reading before you try a direct mail solicitation.

Use the *Direct Mail Planning Guide* (see Figure II-20-2) to help you do it right.

Creating the Direct Mail Piece

Direct mail solicitation is a different kind of a fundraising technique. You are not getting face-to-face with the donor to ask for the gift. So the piece you send has to carry as much personality as you can put into it. It has to look as professional as you can make it without looking glitzy. You have to get the person who receives the mailing to open it or you have wasted your money.

Start with the envelope. Any mailing from the library will probably be opened. Recipients may be glad it is not an overdue notice.

The letter is the most important part. The letter is your appeal. It has to be enthusiastic, yet warm. It has to grab the reader with the first sentence and draw him or her quickly into the message. It has to look good at first glance because appearance is just as important as anything you say.

Creating the Perfect Letter

Let's analyze the letter in greater detail since it is the main part of your appeal.

The salutation. If you can personalize it, do it. Computers and word processors are great for personalizing mass mailings.

The lead. Your first sentence has to stand out like a friendly smile in a hostile crowd. Say something that will make them feel good about the library and your request that will follow.

The body. The body has three parts:

- A statement of your case or why you need the money.
- The appeal based on benefits to the reader or the community.
- The gift request. Don't be subtle; ask for the gift several times.

Express a sense of urgency. Friends, who already know and love the library, will respond well to a straightforward summary of the library's need.

Explain the benefits. The reader doesn't always have to be the direct beneficiary of the gift. Most people don't give because they want a tax write-off equal. They usually give because of some benefit to the community.

Ask for the money. The point of the letter is to get the reader to give money to the library. "Please give" is a simple yet effective way to ask. If you don't ask for the gift they will miss the point of the letter.

Style. Involve your reader as often as possible. Write from the reader's point of view. Align yourself with your reader by making assumptions for the reader. For example, "I am sure you would like to see a big new beautiful library just as much as I would."

Create vivid word pictures. Use graphic colorful words. What do you see when you read, "Our library is a ghetto for books"? Or "Using our library is like crowding two people into a phone booth."

Be yourself. Relax. Put yourself into the picture. Good writers are always visible just behind their words. If you don't care about your need, your reader won't care either.

Be direct. Eliminate clutter from your writing. Don't be wishy-washy. Don't use weasel words. Your fundraising letter will be more effective if you keep it short. Andy Rooney said, "Unclear writing is a result of unclear thinking."

The close. Repeat your strongest plea for money. You want your donor to take out his or checkbook the minute he or she finishes reading your letter and write a check and put it in the mail. Say: "Please give a hundred dollars or whatever you can afford. Do it today!"

Closing salutation. The person who receives the letter needs to feel a kinship with the person who wrote it. Any tasteful closing salutation will do.

Ending postscript. A postscript at the end of the letter will get results. It is the last impression you leave with the person who has read your letter. When a person opens a letter, the first thing they look for is their name at the top. Then they will glance at the signature to see who wrote it. That is when they see your "P.S." While it may appear to be your last chance to convince them to give money, it may be your first chance to tell them your purpose.

Overall the fundraising letter has to be short, direct, and filled with zippy words that carry the fact of the appeal as well as its emotion. It has to grab the reader from the beginning and keep him or her until the end. It has to make him or her want to write a check and send it right away.

Donation Form. Every direct mail fundraising letter must have a donor form. You can put your donation form on the other side of a window envelope. If someone forgets to fill out your form you will still have the donor's address.

The donation form must have the categories of suggested giving. Never suggest less than $50.00. On a one percent return, a gift of $25.00 is the break-even point. Include giving categories that go up to $500 and $1,000.

Return Envelope. Enclose a return envelope that includes permit postage. This added convenience for the donor is proven to produce more gifts. But I don't recommend it for small libraries. The investment in special postal permits and charges for return postage may not be worth the cost.

Premiums. Premiums are an effective way to increase the number and size of the gifts. You offer to give the donor something in exchange for a gift. The premium is worth only a fraction of the value of the gift. Coffee mugs, tote bags, caps, and blankets with the library's logo on them are common examples of premiums.

Too often the premiums you can afford will be tacky and detract from your appeal. Don't use them unless you have something tied especially to your library, or if you have something as unique as my homemade bread.

Package. Everything you do with direct mail must work as a single unit. The envelope should involve the reader enough to make him or her want to open it. The letter should make the reader care for your cause enough to give money. The donation card should make it easy to give. Enclosing a self-addressed envelope makes it even easier.

Ask a friend to look at your direct mail piece through the eyes of someone who uses your library once in a while. Try these questions:

- What words or phrases do you remember?
- How would you restate what you just saw in one sentence?
- As you read this piece, what were your unanswered questions?

If your friend takes out his or her checkbook and writes a check for $100, you know you have a winner. Mail the package and wait for the money to come in.

Mailing the package. Check with the post office to learn about your options. It is better to put a stamp on your mailing piece than to use bulk permit indicia. Buying a bulk rate permit won't be worth it if you don't plan to do a lot of mailings. Every mailing must include at least 200 pieces, and each piece must be identical to every other piece. It may be easier and less expensive to use regular first class stamps.

Sample Direct Mail Letter

Mr. and Mrs. Arthur Hillock
2341 31st Street
Great Bend, Kansas 65730

Dear Mr. and Mrs. Hillock:

The library needs your help! Every year it seems that our book budget doesn't go as far as it did the year before, and there are always things we need that we cannot afford.

Last year the carpet in the library turned 30 years old. We need your help to replace it. For a donation of just $30 we can replace a yard of worn-out carpet with a sparkling new floor covering.

The estimated total cost for the project is $300,000, so we will need lots of people in Great Bend to step up to the plate and hit a homerun for us. We need all of the $30 donations we can get, but we also need some $300 gifts and some $1,000 gifts to guarantee that we reach our goal.

Will you please help us by sending a check to the library today? A gift in any amount will be much appreciated.

Thank you.

Sincerely,

Daisy Smith, President
Library Board of Directors

Figure II-20-3 Sample Direct Mail Letter

Mailing list. Send a letter to anyone who might give you money. Start by making a list of persons who have ever given anything to the library before. If they have given books, magazines, memorial gifts, works of art, or furniture, put their name on the list.

Thank you notes. When the money comes in, send thank you notes right away and record the gift in you donor file. Keep a record of everyone who has given to your library. They are your best prospects for repeat gifts. Treat them like good friends because they are.

RESOURCES

A computer and a good word processing program are the best tools you can get. They are a must. You also need a good database management system to maintain your donor list. Specific fundraising software like ResultsPlus!TM (http://rp.metafile.com/), eTapestry.com (www.etapestry.com/), or FundTrack Software (http://fundtracksoftware.com/) are worth considering, though they will be a little pricey if your are running a smaller library. If you have never done a direct mail campaign before get one of the books listed in the bibliography to give you the how-to information you need.

SPECIAL CONSIDERATIONS

You might want to hire a direct mail fundraising professional. Their services will vary, but they know how to get results. You can find them in the yellow pages or by using a search engine on the Internet and typing in "direct mail fundraising." If you don't have the staff or volunteers, hiring a professional firm may be worth it.

On the other hand if your organization is small and your resources are limited, you could make a direct mail activity very personal and produce a good result. Have a special meeting of the people in your group. Pass out nice letter writing stationery. Ask each one to write a personal letter to five friends, outlining the library's need and a request for a donation. Make sure they specify an amount. Enclose a brochure about the project if you have one. Coordinate the effort so that each prospective donor only gets one letter. Repeat the letter writing activity a few times. This is a labor-intensive effort, but it is 100 times more personal and requires fewer resources.

PITFALLS

Before you crank up the mail merge program and start stamping those envelopes you need to know that direct mail is a very expensive method of donor acquisition. I use the term *donor acquisition* advisedly. You are truly acquiring donors you can count on year after year. It usually takes two or more years before direct mail solicitations make money. You have to invest a fair amount of money and wait awhile before you see a return. The key to direct mail is taking those new donors and turning them into bigger donors or repeat donors, i.e. ones who support your annual campaign, will make memorial/tribute gifts, will come to special events, etc. The real work comes on the other side of the direct mail piece. Don't think you can send out a direct mail piece and avoid contacting people and asking them for a gift. Direct mail is primarily a tool for finding people with a charitable intent toward the library. Then you can employ some of the other techniques in this book.

There is a direct mail consortium for larger urban public libraries that helps lower some of the costs through economies of scale.

You need to beware of a few traps you could innocently fall into. Don't use direct mail in a very small town. You will be much better off to organize a few Friends and informally go visit every family and ask them for money. Face-to-face contacts are much more efficient.

Don't expect to raise a lot of money with your first letter. Results take time to measure. You will do well to break even. You can improve the ratio with your first letter if you combine direct mail with other techniques such as follow-up telephone contacts or personal visits.

Check the list to make sure it is socially correct. You don't want to send a letter addressed to Mr. and Mrs. John Jones if they were recently divorced, or one of them has just died. It is just as bad to send a "Mr. and Mrs." letter to people who have been single for years. People care about the way their name is spelled. You should care too.

FOR SCHOOLS AND ACADEMIC LIBRARIES

Direct mail fundraising can work well for school and academic libraries. Answering the questions on the checklist will help you decide how to do it. As with all fundraising efforts in schools and universities, you need to make sure that your effort is aligned with the general fundraising efforts of the institution.

DIRECT MAIL FUNDRAISING CHECKLIST

Use this checklist to help plan your next direct mail campaign.

1. Have you defined the overall purpose of your total fundraising effort?
2. How does direct mail fit into this picture?
3. Is your contact list large enough to warrant a direct mail campaign?
4. What will you do to get prospective donors to open your letter?
5. Have you explained why the library needs the money?
6. What ideas do you have to grab the reader's attention?
7. How much money are you going to ask for?
8. What benefits will you offer your donors? Name on a plaque? A premium?
9. Is there anyone on the list who should receive a personal visit instead of a letter?
10. What form of postage will you use? First class? Bulk rate stamps?
11. How will you handle the thank you notes?

GETTING RESULTS

Direct mail can be a powerful arrow in your quiver of fundraising methods. It can also have a blunt point. If you are going to try this method give it a high enough priority to guarantee its success.

What Do I Do Next?

The most important step is to decide whether or not to do a direct mail campaign. You could spend a lot of time and money and see paltry results. On the other hand I know of a direct mail campaign that produced a few hundred dollars over $1 million. The one million came from one donor and the rest came from a few donors.

If you are serious about direct mail, get one or more of the books on the topic and make sure your understand what you are doing. If you are the librarian, don't try to do this yourself, though it appears that you can. Get some help and spread the load around.

What Are the Policies and Procedures Needed?

Learn about postal options and regulations. It seems like they change every few years and the rates keep going up, which makes direct mail less attractive. Find out if you can use library funds to solicit donations. It is probably not a good idea even if you can. How would you explain using library money on a fundraising effort that didn't break even?

How Much Time Should This Method Take?

Direct mail is a fundraising effort for the long haul. Be ready to do it for several years and have the backing to stay with it if the results of first years are lean. Don't rush into it. Take the time you need to do a good job and organize every thing down to the stamp. A well-planned and thoroughly developed direct mail campaign could take six months or more to organize and a month or two for the money to come in. The real benefit of direct mail is the donors you uncover that can be solicited for larger gifts using other techniques.

When Can I Expect Results?

The money should start coming in as soon as the first batch of letters goes out. However, it could take a year or more to see a worthwhile return on your investment. Don't count on any real money for three to five years, but you could be surprised with a very large gift that will make a believer out of anyone.

What Can I Realistically Expect the Costs to be?

This is not a low-cost fundraising method. Count spending some real up-front money before you ever see a dollar in return. For every mailing piece you plan to send out, count on spending $1.00 to $1.50 for printing and mailing. Besides that you will need office space and staff. You can spend $1,000 or more on fundraising software. You could pay a professional $3,000 or more to develop and write you a mailing piece. Be aware of the costs going in and plan every step carefully. You don't want any surprise costs to foil your efforts halfway into the project.

SUMMARY

Direct mail is a great way to expand your donor base, but the first time out it will probably cost as much money as you make. After you have a list of donors, you can send for renewals and make money. The more often you send a fundraising letter to a donor, the more money you will make. If you are creative in developing new reasons to request money you can send out a letter up to eight times per year and make money each time.

BIBLIOGRAPHY

Kuniholm, Roland. 1989. *Maximum Gifts by Return Mail.* Ambler, Pa.: Fundraising Institute. This book shows you how to write fundraising letters that will get results every time. With hundreds of examples, Roland Kuniholm teaches everything you need to know about writing a successful fundraising letter.

Warwick, Mal. 1996. *Raising Money by Mail: Strategies for Growth and Financial Stability,* rev. ed. Chicago: Strathmoor Press. *Raising Money by Mail* takes an innovative straightforward approach to conducting a direct mail campaign. It will help you build a solid base for a successful future. The format makes it easy to train staff members.

Warwick, Mal. 2001. *How to Write Successful Fundraising Letters.* San Francisco: Jossey-Bass. If you write fundraising letters for a hospital, a college or university, a museum, a health agency, a social service organization, or any nonprofit that needs funds.

Chapter 21

Sponsor Special Events

DESCRIPTION

Special events differ from annual events in that they happen once and may never be used again by the library as a fundraising opportunity. Special events fundraising brings something unique or unusual to the community. They often involve special people, special activities, or special food. People enjoy them, but special events are a lot of work. They usually generate more good will than money. They also transmit valuable facts to the public about your library and its projects. Organizations can and do lose money on special events—especially when the costs are not contained by contract ahead of time.

Most of the time the cost to participate will approximate the actual value of a similar event available locally.

PURPOSES

All special events are designed to give donors a good time in return for their money, even if it is just a chance to win a quilt or a pickup. The main purpose is to raise money for the library—money you can spend for a predetermined purpose.

BENEFITS

People come to special events for the fun of it as well as to give financial support to the library. They also come to see and be seen with the right crowd—that could be their friends or neighbors, their political buddies, or just other people who like to have fun, too. You are just providing a social opportunity for them.

Your event could be an opportunity to train new community leaders, recruit or train new volunteers, find new donors, or to vary the sources of funding.

EXAMPLES

Here is a short list of special events and a brief description of how they work.

- Animal rides—The more exotic the better. Elephants are better than donkeys. You contract with the owner of the animal(s) to give rides to children or adults for a certain number of hours. You collect the money and the profit belongs to the library.
- Art exhibit—The premier showing of a famous artist or a successful local artist is worth something extra. Hold a champagne reception and charge enough to make some money.
- Author book talk—Charge an admission fee or ask the author to donate 20 to 30 percent of the sale of his or her books.
- Casino night—Everybody pays $10 or more to get in. Set up a cash bar and gambling games. Everyone plays with play money. At the end of the evening hold an auction for donated items.
- Circus—Contract with a traveling circus group. Sell tickets and hope enough people come to cover your costs.
- Cruise—Set up a deal with a travel agency. They contact the cruise line and book the rooms. For every eight rooms you sell the cruise line will give you a complimentary room. You sell the free rooms and pocket the difference for the library. Depending on the time of year, destination, and length of the cruise you could make up to $10,000 if 160 people signed up.
- Evening with _____.—Actors portray famous people in history. Abraham Lincoln, Annie Oakley, and Mark Twain are common subjects. Make arrangements with an actor and sell tickets. A reception or book signing will enhance the value of the activity and the cost of the ticket.
- Golf tournament—Find an underwriting sponsor for the tournament. Invite a celebrity golfer to give an exhibition. Ask local golfers to participate. They each pay an entry fee. You give prizes for the lowest scores and a special prize for a "hole in one." Sell tickets to spectators.
- Library night at the _____—Common examples are professional sporting events and the theatre. They are delighted to sell tickets at a discount. The library raises money by charging more than it paid for the tickets—usually 20 to 40 percent more. Another

option is to add value to the ticket with a meal, a reception, transportation, or all of the above.

- Author signing and auction at a local bookstore—Invite local authors to come to a book-signing event. Let the bookstore pick up the cost for advertising and printing. The Houston Public Library makes $10,000 a year from an event like this. The library gets all of the proceeds from the silent auction and the live auction, and then a portion of all the sales of books throughout the night. The bookstore recruits the authors and does most of the work.

- Movie premieres—Make a deal with the movie theatre and sell tickets at a higher than normal price. Include a raffle ticket for something worth a lot of money and double the price of the ticket.

- Musical concert—Arrange with a musical group or artist to do a benefit concert. A home-grown group that has made the big time may be willing to come home and do a free concert. Some musical groups on tour barely make their expenses. A deal for "20 percent after expenses" could leave you holding an empty bag.

- Vehicle rides—Airplane and helicopter rides are popular, but what about a ride in a tank, a harvesting combine, or some other superlarge vehicle. If you can get the owner to donate the use of his or her vehicle, everything you take in is profit.

- Discount to local attraction—The Houston Public Library did a three-way partnership with the utility company who printed discount coupons to the Space Center Houston. These were included in all the utility bills with an article in the newsletter/insert. The coupon was good for $2.00 off the admission price. Each coupon was good for up to six people, and for each person entering with a coupon the library got 50 cents for each coupon used. The library made more than $11,000 off this promotion/collaboration, which lasted three months. They also got tons of free publicity and money.

HOW TO DO IT

Holding a special event is very much like starting a small business. The similarities are striking. For example, put on dinner and you are opening a restaurant for one night. Professionals have a hard time making a go of it. What makes you think you can make enough money to make a difference for your library? Most small businesses expect a three to five-year struggle before they make a profit.

Start by selecting an event that will fit in your community. Sponsor something people like to do. Polka or square dancing is really popular in some parts of Kansas. A night at a Royals baseball game is popular in the Kansas City area. Wine tasting is popular in the Napa Valley of California. Use regular supporters to help you decide on the activity.

Find partners who are willing to help the library because the special event will also benefit their image. If you can find a business that regularly mails a bill to a lot of people in your city, ask them to include a promotional piece for the library's special event—you will save a ton of money on advertising. Partner with another nonprofit group. Share the work. Share the profits and do something that neither of you could do working alone.

Develop various ways to enhance your income from a special event by asking sponsors to pay some or all of the expenses associated with the event. Sponsors can also add experience and expertise. They can provide staffing and donate goods. Their support will add strength and credibility to your special event.

Recruit lots of volunteers to sell tickets and to staff the events.

Advertise every way you can think of. If the event is going on all day try to arrange with a radio station to do a remote broadcast from the event and invite people to come to the event while it is still going on.

Think big. Sometimes librarians and others in small communities get trapped in their small-town mentality. Don't get bogged down thinking you don't have enough time, staff, and resources to put into a special event. You might be surprised to learn what you can do if you get the right kind of help to proceed with confidence.

Do an event feasibility study. Answer these questions as accurately as you can.

- What are the projected personnel costs?
- What are the other big expenses?
- How much net income do you have to clear?
- How much gross income will be required?
- How much income can you count on from underwriters and sponsors?
- How much income can you count on from advertising associated with the event?
- How much income will come from ticket sales?
- How much income will come from door prize drawing, etc.?
- How much income can you count on from sales at the event?

The answers to these questions can help you decide whether to hold a special event or not.

RESOURCES

Because scheduling is critical to the success of your special event, you will need access to the events calendar of other organizations in the community. If you plan to solicit by mail, you will need a good mailing list. The ability to accept credit cards as a form of payment is becoming almost a necessity for fundraising groups. It has been shown to increase the number of sales and the amount of each item purchased.

SPECIAL CONSIDERATIONS

A special event fundraising is an effort to get money from nonconstituents. They want something for their money and they expect a good time. Even though people understand that your special event is a benefit for the library, they expect fair value for their money.

Don't steal a successful idea from another group in your own town or a nearby town. The best way to get the people in these organizations to support your fundraisers is to support their fundraisers.

Sponsors can go to a great deal of trouble to create a memorable evening. You don't have to do that. Instead, let someone else put on the show, and devote the group's energy to selling the tickets.

PITFALLS

If you have to pay individuals to perform at the event, lock in all of your costs, and get sponsors to pay for as many of the expenses as possible.

While some ideas are basically sound, they fail because of inadequate planning and implementation. Not every idea works. It is wisest to avoid altogether some special event fundraisers (see Figure II-21-1).

Reasons for Failure of Special Events

Special events fail because:

- They cost too much to put on.
- The price to participate is not high enough.
- The sponsoring organization doesn't sell enough tickets.
- The group can't pay for up-front costs.
- Nonconstituents are not willing to pay $25 for a $15 dinner.
- What can go wrong will go wrong.

Some Fundraising Activities to Avoid

- Car washes—It is hard to make a lot of money at a car wash. Volunteers get soaked and dirty and the weather can ruin the event before it gets started.
- Slave auctions—They may be embarrassing to the participants and cost the library some valuable public relations.
- Big-ticket raffles—Homes and cars top the list in this category. The organization has to pay for the home or the car and it is difficult to sell enough tickets to recover the costs. Occasionally, someone will donate a car— then you might be able to make some money.
- Gambling—Some people have ethical concerns about gambling in general. This can cause public relations problems. Most states have laws that regulate gambling—even for nonprofit fundraising.
- Jailed local leaders—Someone calls a local leader and gets them to agree to spend an hour in the fundraising jail. The reluctant volunteer has to get his friends to bail him out. The potential for offending someone is high.
- Adult entertainment—While R-rated humor may be acceptable in some circles, the library doesn't need to be exposed to unwanted criticism.

Figure II-21-1 Some Fundraising Activities to Avoid

FOR SCHOOLS AND ACADEMIC LIBRARIES

The fortunes of school and academic libraries can rise and fall with special events just as easily as they can for other libraries. Everything in this section applies equally to all libraries.

CHECKLIST

Use this checklist to pre-assess the success of a planned special event fundraiser:

1. Are there enough people in the community who enjoy doing the activity you are planning to make it commercially successful?
2. Would your activity infringe on a special event of another group?
3. Is the price for participation progressive to allow everyone to participate, yet encourage larger contributions from those who can afford to pay more?
4. Can you lock down your cost from the beginning?
5. Will providers or sponsors underwrite the costs of the event so that all or most of the income will be profit?
6. Do you have enough volunteers to do all the necessary work?
7. Is every one of the volunteers 100 percent behind the activity?
8. Do you have a "Plan B" and a "Plan C" to allow for every contingency?

9. Have you timed your event to fit with other activities in the community?
10. Are people guaranteed to have a good time?

GETTING RESULTS

Holding a special event is always a risk. Even lots of hard work will not guarantee a good result. Every special event is different. It is possible to make a lot of money. It is also possible to lose money.

What Do I Do Next?

Look at your overall fundraising goals. Consider your human and financial resources. Determine if a special event fits with other fundraising efforts. The last thing I want you to face is a bunch of frustrated volunteers who have given their all for the last six months to turn a profit of only a few thousand dollars.

Once you decide to move forward, recruit good leaders and volunteers based on creativity and management skills. Do everything you can to guarantee the success of the special event you have selected.

What Are the Policies and Procedures Needed?

Here again, the issues of sales tax and tax deductions come up. Find out what the rules are and abide by them.

Contracts with well-known performers can be complicated. So can contracts with concert facilities. Count on them being drawn up by a lawyer. Have your lawyer look over your contract before you sign.

How Much Time Should This Method Take?

Most big special events that last for an evening require up to a year of planning. Small special events that use local people can take much less time. If you are going to advertise and sell tickets you need to allow time for the word to get out and give ticket sellers the opportunity to contact everyone who might possibly buy a ticket.

When Can I Expect Results?

Large special events could take more than a year to put on. Others will take much less time. You should see all of the money collected and all of the expenses paid within 60 days after the event.

What Can I Realistically Expect the Costs to Be?

Costs will vary from event to event. In a small town you might be able to rent the local VFW hall for $100 per night for a dance, hire a polka band from the next town over for $400, and print the tickets on the copy machine at the library. If you sell a hundred tickets at $10.00 each everyone has a good time and you make a profit of $500.

A comparable event in a large city renting the ballroom of a swanky hotel with all of the amenities might cost $3,000 or more. Hiring a chamber orchestra from a hundred miles away could cost $7,000 to $10,000 including expenses. You would have to sell a thousand tickets at $20.00 each to make the same margin of profit.

See the list of potential expenses in the section on annual events for an idea on other cost items.

SUMMARY

If you are holding a special event just for the money, find another way to make the money. You will more than likely find that it will be too much work and not enough money. Special events can still be a lot of fun and bring the community together in a social activity that everyone will enjoy. Your event could be an opportunity to train new community leaders, recruit or train new volunteers, or find new donors. Here are the main points of holding special events:

- Special event fundraising is an effort to get money from nonconstituents.
- Special event fundraising brings something unique or unusual to the community.
- People enjoy special events, but they are a lot of work.
- People who come to a special event expect fair value for their money.
- Libraries often lose money on special events despite incalculable hours of hard work by many volunteers.
- Avoid failure by carefully planning everything and then get sponsors to cover the costs.

BIBLIOGRAPHY

Allen, Judy. 2000. *Event Planning: The Ultimate Guide to Successful Meetings, Corporate Events, Fundraising Galas, Conferences, Conventions, Incentives, and Other Special Events.* Toronto: John Wiley & Sons Canada. The helpful insights revealed by the author from her experiences make this book a must-read for every event planner. The author references her Web site, which includes additional advice and insights. If you are thinking about a gala fundraising event, don't do it without this book. The location of your special event is the key to your success. Judy Allen makes that point perfectly clear in this book.

Armstrong, James. 2001. *Planning Special Events*. San Francisco, Calif.: Jossey-Bass Wiley. This book will show you how to produce special events that will make money and expand your donor base. James Armstrong's step-by-step guide will lead you through the maze of managing a special event. It has lots of worksheets and examples to make events planning easier.

Freedman, Harry A., and Karen Feldman. 1998. *The Business of Special Events: Fundraising Strategies for Changing Times*. Sarasota, Fla.: Pineapple Press. This book takes the business of planning a special event and lays it out piece by piece. It covers the full gamut of the topic without leaving out a thing. Full of samples, examples, tips, and suggestions, this book is the last word on special events.

Harrison, Bill J. 1996. *Fundraising; The Good, the Bad and the Ugly and How to Tell the Difference*. Mesa, Ariz.: Bill J. Harrison (P.O. Box 4705, Mesa, AZ 85211-4705). This book addresses a broad range of fundraising topics from special events, to involving board members and volunteers, to soliciting donations from corporations.

Chapter 22

Publish and Sell a Cookbook

DESCRIPTION

Publishing and selling a cookbook is a good moneymaker. Cookbooks are easy to sell because they make nice gifts. Plus, everyone in your organization will want at least one.

Members of the organization gather recipes from all of their friends and type them up on cards and send them to a fundraising cookbook publisher. The publishers offer a variety of bindings including: a looseleaf notebook, a plastic comb binding, or a metal/plastic spiral binding. Publishers charge according to the binding, the number of pages, and the number of copies you order. They often require an up-front commitment of cash, but some publishers will give you a month or so to sell enough of the books to pay for the publishing. When the cookbooks arrive volunteers go out and sell them. Several libraries I know of have made a few thousand dollars from an $8.00 cookbook.

PURPOSES

While the main purpose of publishing and selling a cookbook is to make money for the library, many other positive outcomes are possible. Publishing a cookbook as a group will build a sense of ownership and buy-in for the fundraising effort—especially when everyone submits at least one recipe. In some cases, there is an unspoken competition to submit the most elegant recipe or the recipe to a simple dish that tastes good. The cookbook becomes a community project, and now everyone has to have a copy, even if it is just to see his or her name in print.

BENEFITS

Sometimes Friends groups need something to do to keep them alive. This is a good project for them. Members get involved gathering recipes and selling the books. Idle Friends groups may end up defunct.

Selling cookbooks could be a training activity for other, more difficult fundraising activities like soliciting for money.

The main benefit of publishing and selling a cookbook is the money it brings in for the library. If you haven't tried this one, try it. You will be surprised at the amount of money it will bring in.

EXAMPLE

When the Elroy (Wisconsin) Public Library needed a photocopier, librarian Barbara DeLong put together a community cookbook. The library staff solicited ads from local businesses and recipes from the community. They sold the cookbook for $5.00, netting over $1,300.

They planned it so the cookbook arrived early November for sale as Christmas gifts. The cookbook cover featured a photo of the library as it appeared in 1908. The text featured a short history of the library at the beginning of the book.

HOW TO DO IT

Start by searching the Internet for publishers of fundraising cookbooks. Search on the phrase, "cookbook publisher." Add "fundraising" to narrow the search.

Compare the various publishers you find. They each have their own special services and claim to superiority. Determine the features you want in your cookbook and select the publisher that will best match your requirements.

Pricing will vary. Generally, the cost of each book is based on the number of pages you print, the binding, who does the typesetting, and the cover. The more books you order the lower the unit price.

Request or order a getting started kit. This kit will detail your options, including pricing, binding and cover options, paper and graphic choices, and preferences for typesetting. This kit will give you step-by-step guidance to help you design your book, collect and organize the recipes, and prepare your book for publication. Review your options carefully and with the group and set a tentative goal for the number of recipes/pages and the number of books you plan to publish. Estimate the number of recipes you will need from each member of the group or set a limit if you have a large group.

Collect the recipes from your group. Make it easy for them to submit their recipes. You could eliminate a lot of old favorite recipes, if you require them to be typewritten or in electronic format. Give or send recipe forms to everyone who is invited to submit recipes, and make it easy for your members to return the forms.

Decide who will set the type. Some publishers give you the choice of doing it yourself or letting them do it. It will cost you more money to let them do it, but the book will probably look better if they do it. If they request that the text be submitted in electronic format, it could cost you less. If you decide to do the typesetting yourself do it on a computer, using a standard word processing program and a laser printer. If you send the publisher camera-ready copy they will take a picture of each page and print it the way the camera sees it—misspelled words and all.

Once you have all the recipes together and you have decided how the type will be set estimate the number of pages and make a decision about the length of the cookbook and the number of copies. A cookbook with less than 200 recipes is considered the minimum size worth printing. The least number of books considered economical to print is in the range of 250 to 350 books. Prices for books of this size in these quantities will cost between $2.50 and $3.50. They can be sold for between $6.00 and $8.00. I do not recommend going this small. If you are going to all the work to produce a cookbook, think bigger.

Estimate the number of books you can sell by multiplying the number of people who are going to sell the book by ten. Some people will sell more than others, some will sell less. It might take you a while to get rid of all the books, but think of all the money you will make when the last one is sold. If you have a group of 100 people order 1,000 books. A thousand books with 500 recipes will cost between $3.00 and $4.00, and you can sell them for between $8.00 and $12.00. Your profits will range from $4,000 to $9,000. All of this depends on a lot of variables you select.

Do something special to make your book one-of-a-kind. Include a picture of the library, a history of the library, or something else that will make people want to buy it for more than just the recipes. Work with the publisher to make it unique. If you want to use photos send the original to the publisher to get the very best reproduction possible.

Pay particular attention to the cover. A colorful plastic cover will attract more buyers and make a nicer looking gift. If you are selling the book to be a gift to others, people will pay more for an attractive professional-looking book. They won't buy it at all if it looks cheap or home-made. Most publishers offer a hardcover with any of their bindings for a little more money.

Cookbooks take a lot of wear and tear, and often get stained. Have the book printed on top-quality, acid-free, 60-pound offset paper. This will make the book more appealing to buyers.

Type size and face can make a difference. If you are planning to sell it to senior citizens do them a favor and use 14-point type. This will increase the cost, but you could sell it as a large print cookbook. A serif-type like Times Roman is easier to read. San serif type fonts like Helvetica and Arial are more difficult to read.

I cook a lot and I hate cookbooks that don't lay open flat on the counter when I am putting a dish together. This is an essential consideration for the binding of a cookbook. Loose-leaf notebooks, plastic comb, and spiral bound books will all lay open flat.

Once you have your cookbook designed the way you want it, get a final quote from more than one publisher. You may be surprised at the difference. If you lack the up-front money that some publishers require, you may have to go with a publisher who will give you 30 days before the first payment is due.

The best time to sell a cookbook is a month or more before the holidays. People are usually in a generous mood and will be glad for the opportunity to buy a gift for less than $20. Time your order with the publisher to make sure your cookbooks are delivered around the first of November.

RESOURCES

Use the Internet to help you find publishers and ideas for your cookbook.

Obtain a planning packet from several publishers of cookbooks. These kits will be your best resource. They will take you through the process one step at a time.

Count on members of your group for recipes and help to compile the book. Committed enthusiasm is always a great resource for any fundraising activity.

Get access to a computer with a powerful word processing program, like Microsoft Word or Word Perfect. If you are not using a computer you are working hard and not smart.

SPECIAL CONSIDERATIONS

Publishing and selling a cookbook will not solve all of your fundraising goals, but it can be a significant arrow in your quiver. Here are a few tips to consider as you plan your cookbook:

- Order more cookbooks than you think you can sell. Every cookbook project will have a break-even point—the point at which the profit from the books you have sold covers the cost of all the books. Beyond that point every one you sell is pure profit.
- Make sure that you have recipes from every member in your group—even if you have to visit him or her at home and wait while he or she writes out the recipe. Everyone likes to see his or her name in print.
- Carefully consider whether or not you want advertising in your book. The revenue from advertising may not offset lost sales because it contains advertising. Remember that school yearbooks have advertising and most students still buy one.
- Make sure your book is as near perfect as you can make it. You will sell more books and make more money.
- Find a place for passive selling like on a shelf behind the circulation desk. Your patrons may see the book and want a copy.

PITFALLS

A cookbook project is almost foolproof, but there are a few things to avoid. These tips will help you maximize your profits:

- Don't slap your cookbook together and call it good or try to get by cheaply. Cheap is often very expensive.
- Don't use every recipe you receive from your members. Set guidelines ahead of time and follow them. Some recipes may be too complicated, difficult to follow, or too easy like opening three cans of something and heating them in a microwave.
- Don't count on every member to sell his or her quota of books. Better yet don't set quotas at all. Every person has a different circle of friends and has a different comfort level of selling things to his or her friends.
- Don't order way too many books from the publisher. You can always submit a second order when the first order runs out.
- Don't set the price of your cookbook too low. People who buy it will know that it is a fundraising project for your library and will be willing to pay a little more, even though they could buy a com-

parable book for less in a store. The hook is they are buying a unique item.

- Don't finalize a cookbook project if you don't have the united support of everyone in the group. Your effort could fall flat on its face if no one wants to sell the books when they come in.

FOR SCHOOLS AND ACADEMIC LIBRARIES

A school library could try a cookbook project, but I would leave this one to the parent-teacher organization. They will have a larger constituent base. Maybe they will give the library some of the money they raise.

I believe there are better ways for an academic library to raise money. The effort spent on a cookbook could be redirected toward more profitable fundraising projects.

CHECKLIST

Here is a planning checklist for publishing and selling a cookbook.

1. Do you have enough members in your organization to compile and sell the cookbook?
2. Does the leadership of the organization have the drive to make it happen?
3. Have you done the necessary research to make decisions for success with the cookbook?
4. How will you get the recipes?
5. What format will you accept?
6. How many recipes will the book have?
7. Will you set the type or have the publisher do it?
8. How many copies will you have printed?
9. What will you do to make your book unique and attractive as a gift?
10. Are all of the members of the group willing to go out and sell the book?

GETTING RESULTS

Of the entire list of moneymaking projects mentioned in this book, I like this one the best. It is a relatively easy project to accomplish, and it has the best potential for making a lot of money.

What Do I Do Next?

Gather information from several cookbook companies and present this to the group as a possible fundraising activity. Make sure everyone is aware of the work involved and the commitment he or she will have to make. Once the group selects a publisher, get a copy of their startup kit and full steam ahead using the "How to do it" section of this chapter.

What Are the Policies and Procedures Needed?

Copyright issues could be a problem, though it might be difficult to prove that someone from your organization decided to include a recipe from a recent issue of *Good Housekeeping*.

You will need to set up procedures to gather and sort the recipes. If you want to have the right to not include some recipes, make sure everyone understands the selection criteria in advance.

Again, sales tax laws may apply. Find out and make sure everyone who sells books understands the law.

How Much Time Should This Method Take?

To do a good job with a cookbook, count on spending a year—six months to get it published and six months to sell it. It may even take longer to sell the last few cookbooks.

When Can I Expect Results?

If you plan to pay $5.00 for each cookbook and sell them for $10.00 the group doesn't make any money until they have sold half of all the cookbooks. From then on every book you sell is 100 percent pure profit. Selling them all could take more than a year.

What Can I Realistically Expect the Costs to Be?

The up-front costs are negligible. Most publishers will give nonprofit groups a month or two after the books are delivered before the first payment is due. You might have some expenses connected with typesetting the book or gathering the recipes. You can expect to clear anywhere from a few thousand dollars to over $10,000 with a cookbook.

SUMMARY

Cookbook projects are good moneymakers and can be a lot of fun. Cookbooks are easy to sell because they make nice gifts. Selling cookbooks could be a training activity for other, more difficult fundraising activities like soliciting for money.

Using the Internet as a research tool is a good place to start. You will find several reputable publishers who provide lots of ideas to make your project successful. Buy a few kits to help you survey the landscape of cookbook publishing.

Basically, a cookbook project involves:

- Gathering recipes from members of the organization.
- Sorting and organizing the recipes.
- Putting the recipes in an acceptable format to send to the publisher.
- Deciding how many pages the book will have and how many copies of the book to order.
- Contracting with the publisher.
- Selling the books and paying for publication costs.

You can make from $1,000 to $10,000, depending on the size and number of cookbooks. The more books you can order and sell, the more money you will make.

BIBLIOGRAPHY

Beahm, George W. 1985. *How to Publish and Sell Your Cookbook: A Guide for Fundraisers*. Hampton, Va.: GB Publishers. This book is for fundraisers who want to publish a cookbook. The ideas included are worth seeing before you start work on your cookbook.

Schmidt, R. Marilyn. 1995. *How to Write and Publish a Family Cookbook*. Barnegat Light, N.J.: Pine Barrens Press. Written for individuals who want to publish their own cookbook, this book has some good suggestions for any fundraising group planning to publish a cookbook.

Chapter 23

Organize a Used Book Sale

DESCRIPTION

Successful book sales require getting used books from almost everyone in town, picking out the best ones for the sale, and selling them for as much money as you can get. It takes a lot of hard work from a lot of volunteers. Think big and involve everyone who will volunteer. Book lovers enjoy handling and rummaging through old books. A book sale is a ready-made activity for the Friends of the Library. Why not turn your sale over to them? They will have a ball. A book sale is fun for them and good publicity, too. It can be a great tool for the Friends to recruit new members. When it is done right, it could be the big annual event for the Friends.

PURPOSES

The proceeds of a used book sale can be spent any way you want, unless the proceeds go to the treasury of the Friends of the Library. If they do all of the work they should get all of the money. If the library contributes the books, then maybe they should split the money based on a prearranged agreement. It doesn't pay to quibble with the Friends over the proceeds of a book sale. The library and Friends should already be on the same page.

BENEFITS

The public relations value of a book sale is immeasurable. It is truly a win-win situation. The donor gets rid of books he or she no longer wants. The buyer gets a bargain. The library gets a few books it can add to the collection. The Friends get a lot of visibility and new members. The library benefits from the fundraising effort. The whole town feels good about it.

EXAMPLES

You don't have to be in a large town to make money from a used book sale. The library in Cooperstown, New York (population 2,500), earns more than $2,000 each year with their Fourth of July book sale. A dollar per capita isn't bad for a book sale.

The Friends Book Fair of the St. Charles City County (Missouri) Library is the next to largest used book sale in the St. Louis area. They boast over 300,000 items in their sale. All items are sorted into standard categories. Hardbacks sell for $2.00 and paperbacks sell for $1.00 each. Prices are reduced on Saturday, and on Sunday, books sell for $3.00 for a full grocery bag. The Friends give all the money to the library.

HOW TO DO IT

You start by encouraging people to bring their used books to the library. Of course the library always gets "first dibs" on any books that fit the criteria for its collection. You can fill in missing periodicals, restock the paperback racks and fill in a special collection with donated books.

Most libraries accept gifts with the understanding that books donated to the library, but not used in the collection, will go to the book sale or whatever is best for the library.

Someone has to be in charge of the book sale. Unlike the chair of a capital campaign, the chair of the book sale doesn't have to give money or even give books. He or she has to be willing to work and be able to tell others what to do. It helps to have a set of grubby clothes because used books can be dusty. The planning guide in Figure II-23-1 will help the committee organize their efforts.

Getting the Books

Once you have made the decision to hold a book sale, the next step is to get some books to sell. Make it easy for people that have books they don't want, but can't bear to throw away. Write a story for the local newspaper about the sale, telling how to donate books. Place a classified ad with the garage sale notices to bring in garage sale leftovers.

Make up a flyer telling what you will accept and where to bring the books. Mention that the donation is tax-deductible as a charitable contribution. Whatever you use, make it clear how to get the books to you.

Planning Worksheet for a Used Book Sale

1. Who will be in charge?

2. What committees will you have? (Publicity, sorting, pricing, hauling, set up, take down, recruiting volunteers, securing books, etc.)

3. Who will head each of these committees?

4. When will you have it? (Spring, Summer, or Fall? In conjunction with something else?)

5. Where will you have it? (At the library? Indoors or outdoors?)

6. Where will you store the books before the book sale?

7. How will you display them? (Shelves, tables, boxes?)

8. How will you advertise to get books?

9. How will you advertise to get customers for the sale?

10. What will you accept as donations?

11. How will you handle thank you notes and receipts?

12. What will your price range be?

Figure II-23-1 Planning Worksheet for a Used Book Sale

Staff members and volunteers who accept donations have to have receipt forms to give donors for income tax purposes. When you issue a receipt for used books, do not place a dollar value on the donation. The IRS says that the valuation is the responsibility of the donor. You are best off issuing a receipt that states the number of hardback books, paperbacks, and any other materials donated. Don't forget to say thank you and put their names on your donor list.

In your publicity, stress the following:

- What the library will accept.
- How to get it to the library.
- The donation is tax-deductible.
- All proceeds benefit the library.

If you decide to include discarded books from the library collection, make sure you can do it legally. If it is all right, mark the books in several places with one inch high letters that say something like this, "NO LONGER THE PROPERTY OF LITTLETOWN PUBLIC LIBRARY." After the library staff has gone to the trouble of withdrawing the book from the shelves and removing the bibliographic record from the catalog, you don't want the book to find its way back in the library.

Sorting and Pricing

The success of your book sale will depend on the amount of sorting and organizing you do. If your book sale brings in $10,000 to $30,000 per year, sorting and pricing will go on year-round. Yes, people do like to browse and find hidden treasures at book sales, but with 20,000 to 30,000 books to look through, they will appreciate whatever sorting you do ahead of time.

Try separating the paperbacks into westerns, romances, children's books, nonfiction, and novels. Do the same for the hardbacks. Organize the hardback nonfiction into the ten Dewey Decimal classes. Make a special display for science fiction, westerns, and children's materials. They always sell out.

Before the sale, eliminate from the sale books that are damaged, falling apart, or smell bad. Eliminating the really unsightly and out-of-date items from the tables and shelves makes the rest of the books in the sale more attractive.

You may also find some very valuable books. You will want to handle them separately. Put aside books on your home state or books by local authors. Display these books in a special way and charge more for them. Do the same with "almost new" books. Hold a silent auction for them.

First editions of famous authors, books autographed by the author, or anything that looks special to you, can claim a premium price. Make it as easy as possible for your buyers to find what they want, if you have it.

Train the people who will be selling the books and give them enough change to work with. Make sure you have plenty of plastic bags for people to carry their books home in.

Early Considerations

If you want to try a book sale, some early decisions include:

- When will you hold the sale?
- How long will you hold the sale?
- Where can you hold the sale?
- Will you have to pay rent, supply your own tables?
- Will you have adequate time beforehand to set up and afterwards to clear out?
- Will you be accessible to the disabled? Will you have enough room in the library for sorting books?
- Who will help you? You will need people to move the books around and people to sort and price. You will need publicity people to solicit donations and promote the sale.
- What materials will you accept? Besides books, you can ask for and sell magazines, records, tapes, art prints, sewing patterns, maps, games, and puzzles. You will be surprised at what people will buy if they think they are getting a bargain.
- How much will you charge? Pricing is the key to the success of your book sale. Charging too much will cost you sales and you could be stuck with books that didn't sell. If you charge too little, your profits will suffer.
- Will you charge admission for a preview to the book sale? Most people who make the effort to come to a book sale will be glad to pay a dollar or two to get first pick at the books. Many Friends groups use the book sale as a membership perk and to solicit new memberships.

RESOURCES

Books are heavy and the best tools you can have are several hand trucks or other devices to move the books around. Of course you will need lots of volunteers with strong backs to haul the books. You will also need lots of room and plenty of tables for the books.

SPECIAL CONSIDERATIONS

- If a customer really wants a book he or she will buy it for a dollar as readily as for a nickel. If she doesn't want it, she won't carry it home as a gift.
- Customers adjust their thinking to whatever price range you establish. If most books are 5 cents, a book for 25 cents becomes something to think about twice. If most books are $1.00, a book for 50 cents is a bargain.
- A book valued at $20.00 by a dealer won't sell for 20 cents, unless someone who wants and values its content comes to your sale.
- Small increments in price usually are meaningless and make life harder for the workers. What is the difference between a 35-cent book and a 40-cent book? Try pricing everything in 25 cent or 50 cent increments.

PITFALLS

Since you only earn about $5.00 for every hour spent on a book sale, it doesn't pay to assign staff members to work the book sale as part of their work for the library, although someone from the library has to go through the books as they come in to determine if the library can use some of the better ones.

FOR SCHOOLS AND ACADEMIC LIBRARIES

I don't recommend used book sales for school libraries. If they can get worthwhile books donated in sufficient quantities they may be able to make it work. Discarded books from a school library probably won't be worth very much. I would recommend a new book sale instead.

Academic libraries rarely discard books. They can find better ways to bring in extra money.

CHECKLIST

Once you decide to hold a book sale, answer the questions in Figure II-23-1 before you move ahead.

GETTING RESULTS

In many libraries the used book sale is an annual event. The level of success depends on the number and quality of books for sale.

What Do I Do Next?

Set a date for the book fair, advertise for books, and line up volunteers to help. Of course you will accept used books as gifts all year long. Once you have scheduled the book sale organize the committee and let them help sort and price the books. Or better yet, turn the whole business over to the Friends of the Library.

What Are the Policies and Procedures Needed?

You can give a receipt to people who donate books, but you cannot put a value on the donation. They have to do that. People who buy books at the sale get no tax deduction. Again, sales tax laws may apply but they may not because the books are used.

Books selected to be added to the library's collection should meet the same standards for condition, content, etc. as any other book added to the collection.

How Much Time Should This Method Take?

It takes about a year to gather enough good used books to have a sale worth the effort. Try to schedule the library's used book sale about the same time every year.

When Can I Expect Results?

You can expect to spend the money every year right after the book sale. Unless you have designated the book sale money for something specific like new books, you can spend it for whatever the library needs most.

What Can I Realistically Expect the Costs to Be?

A book sale is a low-overhead project. Your inventory is free. Your expenses are low, and you can realize about $5.00 for every volunteer-hour spent on the book sale. The cost for advertising is the only major expense. Count on spending between 3 and 5 percent of your expected income for advertising. Refreshments for volunteers might run a dollar per person.

SUMMARY

Successful book sales require getting used books from almost everyone in town and then sorting and displaying them attractively. People who love books enjoy handling and rummaging through them. Here are the main points to having a used book sale:

- A book sale is a ready-made activity for the Friends of the Library.

- A book sale is fun for the Friends and good for publicity, too.
- The public relations value of a book sale is immeasurable.
- The library gets a few books it can add to the collection.
- Most libraries accept gifts with the understanding that books do-nated to the library but not used in the collection will go to the book sale.
- Before the sale discard books that are damaged, falling apart, or smell bad.

Since you only earn about $5.00 for every hour spent on a book sale, it doesn't pay to assign staff members to work the book sale as part of their work for the library.

BIBLIOGRAPHY

Dumas, Jo Ann, and Pat Ditzler. 1999. *Book Sale Survival Kit: A Step-by-Step Guide to Used Book Sale Success*. Lancaster, Pa.: Treetops Press. One of only a few resources on used book sales, this work gives you the tools to hold a book sale and survive the experience. It has wonderful suggestions on how to get book donations, how to recruit volunteers, how to organize the book sale committee, how to sort the books, and how to price them to sell.

Chapter 24

Hold Food Events

DESCRIPTION

Food events are a lot of work with little return, but they can bring a small community together. At food events you sell something to eat to make money for the library. Food events can be annual events or one-shot wonders. They can also be one-shot flops, if you don't get most of your expenses donated. These events can range from occasional ice cream socials to elegant chocolate festivals. They can be soup suppers or $100-a-plate extravaganzas. They all have something in common—food. The fact that you are selling anything to donors suggests that you are making an effort to get money from nonconstituents. You will have to tailor your event to the community.

PURPOSES

The main purpose of a food event is to raise money for your library. The money can be used for whatever the library deems necessary. I have seen new libraries built with funding from soup suppers and bake sales. Every $1,000 counts, and food events can be an integral part of an overall capital campaign.

BENEFITS

Food events help the library maintain a public awareness that the library needs money for one or more projects. Food events can bring like-minded people or people from various groups together for social interaction.

EXAMPLES

Pancake Feed

The Noon Kiwanis Club in Great Bend, Kansas, has perfected the art of the pancake supper. Without increasing the price of their tickets for 20 years they have doubled their income from one food event. They must be doing something right.

They don't buy anything they can get donated. Everything from sausage to syrup, pancake mix to coffee is donated. Members of the club contact local merchants and ask them to furnish the food products they need.

Members compete at selling tickets. The winners get a steak dinner—all donated, of course.

They rent the gymnasium and kitchen of the local Catholic church/school for the event and start serving at 11:00 A.M. They serve pancakes, sausage, and coffee, tea, or orange drink. Even though serving runs smoothly, the serving line rivals queues at Disneyland in August.

Every member participates. Doing everything from taking tickets to refilling coffee cups. All the food is served on plastic, so cleanup is easy and carryout is a snap.

Chili Supper

Every year the Great Bend High School A Capella Choir holds a chili supper in the high school cafeteria just before the high school homecoming football game. The money is used for a trip for the choir. Parents of juniors and seniors organize and run the event. The parents of juniors are in training for next year's event. The school district's food service provides the food at cost. Choir students sell the tickets. All of the parents participate on committees from taking tickets to cleanup. Students are also expected to help if they are not involved in the game. The choir of 80 members nets about $3,000 every year. Here are some of the things that make it a success:

- They sell lots of tickets to people who don't come to eat the chili.
- They allow for carryout.
- They serve homemade cinnamon rolls with the chili.
- They have streamlined the process to serve a lot of people in a short time.
- They have many volunteers—all of the choir members and all of their parents.
- They have it on a night when more people will be at or near the school for another event.

- They have it in a convenient location.
- They serve food that is safe to eat in a location that is inspected by health officials.

Dinners

The Arcade (New York) Free Library needed to purchase some computer furniture. They held a series of salad luncheons to raise the money. The library staff, volunteers, and Friends of the Library agreed to set a specific number of tables and provide a variety of salads. The people who prepared the food also sold tickets. Selling out every time, they raised $1,000 at each luncheon.

The setting was quite elegant. Part of the library was the first floor of a former residence. They use the former living rooms and dining area for reading rooms, meeting rooms, and cultural activities. They suggest you check with other groups in the community so your event does not conflict with another fundraiser.

HOW TO DO IT

Start with a successful experience. Decide what you want to do and organize with proven leadership. Make sure you have lots of volunteers. Early on you will have to decide on some critical issues that will determine how much money you will make. Try as many of these as you can:

Location:
- Hold the event in a facility where everybody knows and feels comfortable.

Date:
- Hold your event right before or in connection with a sports event that will attract a large crowd, unless of course your event is so big that it will attract its own crowd. Some groups have been successful at serving breakfast at 4:30 A.M. the opening day of pheasant season.

Cuisine:
- Select a meal that has many components. It makes it easier to ask for donations from several different suppliers.
- Keep the meal simple and easy to prepare. Remember that amateurs are doing the cooking.
- Don't give choices. Choices complicate preparation and slow down the serving line.

Product acquisition:
- Don't buy anything you can get donated. If you can't get it free, get someone to underwrite the cost or get it wholesale. If you have to pay retail, make another meal.

Pricing:
- Calculate the cost per meal and charge four to six times your cost, unless all of the food is donated. Then price your tickets similar to the cost of a comparable meal in a restaurant.

Advertising:
- Use every possible opportunity to advertise your event. Put ads in the newspaper, on the radio, and on television. Also ask for public service announcement time and space.

Tickets:
- Try to sell them in books of ten and include a chance on something nice with each book of ten tickets.
- Encourage competition between teams. Give prizes to the team and the individual that sells the most.

Cleanup:
- Leave the place better than you found it. Hire the person whose job it normally is to clean the facility you are using to supervise the cleanup and make sure everything is in order before you leave.

Evaluation:
- Count the money and subtract the expenses to figure out how much money you earned.
- Write up the suggestions for the leaders of the next food event.

RESOURCES

The best resource for a food event is donors who will either donate the materials you need for the meal or some within the organization to underwrite the cost of the stuff you need. Next to getting the products for nothing, many volunteer workers are needed to guarantee the success of the event. You also need an army of ticket sellers. The more tickets they sell the more money you will make.

Figure out a way to get the tickets printed professionally—especially if you are going to use consecutively numbered stubs to give away a door prize.

You will need a good planning calendar to keep the committee on task and know what needs to be done next.

SPECIAL CONSIDERATIONS

Large gala banquets that cost over $50 per person are in a league all by themselves. Work with the sales representative of the venue for the event and hire a professional events planner to make sure everything goes the way you want it to happen.

Restaurants go out of business all of the time. If you are going to succeed where they fail, you are going to have to do something better than they are doing. They are professionals. You are amateurs. The best ways to overcome the gap in experience are:

- Play to the charitable nature of your event and the benefit to the library.
- Get the food and other products donated to keep costs down and increase profits.
- Do all of the work with volunteers.
- Sell lots of tickets.
- Charge more than you need to, but not so much that nobody will buy them.

PITFALLS

Most states have strict laws regarding the preparation and selling of food. Food prepared in homes for an occasional event is usually all right, but if you do it frequently and on a regular basis, you may be violating the law. Food prepared at home and brought to a different place to be served should be protected from spoiling, which can happen in just a few hours if left at room temperature. Keep hot things hot and cold things cold.

If possible use the facilities of an organization that already has a place to prepare and serve food for large numbers of people, like a school cafeteria.

Many successful food events are held in banquet facilities of large hotels. Hotels will negotiate a price and take care of the whole event. This is a safe way to handle the event and will save the library lots of work, but don't count on making a lot of money unless you charge $100 a plate for a meal the hotel charges you $20 for.

FOR SCHOOLS AND ACADEMIC LIBRARIES

School libraries should stick to chili suppers held in the school cafeteria if they do it at all. School librarians would do better to have a book fair than a food event. People associate libraries with books and will buy books to help the school library.

Academic libraries might be successful with a large banquet in a hotel. The main catch is selling the tickets. Who is going to do it? There are probably better ways to raise money for an academic library than to hold a food event.

CHECKLIST

Sponsoring a food event requires planning and organization. Here is a checklist to help you do both.

1. Is the committee made up of experienced hands and people who are still learning?
2. Do you have enough volunteers to get all of the work done without putting too much of it on just a few people?
3. Is the work of the committee divided into manageable tasks?
4. Is the cuisine unique but familiar enough to attract a broad range of customers?
5. Do you plan to have door prizes or a raffle drawing associated with the food event?
6. If you plan to give prizes what will they be and how will you obtain them?
7. How will you print the tickets and who is going to do it?
8. Who is going to sell the tickets and how long will they have to do it?
9. What will you do to streamline serving the food?
10. Who, specifically, will be on the cleanup committee?

GETTING RESULTS

Many small libraries thrive on food events. The key to getting good results is community participation.

What Do I Do Next?

It will probably be easier to organize more people behind a food event than to get them to go out soliciting door-to-door for donations. I have known librarians who tried to do all of the cooking for a food event and they told me they would never try it again. It was too much work and not enough money. If you are obliged to do a food event, find lots of volunteers to help. Leave the cooking to the pros—though I suspect that after cooking 4,000 pancakes once a year for 20 years you might get pretty good at it.

What Are the Policies and Procedures Needed?

Make sure you follow the health regulations for food preparation. Collect and pay sales tax if you are required to.

How Much Time Should This Method Take?

Organizing and planning a food event should take about three months. Allow at least a month for advanced tickets sales.

When Can I Expect Results?

You can spend the money as soon as you have paid all of the bills.

What Can I Realistically Expect the Costs to Be?

Expect to pay $50 to $200 for a room that will hold a hundred people. Expect to pay about a dollar in food costs for every $4.00 ticket you sell.

If your food event is built around volunteers preparing the food at home and donating it to the cause your costs will be minimal. On fancy meals you take your chance with breaking even.

Do a projected budget and set sales goals before you decide to proceed with a food event.

SUMMARY

Food events can range from occasional ice cream socials to elegant chocolate festivals. The main purpose of a food event is to raise money for your library. They can be annual events or one-shot wonders. Food events can also fall flat on their faces.

Food events help the library maintain a public awareness that the library needs money for one or more projects. Food events can bring like-minded people or people from various groups together for social interaction.

The main elements of a successful food event include:

- Organization
- Planning
- Volunteers/workers
- Date
- Location
- Cuisine
- Pricing
- Ticket sales
- Streamlined serving

Gala events are best left to the professionals. Elegant people who pay elegant prices want everything to be elegant. Unless you have a real flair for being elegant, let those who do it for a living do it for you.

BIBLIOGRAPHY

Stallings, Betty, and Donna McMillion. 1999. *How to Produce Fabulous Fundraising Events: Reap Remarkable Returns with Minimal Effort: Includes Step-By-Step Guide to the Perfect Fundraising Event.* Pleasanton, Calif.: Building Better Skills. Nonprofit volunteers and staff should get this book and read it. The authors have clearly defined what makes events successful, and they have provided an insider's guide to a foolproof fundraiser. This is a fundraising book that truly emphasizes the importance of volunteers and the principles of volunteer management.

Chapter 25

Solicit Memorial Gifts

DESCRIPTION

When someone dies, friends and relatives send tokens of remembrance—usually flowers or gifts to the family or next of kin. The flowers wilt and the gifts are soon forgotten. A memorial-giving program creates the opportunity for donors to invest in the future of the library and extend the memory of the one who has died. It allows your donors to support your library and fulfill a social obligation at the same time. They send a gift to the library in honor of their friend or loved one. You send an acknowledgment to the family and a thank you note to the donor. Everyone feels good for the effort.

Memorial giving is not limited to remembering someone who has passed away. It is also a very appropriate way to honor a person for an achievement or milestone, such as winning a contest, having a birthday or anniversary, etc. When you receive a gift honoring someone who is still living, it is very honoring to invite him or her to help you select the book in their honor and then offer to let them be the first to borrow it. Of course, a thank you note is sent to the donor, but the acknowledgment is sent to the person being honored.

PURPOSES

For the library, the main purpose for memorial giving is to get more money for books or other library materials. Large gifts may be put in a savings account to accumulate interest and be comingled with other gifts to pay for something big. Sometimes a donor will want to honor a loved one by making a gift to purchase a piece of furniture or equipment and having the library put a memorial plate on it.

For the donor, the main purpose for memorial giving is to remember a loved one in a lasting, tangible way. Both the donor and the librarian need to agree on the method or form of recognition.

BENEFITS

Memorial giving is tailor-made for libraries. It provides immediate cash, not just pledges of future giving. Depending on how you set it up, you can spend the money on books or anything else you want. It is extra money for you. The donor would probably spend the money some other way (flowers or gifts) if he or she didn't give it to the library. Memorial giving is not subject to seasonal fluctuations, but it is unpredictable. Deaths, birthdays, and anniversaries occur all year long. Memorial giving will grow as people become more aware of your program. Once you motivate a donor to use your memorial program he or she will tend to use it over and over to honor other friends as they pass away. Small memorial gifts can lead to larger gifts, even major bequests, as you develop your relationship with donors. Set up a list of all your donors and stay in touch with them with regular information about the library. This could lead to a very high return on your investment.

You can't use memorial money for the light bill or other ongoing expenses, but it is good to have it for books and other materials.

EXAMPLES

Several years ago I created a half-page flyer that was a passive appeal for memorial gifts. The headline read: "Some people believe this is a great way to honor a loved one . . . It is." A sample memorial bookplate with a donor's name and the person being memorialized was placed to the left of the words. The flyer also had a reply coupon with lines for names, addresses, etc. We put these flyers at the front desk for people to take. We also gave a few to funeral homes to give to families, hoping they would list the library as a memorial recipient in the obituary.

When Bastrop, Texas (population 4,000) built a new library, they created a memorial gift "Wish List" and raised $65,000 in memorial gifts. The wish list read, in part, like this:

- Book shelving $40,000 (3 feet = $300).
- Table, seat /4 5@ $500 each.
- Reference Desk $3,000.
- Book Drop $1,000.
- Copier $ 4,500.
- Reading room chairs 37 @ $180 each.

Great Bend Public Library
Great Bend, Kansas 67530

❖

Presented by
Charlotte Taylor

In Memory of
Eunice Farmer

Some people believe this is a great way to honor a loved one.

It is.

The Great Bend Public Library's Memorial Program is a practical, gracious, great way to pay a lasting tribute to a loved one.

You simply request that a book be added to the Great Bend Public Library in memory of a person you designate ($25 = 1 book). The library completes a memorial bookplate and secures it to the inside front cover of the book purchased with your contribution.

Result: A living memorial that will endure for years.

Complete the coupon below and mail with your check to:
Great Bend Public Library
1409 Williams
Great Bend, Kansas 67530

Enclosed is $_____ as a gift to the Great Bend Public Library. The name of the person I wish to memorialize is _____.

Please send acknowledgment to _____,
whose address is _____.

Donor's Name: _____
Donor's Address: _____
City: _____ State: _____ Zip: _____

Please make checks payable to Great Bend Public Library.
All contributions tax-deductible.

Figure II-25-1 Memorial Giving Flyer

They were very successful in furnishing their new library.

HOW TO DO IT

If you are not actively seeking memorial gifts, you are missing out on one of the best, most passive, yet productive, fundraising opportunities you can do. Most libraries have de facto memorial programs, but they could do much more to increase memorial giving. Here are a few suggestions.

Start by creating a brochure. Place copies at the circulation desk of the library. Take the brochure to the funeral homes and ask the funeral directors to suggest the library to families as a possible recipient for memorial gifts.

You might also try leaving copies in:

- Hospitals
- Drug stores
- Nursing homes
- Bank lobbies
- Hospices

Ask the Friends of the Library to publish the memorial-giving coupon as part of their newsletter. Make a list of everyone who has ever given money to your library and send him or her a copy once a year. Send your brochure with a letter to everyone on your mailing list inviting them to donate to the library's memorial-giving program.

Spreading the Word

Advertise on the obituary page of your local newspaper. This will get your message before the public and remind them often. Most newspapers will give you a discount if you run the same advertisement every other day for a month. You can change the ad every month to create new interest.

Once a month publish a list of donations to the library with donors in the newspaper. Unless they request otherwise, donors like to see their names in print.

You could also establish a memorial-giving registry. Write the name of the donor and the name of the person memorialized in a special book you keep on display in a prominent place in the library.

Use your memorial program to cultivate the next-of-kin as donors. After a few weeks you can send them a brief letter offering to acquaint them with the library's memorial-giving program. You could say something like this: "Recently, a generous memorial contribution was made

---

Sample Memorial Solicitation Letter

Dear Mr. and Mrs. Robert Cuthbert,

We have a wonderful way to honor a loved one and invest in the future of the library at the same time. Your memorial gift in the amount of $25 or more will buy a book for the library with a bookplate honoring someone you care about.

You will enjoy the privacy of giving without revealing the amount to others. You will have the satisfaction in knowing that your gift serves a dual function. It will be helping the library and at the same time you will be remembering a friend or loved. Your memorial gift to the library is a convenient way to satisfy a social obligation and tell others you truly care.

A memorial gift can also be a way to honor a special occasion or achievement of a friend or loved one. You could say congratulations for having an anniversary or birthday. We would be happy to honor them even further by letting them help select the book to be purchased in their honor.

Please keep this letter and memorial coupon for future use. The next time you want to remember a loved one in a lasting way, think of the library. Fill out the donation form and send a check for $25 or more.

Sincerely,

Librarian

Figure II-25-2 Sample Memorial Solicitation Letter

to the library in the name of _____, and we thought you might be interested in knowing more about the library and our memorial-giving program. Let us know if we can help you." And so on . . . . This type of communication can lead to larger gifts, and even a bequest in their will.

RESOURCES

The best resource you can have to help with memorial giving is a printed flyer to make people aware of the opportunity to make a memorial gift to the library. The next best thing you can do to insure success is to have a mechanism that works well for acknowledgments receipts and thank you notes. If you have these two things in place and they are working well, you should receive your share of the memorial giving in your community.

SPECIAL CONSIDERATIONS

Extreme care must be given to avoid injuring the tender feelings of those who have lost a loved one. They are still going through the grieving process. You never intend to hurt anyone's feelings, but a word carelessly spoken or the *way* something is done can lead to misunderstandings and bad public relations for the library.

If money has been given for books and you know the reading interests of the deceased, try to find a book you think he or she might have liked to read. This will make the family feel good.

PITFALLS

Control of the memorial money sent to funeral homes then forwarded to the library is one of the most difficult issues to swarm around memorial giving. It is wise to have a policy on the issue.

The family of the deceased often wants to dictate how the money should be spent. If that is the way you want your policy to read, write it that way and let it go. If the donor has not said how his or her gift should be spent, then the librarian should have the discretion. The rub comes when the relatives of the deceased want to assume control over the money given by others and thereby direct how the money is spent. The librarian and the family could find themselves at cross-purposes.

The best policy in most cases is this: "The library accepts gifts on the basis it can use them. If the library cannot use a gift it retains the right to dispose of it in any manner its employees choose. Money gifts will be used, whenever possible, for the purposes designated by the donor."

Don't leave the thank you notes and acknowledgments to chance. Assign someone in the library to do it immediately upon receiving the gift. From *Thanking Miss Daisy: A Study of Donor Attitudes Relating to Recognition*, by Kathleen M. Clark, we learned that donors want to know for sure we got their gift. At the Great Bend Public Library we have developed a form for all donations, which includes a space for the staff person responsible for sending the thank you note and acknowledgment to sign when the task has been completed.

FOR SCHOOLS AND ACADEMIC LIBRARIES

Memorial giving is important to most college and university libraries. Gifts can be relatively small but still make a difference to the library. Get the alumni newspaper or magazine to include the library's solicitation for memorial gifts in their publications. Pay for it if you have to.

School libraries can benefit from memorial giving, too. You will have to be careful if a child in the school dies. There is a fine line between offending loved ones and giving them an opportunity to remember their child. It is probably best to create a public awareness of the library's memorial-giving program before a death occurs.

CHECKLIST

Here is the checklist for organizing and promoting a memorial-giving program.

1. Do you have a gift policy in place that includes a section on memorial giving?
2. Do you have a policy on recognition of donors that is tied to the size of their gift?
3. Do you have a flyer or promotion piece that explains your memorial-giving program and includes a donor coupon to submit with the gift?
4. Is the staff trained on how to accept gifts for the library?
5. Is one or more staff members assigned the responsibility of sending receipts, acknowledgments, and thank you notes?
6. Do you have a plan to promote memorial giving?
7. Have you implemented the plan and is it working?
8. Have you distributed your memorial flyers to places like funeral homes, hospitals, or doctors' offices?

GETTING RESULTS

Memorial giving is a good source of revenue even though it is not very predictable. You can increase your chances for good results if you will be more proactive in asking.

What Do I Do Next?

Many memorial gifts come in without being solicited. If you want more money to come in from memorial giving you have to be more proactive. Create a brochure or a flyer like the one on page 363. Let people know that the library will put a person's name in a book if they will give enough money to buy the book.

When you give talks about the library, mention the memorial-giving program. Include information about memorial giving on the library's Web site.

What Are the Policies and Procedures Needed?

Follow the library's policy on giving. You may have to establish procedures for soliciting and handling memorial gifts. Be sure to include a section on who controls the expenditure of the money.

How Much Time Should This Method Take?

You could put a stack of memorial-giving flyers on the circulation desk tomorrow and receive ten gifts the next day or you could wait 10 months to receive the first gift. One of the problems with passive fundraising is its unreliability. It could take years to build community awareness about the library's memorial-giving program.

When Can I Expect Results?

About the time you think you are never going to get a memorial gift ten checks will come in because a grieving family designated the library as a memorial recipient.

What Can I Realistically Expect the Costs to Be?

The cost for a thousand brochures or flyers will be $100 to $200.

SUMMARY

Some may think it uncultured for a library to capitalize on the death of someone, but the library is in a unique position to offer an opportunity for lasting remembrance. Are you missing out on a steady flow of money into your library because you don't have a memorial-giving program? Here are some ideas to remember as you set up a memorial-giving program or revamp the one you have:

- Memorial giving provides donors with the opportunity to make a lasting gift to the library and keep the memory of a loved one alive.
- Large gifts, even major bequests can start out as memorial gifts.
- Start a memorial-giving program by creating a half-page flyer that is a passive appeal for memorial gifts. Put it out where people can see it and then advertise the library's memorial-giving program.
- Don't reserve the memorial-giving program for the deceased. Offer it to anyone who wants to honor a friend or loved one's special occasion or achievement.
- Recognize donors and honorees appropriately and promptly.

Memorial giving can be a steady source of income for your library. You just need to tap into it.

BIBLIOGRAPHY

Jordan, Ronald R., and Katelyn L Quynn. 2001. *Invest in Charity: A Donor's Guide to Charitable Giving*. New York: Wiley.
This is the only book that furnishes information about charitable giving for donors. It shows them the strategies they can integrate into their overall tax, estate, and financial plans. This could be a good tool if planned giving is part of your fundraising plan.

In Conclusion

Fundraising for libraries is not just about money. It is about people and the way we treat them, the way we serve them, and the way we meet their needs. Fundraising for libraries is about looking for opportunities—opportunities to serve others and opportunities to allow others to serve libraries. By doing so, we build relationships of trust and empowerment.

Fundraising for the library is not a task we tack on to the job description of the library director or the person in charge of public relations. Fundraising has to become the warp and weave of the fabric we are made of. Everything we do every day can be seen as a fundraising activity. Fundraising for the library is just as important for the president of the board as it is for the high school student who puts the books back on the shelf. Who knows when a kind act will produce a million-dollar gift—or even a $10 gift?

Fundraising challenges us to step outside of our comfort zones and approach people and ask them for money. We shy away from this task because we think they don't want to give to the library. The truth is most people are willing to give something to help the library do its job. Our job is to remember the four most important words in fundraising—ask for the gift.

When we ask for the gift, I hope we set our sights high and go for the brass ring. Who knows we might catch it.

Appendix I

Sample
CONSTITUTION AND BY-LAWS
FOR
FRIENDS OF THE HAPPY HOLLOW PUBLIC LIBRARY.
CONSTITUTION

ARTICLE I - NAME

The name of this organization shall be Friends of the Happy Hollow
Public Library.

ARTICLE II - PURPOSE

The purposes of this organization are as follows.
(A)   To maintain an association of persons interested in the Happy
Hollow Public Library.
(B)   To promote and stimulate the use of the library's resources
and services.
(C)   To make the public aware of the Friends of the Happy Hollow
Public Library and the services they perform.
(D)   To encourage and receive gifts and bequests to the library.
(E)   To support and cooperate with the library in developing library
services and facilities in the community.
(F)   The purposes of the organization shall be limited to charitable
and educational purposes within the meaning of Section 501 (c) (3) of
the Internal Revenue Code.
No substantial part of the organization's activities shall involve at-
tempts to influence legislation except as allowed under the provisions

of Section 501 (h) of the Internal Revenue Code. The organization shall not carry on propaganda or intervene in any political campaign (including the publishing or distributing of statements) on behalf of any candidate for public office.

The organization shall not carry on any other activities not permitted to be carried on by:

(1) an organization exempt from Federal Income Tax under Section 501 (c) (3) of the Internal Revenue Code of 1954 (or the corresponding provisions of any future United States Internal Revenue Law);

(2) an organization, contributions to which are deductible under Section 170 (c) (2) of the Internal Revenue Code of 1954 (or the corresponding provisions of any future United States Internal Revenue Law).

ARTICLE III - MEMBERSHIP

Section 1:   Membership of this organization shall be open to all persons interested in the library.

Section 2:   Each membership shall be entitled to one vote. A family membership entitles each member of the family to one vote.

Section 3:   The membership shall have the option to sponsor a Junior Friends group involving young people up to the age of eighteen.

ARTICLE IV - OFFICERS AND ELECTION

Section 1:   The officers of the organization shall be vested in a Board of Directors which shall consist of three (3) Directors and a President, Vice President, Treasurer, and Secretary.

Section 2:   Terms of Office

(A) All officers shall be elected for a one-year term.

(B) The election of officers and directors shall be held at the annual meeting, and they shall assume the duties of that officer immediately following election. Officers and directors shall be elected by a majority vote of those present at the annual meeting.

Section 3:   Officers and directors shall be nominated by a nominating committee appointed by the president with the consent of the Board of Directors, such nominating committee to consist of one member of the Board of Directors and two persons appointed from the membership at large. The nominating committee shall not nominate any person who does not consent to such nomination. Nominations shall be submitted to the membership in writing at least two weeks prior to the annual meeting. Additional nominations may be made from the floor with consent from the nominee.

Section 4:   Officers and directors shall be elected by a majority vote of those present at the annual meeting.

Section 5:   Vacancies occurring on the Board of Directors shall be filled for the unexpired term thereof by a majority vote of the remaining members of the Board of Directors.

ARTICLE V - AMENDMENTS

Section 1:   This Constitution and By-Laws may be amended by the majority of the members voting on such an amendment.

ARTICLE VI - FINANCES

Section 1:   Moneys received from memberships, projects, gifts, and memorials shall be used to further the purposes of this organization.

Section 2:   All funds of the organization shall be deposited from time to time to the credit of the organization in such banks as the Board of Directors may select.

Section 3:   All expenditures from these funds shall be approved by the Board of Directors.

Section 4:   The fiscal year shall be from January 1 through December 31 of each year.

Section 5:   No part of the net earnings of the organization shall inure to the benefit of, or be distributable to, its members, trustees, officers, or other private persons, except that the organization shall be authorized and empowered to pay reasonable compensation for services rendered.

ARTICLE VII - DISSOLUTION

Upon dissolution of the organization the Board of Directors, after paying or making provisions for the payment of all of the liabilities and obligations of the organization, shall transfer or convey all remaining assets to the Happy Hollow Public Library.

If the Happy Hollow Public Library is no longer in existence or is unable or unwilling to receive the assets, the remaining assets shall be distributed to an organization which at the time qualifies as an exempt organization under Section 501 (c) (3) of the Internal Revenue Code, or to a governmental unit for a public purpose.

BY-LAWS

ARTICLE I - MEETINGS

Section 1:   The annual meeting shall be held in December. Members shall be notified in writing at least two weeks prior to the date of the meeting.

Section 2:   Meetings of the Board of Directors shall be held throughout the year on specific dates agreed on by the Directors.

Section 3:   A simple majority of the Board of Directors shall constitute a quorum.

Section 4:   The agency head or a delegated representative shall be present at all meetings.

Section 5:   All meetings shall be open to the public.

ARTICLE II - DUTIES OF OFFICERS AND DIRECTORS

Section 1:   The President shall:

(A) Preside at all meetings.

(B) With the consent of the Board of Directors, appoint all committee chairpersons and coordinate their activities.

(C) Represent the Friends before any group requesting presence of the Friends, or delegate a representative.

(D) Be an ex-officio member of all committees except the nominating committee.

(E) Prepare a brief annual report to include information on the activities of the past year and an announcement of the date of the annual meeting in October.

(F) Appoint with consent of the Board of Directors a representative and an alternate to the Friends Council to serve for one year.

Section 2:   The Vice President shall:

(A) Preside at meetings and perform the duties of the President in the absence of the President.

Section 3:   The Secretary shall:

(A) Keep the minutes of all Board and Annual meetings and distribute them to all Board members, the community librarian, and the Executive Board of the Friends Council.

(B) Conduct all correspondence as directed by the President.

(C) Perform such other duties as are customary of the office of Secretary

Section 4:   The Treasurer shall:

(A) Be the chief financial officer of the organization.

(B) Make regular financial reports to the Board of Directors.

(C) Keep an account of all money received by the organization and deposit the same in the bank designated by the Board.

(D) Pay all bills as approved by the Board of Directors.

(E) Act as membership chairman, collect all dues, maintain a current list of paid members, and regularly inform the Board of the status of the membership.

(F) Perform such other duties as the Board of Directors may from time to time prescribe.

ARTICLE III - DUTIES OF STANDING COMMITTEES

Section 1:   The Program Chairperson shall:

(A) Cooperate with the librarian in the selection and presentation of informational, educational, recreational programs and events according to the guidelines set forth in the Happy Hollow Public Library Programming Policy. Approval of sponsorship and/or events shall be granted by a majority vote of the Board of Directors.

(B) Act as hospitality chairperson in coordinating all social arrangements, welcoming speakers and guests, and performing other duties as directed by the President.

Section 2:   The Telephone Chairperson shall:

(A) Notify and/or remind members of meetings, call for volunteers from the membership when needed for special projects, and aid the Treasurer in organizing membership drives.

Section 3:   The Special Projects Chairperson shall:

(A) Initiate special community-oriented projects with the approval of the Board.

(B) Organize committees to carry out projects.

ARTICLE IV - DUES STRUCTURE

Section 1:   Dues shall be payable annually.
Section 2:   Dues shall be:
    Individual $ 5.00
    Junior Friends   1.00
    Family   7.50
    Sustaining
    Business and Organization
    Life Membership   100.00

Appendix II

Sample Document
BYLAWS
OF
THE SINGING ROCK PUBLIC LIBRARY FOUNDATION

ARTICLE I

NAME AND LOCATION

Section 1.   The name of the corporation is the Singing Rock Public Library Foundation.

Section 2.   General Office. The general and principal office of the Foundation in this state shall be located at the Singing Rock Public Library, 1409 Williams, Singing Rock, KS 66679.

Section 3.   Other Offices. In addition to its principal office in this state, the Foundation may maintain offices at any other place or places designated by the Board of Trustees within the State of Kansas.

Section 4.   Corporate Seal. The Foundation may have a seal upon which shall be inscribed its name and the words "Corporate Seal."

Section 5.   Resident Agent. The name and address of the resident agent of the Foundation is _____, 1409 Williams, Singing Rock, KS 66679.

ARTICLE II

PURPOSE

Section 1.   Basic Purpose. The Foundation shall have as its basic purpose the promotion of the continued growth and improvement of the welfare, general public relations and for increasing the size and number of the holdings of library materials of the Singing Rock Public Library.

Section 2.   Ancillary Purposes. The Foundation shall, in pursuit of its basic purpose, engage in the following pursuits:

(a) To establish and maintain an endowment fund for the benefit of the Singing Rock Public Library.

(b) To encourage individuals and organizations to make financial contributions to support the Singing Rock Public Library, and to accept, acknowledge and approve each and every gift either in money or material regardless of size or form.

(c) To establish, promote, maintain, endow and render aid and assistance, financial or otherwise, to the Singing Rock Public Library.

(d) To establish certain memorials in cooperation with the donors.

(e) To purchase, for the Singing Rock Public Library, library materials, or to make funds available for such purposes.

(f) To accept only such gifts of property or material as the donor may consent to the Board of Trustees converting into money.

(g) To establish two types of funds. The first and primary fund shall be the endowment fund or funds, which shall be invested for the highest possible income of good security, the income of which only shall be transferred to the second fund. The second fund shall be the working fund from which all purchases and expenses shall be paid. It shall receive the earnings of the endowment funds and all such incidental gifts and income that may be found to be too small to constitute the formation of an endowment fund and whose donors have expressed no desires as to the disposition of such funds.

(h) In the event of dissolution, to make contributions to organizations that qualify as exempt charitable, educational, or scientific organizations under Section 501 (c) (3) of the I.R.C. of 1954 (or the corresponding provision of any future U. S. Internal Revenue law).

ARTICLE III

TRUSTEES

Section 1. The business and property of the Foundation shall be managed by the Board of Trustees as stated in the Articles of Incorporation. The Board of Trustees shall be composed of at least seven (7) individuals, elected by the Board of Directors of the Singing Rock Public Library at the annual meeting of said board. Trustees' terms shall ordinarily be for three (3) years. The terms of the Trustees shall be staggered so that at least two Trustees are elected at each annual meeting. The number of terms that a Trustee may serve is unlimited.

Section 2. Trustees shall be residents of the State of Kansas. Trustees shall have served or be serving on the Board of Trustees of the Singing Rock Public Library.

Section 3. An annual meeting of the Board of Trustees shall be held each year upon the call of the chairman.

Section 4. A special meeting of the Board of Trustees may be called at any time or place by the chairman or vice-chairman, or in their absence or inability to act, the same may be called by any two members of the Board. By unanimous consent of the Trustees, regular or special meetings of the Board of Trustees may be held without notice of any time or place.

Section 5. Notice of all regular and special meetings shall be mailed to each Trustee by the Secretary at least two days previous to the time fixed for such meeting. All notices of special meeting shall state the purpose thereof and the time and place where the meeting is to be held.

Section 6. A quorum for the transaction of business at any meeting of the Board of Trustees shall consist of the majority of the members of the Board; but the Trustees, although less than a quorum, shall have the power to adjourn the meeting from day to day or to some future date.

Section 7. Whenever a vacancy shall occur in the Board of Trustees by death, resignation or otherwise, the same shall be filled without undue delay by a majority vote of the Board of Trustees of the Singing Rock Public Library.

Section 8.   Any Trustee may be removed, with or without cause, by the vote of two-thirds (2/3) of the members of the Board of Trustees of the Singing Rock Public Library at any special meeting called for the purpose, at which meeting any vacancy caused by such removal may be filled.

ARTICLE IV

OFFICERS

Section 1.   The officers of the Foundation shall consist of a chairman, a vice-chairman, a secretary and a treasurer, and such other officers as shall, from time to time, be provided by the Board of Trustees. The office of secretary and treasurer may be held by the same person.

   The officers shall be chosen from among the Trustees. All officers shall be chosen by the Board of Trustees of the Foundation at the annual meeting of such Board, or at such other meeting of said Board as may be called for that purpose. The chairman and vice-chairman shall hold office until the next annual meeting of the Board of Trustees and until their respective successors are elected and qualified. The chairman and vice-chairman may serve unlimited consecutive terms. All other officers of the Foundation shall hold office at the pleasure of the Board of Trustees.

Section 2.   Chairman. The chairman shall preside at all meetings of the Board of Trustees and shall have general supervision of the affairs of the Foundation and shall see that all orders and resolutions of the Board are carried into effect.

Section 3.   Vice-Chairman. In the absence, disability or under the direction of the chairman, the vice-chairman shall be vested with all the powers and perform all the duties of the chairman, and shall have such additional powers and perform such additional duties as shall be ordered by the Board of Trustees.

Section 4.   Secretary. The secretary shall give or cause to be given all required notices of meetings of the Board of Trustees, except as otherwise provided in these Bylaws; shall record all proceedings at the meetings of the Board of Trustees in a book to be kept for that purpose; and shall perform such other duties as may be assigned to him by the chairman or Board of Trustees. The secretary shall have custody of the seal of the Foundation, if one is issued, and shall affix the same to all instruments when duly authorized to do so and attest to same, and do and perform such additional duties as may be ordered by the Board of Trustees.

Section 5. Treasurer. The treasurer shall have the custody of all moneys, valuable papers and documents of the Foundation, shall place the same for safekeeping in such depositories as may be designed by the Board of Trustees. The treasurer shall expend the funds of the Foundation as directed by the Board of Trustees, taking proper vouchers for such expenditures, shall keep or cause to be kept, a book or books setting forth a true record of the receipts, expenditures, assets, liabilities, losses and gains of the Foundation and shall, when and as required by the chairman of the Board of Trustees, render a statement of the financial condition of the Foundation and cause to be filed appropriate tax returns. As a requirement to serve as treasurer of the Foundation, the treasurer shall procure an appropriate bond in an amount to be determined by the Board of Trustees, from an insurer authorized to transact business in this state.

ARTICLE V

ADVISORY BOARD OF TRUSTEES

Section 1. Advisory Board: There shall be a committee known as the Advisory Board of Trustees consisting of not less than one (1) nor more than nine (9) persons of varied ages and abilities, appointed by the Board of Trustees for terms of one (1) year or until successors are chosen.

Section 2. The Board of Trustees shall select individuals interested in the promotion and improvement of the Singing Rock Public Library as Advisory Trustees.

Section 3. Said Advisory Board of Trustees shall meet at least annually on the call and proper notice of the chairman of such Advisory Board of Trustees.

Section 4. The purpose of the Advisory Board of Trustees shall be to give to the Board of Trustees reports and suggestions as to the continued and future efforts of said Foundation.

Section 5. The Board of Trustees shall appoint a chairman of the Advisory Board of Trustees. The Advisory Board of Trustees shall select a vice-chairman and secretary from its members.

ARTICLE VI

Section 1. These Bylaws may be amended upon a vote of the majority of a quorum of the Trustees of the Singing Rock Public Library present at any annual meeting of such Board, or at any special meeting thereof, when proper notice of such proposed amendment has been given.

References

ALA/LAMA. 1995. [Online]. Available: www.ala.org/lama/publications/leads/leads3/LEADS.V3.N08.html [2001, October 10].

Escoffier, Al. 2000. E-mail message to author dated December 6.

Friends of Libraries USA. 2002. [Online]. Available: www.folusa.com [2002, February 18].

Gannett Foundation. 2002. [Online]. Available: www.gannettfoundation.org/ [2002, February 18].

Grosse Point Public Library. 2000. 1999-2000 Annual Giving Roll of Honor [Online]. Available: www.gp.lib.mi.us/fundraising/honorroll.html [2002, February 17].

Hartsook, Robert. 1989. Fundraising workshop, Topeka Public Library, Topeka, Kansas.

Hillman, Howard, and Karin Abarbanel. 1975. The Art of Winning Foundation Grants. New York: Vanguard Press.

Krotz, Leah. 2001. E-mail message to author dated October 11.

Lapsley, Andrea. 2001. E-mail message to author in March.

The Library Shop at the Library of Virginia. 2002. [Online]. Available: www.lva.lib.va.us/sb/shop/index.htm [2002, February 18].

LSTA goals. 2001. [Online]. Available: www.imls.gov/grants/library/index.htm [2001, September].

Lutheran Brotherhood. 2002. [Online]. Available: www.luthbro.com/index.html [2002, February 18].

National Press Club. 2001. The 24th Annual National Press Club Book Fair and Authors' Night [Online]. Available: http://npc.press.org/programs/2001bookfair.shtml [2002, February 18].

Peters Township Public Library. 2002. [Online]. Available: www.ptlibrary.org/Fundraising.html [2002, February 18].

Runion, Joanna. 2000. LSTA grant proposal.

San Antonio Public Library. 2001. [Online]. Available: www.sat.lib.tx.us/html/cellar.htm [2001, October 10].

Sara Lee Foundation. 2001. [Online]. Available: www.saraleefoundation.org/ci_grants.html [2001, October 10].

Swan, James. 1990. *Fundraising for Small Public Libraries*. New York: Neal-Schuman.

Sweitzer, Sandy. 2001. E-mail message to author dated September 15.

Trotta, Marcia. 2001. E-mail message to author in September.

Index

About the Author

JAMES SWAN has worked in school, academic, or public libraries since 1959. He has been the director of the Central Kansas Library System and the Great Bend Public Library since 1977. He has spoken and written books for librarians on a wide variety of topics. *Fundraising for Libraries* is his fifth book. He holds a BA and MLS from Brigham Young University.